THE COUNTERFEIT SPY

THE
COUNTERFEIT
SPY

Sefton Delmer

1817

HARPER & ROW, PUBLISHERS

NEW YORK • EVANSTON • SAN FRANCISCO • LONDON

FIRST U.S. EDITION

STANDARD BOOK NUMBER: 06-011019-8

LIBRARY OF CONGRESS CATALOG CARD NUMBER: 71-95948

This book is dedicated to the memory
of Donald Harvey McLachlan, OBE,
who first introduced the author to
the labyrinth of Storey's Gate.

Acknowledgements

Foremost among the friends, old and new, who helped me with their recollections and advice for this book is Colonel N. W. Wild who commanded the Anglo-American deception unit. While I take full responsibility for everything I have written, I am only too happy to acknowledge my great debt to Colonel Wild for the information, advice, and encouragement he has given me. The officers of the Military Archives of the German Federal Republic in Freiburg most generously allowed me unrestricted access to their extensive files which now include many records of the German intelligence services captured by the Americans, and later returned by them. I recall with special gratitude the help of Frau Luise Jodl, widow of Colonel-General Jodl, an honourable officer and a gentleman who was made a scapegoat for the crimes of the Third Reich. I would have found it understandable if Frau Jodl had refused to have anything to do with a writer whom many Germans dislike for his outspoken criticism of their attitudes. Instead she introduced me to former members of the intelligence branch of Hitler's General Staff and assisted me in deciphering some of her husband's handwritten notes. I only hope she will not regret her kindness when she reads this book. I must also thank Andre Deutsch Ltd. for permission to quote an extract from the German edition of Schellenberg's *Memoiren*, the Viking Press for a quotation from General John R. Dean's *The Strange Alliance*, Deutsche Verlags-Anstalt for a quotation from Helmut Heiber's *Lagebesprechungen*, and the Bundeszentrale Für Heimatdienst for excerpts from *20 Juli, 1944*. I must again thank the librarians of the Royal Institute for International Affairs, the London Library, and the Weiner Library for their help, and my old friend Ursula von Krosigk for the promptness with which she and her Berlin bookshop have always dealt with my many requests.

Contents

Storey's Gate

I had been for a stroll across St James's Park and was just going to pass the government buildings in Storey's Gate when I caught sight of the tourists. A gaggle of them was preparing to descend into that bomb-proof catacomb which during the war had been Winston Churchill's equivalent to Hitler's Führerhauptquartier.

Could it be that unbeknown to me the place had been preserved as an historic monument and was now open to the public? A white-haired old man seemed to be shepherding the tourists. So I went across and asked him. Yes, sure enough, I was right. The place was open to the public and even though there had been no publicity, it was attracting many visitors, more than five thousand already this year.

'Come along too, if you like, sir,' the old man invited me. I liked.

Two floors down we went, both below street level. As we descended the stairs I talked with our guide. His name he told me was Trigger and he had worked in the building, though not in Churchill's time. First, he had been a messenger, then a store-keeper. Now he was on a pension. Showing people around the place from which for the best part of five years Churchill had planned and directed the struggle against Nazi Germany was his hobby.

Mr Trigger produced the keys and unlocked the heavy door which, when I was last here during the war, had been guarded by Royal Marines.

The first things Mr Trigger pointed to in the low-ceilinged vault with its heavy steel girders and stout timber reinforcements were the maps and charts on the walls and the myriad pinpricks left in them like so many woodworm borings by the coloured pointer pins of Churchill's staff officers.

Lovingly he fondled the smooth surface of the enormous mahogany table round which Churchill used to meet the ministers and service chiefs of his War Cabinet. Name-plates still marked where they sat . . . Eden, Bevin . . . Beaverbrook—and the rest. In every place lay Stationery Office blotters and pencils as though the War Cabinet were just about to meet. Even the stern notice in heavy black type forbidding defeatist talk and thought was still where Churchill had placed it during one of the early crises. It quoted a Draconic ukase by Queen Victoria, though without giving its date or the ocasion which had prompted it.

Please understand there is no depression in this house and we are not interested in the possibilities of defeat. They do not exist.

Victoria, R.I.

Mr Trigger showed us Churchill's emergency bedroom. Here Winston used to spend the night, if the Blitz became too thick or the need for decisions too pressing for him to be absent from the bridge for even the short time it would take him to commute through the specially constructed tunnel to his official residence in nearby Downing Street. The narrow bed under the omnipresent steel girders and the austere chairs provided by the Office of Works looked singularly out of keeping with what one knows of Churchill's ideas of bedroom comfort.

For the benefit of the two Americans in the party Mr Trigger unlocked the sound-proof telephone room used by Churchill for his transatlantic conversations with Roosevelt. Churchill and Roosevelt talked freely over that telephone in the full confidence that what they said was protected by the 'scrambling' device. They had been assured that the 'scrambler' distorted speech and made it unintelligible for all ears but those of the principals. As we know today it did not. In fact Hitler's listening post at Eindhoven in Holland unscrambled the scrambler and bugged the talks.*

What intrigued me most among Mr Trigger's treasures were the charts showing the disposition of the RAF and the US Air Force on their airfields in Britain just before the invasion of France. There it all was! The complete order of battle for D-day. What would not Colonel 'Bulle' Dewitz and Hitler's other air intelligence officers

---

* David Kahn, *The Code-Breakers*, page 556.

have given for a sight of these revealing charts! But on second thoughts I wondered—would they?

Would they have accepted them as the truth? Or would they, as I suspect, have dismissed them as a fake intended to mislead and deceive them? During the months before the invasion a false picture of the Allied dispositions had been planted bit by bit on the German intelligence staffs. They had accepted it completely. And once an intelligence officer, German or Allied, had made up his mind and committed himself to the reliability of a 'trusted source', it was almost impossible to shake his conviction. This infallibility complex seems to be an occupational psychosis common to all intelligence officers, but those serving Hitler's totalitarian Third Reich were the most prone to it. Yes, I am pretty sure that even in the presence of the truth they would have loyally preserved their faith in the fake.

What an ironic quirk, too, that the team of British staff officers, who with their American partners planned the hoax which deceived Hitler (and thus not only assured the success of the invasion but saved thousands of British and American lives) worked in an office in these caverns only a few doors removed from the 'joint planners' of Churchill's War Cabinet Office. Although, of course, when you think of it, it was logical enough that the designers of the bogus plan should co-ordinate their scheming most carefully with the authors of the genuine one.

That, too, is why their chief, the British Colonel J. H. ('Johnny') Bevan, could have been seen in Churchill's catacombs most days, sauntering along their passages on his way to consult with his neighbours. And so too could Noël Wild, the incisive little colonel of hussars, who headed Eisenhower's deception team at SHAEF. Colonel Wild was so much of a regular at the War Cabinet Offices that he was made an honorary member of the planners' mess.

My own war job—I was in charge of a Psychological Warfare campaign to soften up the German forces in the invasion area in readiness for D-day*—had caused me to pay frequent visits to the colonels in their underground lair next to Churchill's.

As Mr Trigger took us below to show us around I looked for the

* See my *Black Boomerang*—Secker and Warburg, London, and Viking, New York.

colonels' old headquarters. It was shut, and Mr Trigger had no key to it.

'Seems to be uninhabited. Some sort of a storeroom now used by the Treasury, I would say, sir,' suggested Mr Trigger, and called my attention to the notice on the door. 'Treasury Press Registry' it said.

Excellent cover that would be, I thought, if a successor to the colonels was carrying on the good work. And why shouldn't there be? After all, the Russians were still hard at it. The KGB had its 'Disinformation' sections planting deception all over the world.

But then as usual came second thoughts. I was being too romantic, I told myself. Deception of our adversaries was not a game that Britain, let alone the NATO Alliance, could play in peacetime. We are all of us democracies. Only in times of war can we suspend civil liberties and impose the kind of security restrictions and secrecy without which deception policies could not possibly succeed. No, that notice on the door told the truth, I felt sure. It was inevitable that the office from which Hitler was conned into defeat should have become a dump for old newspapers and yellowed press cuttings.

As I followed Mr Trigger and the tourists, I made a resolve. The story of the plans made and the decisions taken in Churchill's underground war room has been told in countless biographies and memoirs. The secret history of the men who wrong-footed Hitler is in danger of being buried for ever in a cellar filled with lumber. Let me try to tell what I have been able to dig out about it before it is too late.

For even if the story serves no other purpose than to make the new generation of Western intelligence-getters a little more aware of what can be done by deception in planting false trails, it will have served a valuable purpose. Especially in this age, when our Western intelligence agencies, as starved comparatively of detailed information about the Soviet Union and China (despite observation by satellites and U2 planes) as was Hitler about Britain in 1944, seem only too ready to gobble up every crumb of bait thrown their way and celebrate it as a world-beating scoop.

I

Dupe in a Chalet

Colonel Friedrich-Adolf Krummacher was Hitler's very own personal intelligence officer, and he hated it. He hated having to provide intelligence which fitted in with the wishful thinking of Hitler's 'divinatory intuition'. He hated the toadying intrigues of the Führer headquarters, the obsequious yesmanship of the officers who formed Hitler's headquarters staff, the so-called Wehrmachtführungsstab.

Krummacher was forty-seven years old in 1944 and a veteran artillery officer of the First World War. He had drifted into intelligence work after leaving the Weimar Republic's Reichswehr and serving for eight years in China (from 1930 to 1938), as adjutant to successive chiefs of the German military mission to Chiang Kai-shek.

He had never been trained as an intelligence officer. He had never been an officer of the General Staff or attended the staff college. But he did have friends among the senior officers of the Abwehr, the Secret Service under Admiral Wilhelm Canaris. To give him a job they had attached him to the High Command as a liaison officer, first with the Abwehr and later with Himmler's Sicherheits Dienst (Security Service), after Himmler had taken over the Abwehr. Now he was what the British and Americans would describe as the G2 in the Wehrmachtführungsstab that accompanied Hitler wherever he established his headquarters.

On this morning of June 9, 1944, the Führer headquarters was in Hitler's Berghof, the oversized multi-millionaire's chalet the dictator had built himself on his beloved Obersalzberg in the Alps above Berchtesgaden. Krummacher and other members of the Wehrmachtführungsstab had been assigned offices in the infantry barracks at Strub, a northern suburb of Berchtesgaden.

---

* Armed Forces Operations Staff.

And that is where we may assume he found himself at this moment, sitting at his desk, his plump round head with its stubble of close-cropped grey hair bent in frowning concentration over the papers in front of him: intelligence dealing with the Anglo-American landing, now in its fourth day.

Krummacher had the reputation with his comrades in the Wehrmachtführungsstab of being *stinkfaul* (stinking lazy). And so I can well imagine him, as he has indeed been described to me, constantly looking at the clock and then at the pile of papers in his 'In'-tray and groaning. Even for an officer of a less phlegmatic temperament than Krummacher's all that paper was too much. Too much for him and his assistant Major Borchers to cope with on their own—the Russian fronts, the Balkans, Italy, and now Normandy. Hitler was unwilling to assign him more staff. The Führer paid no great regard to intelligence. Indeed, until things began to go wrong on the Russian front he had had no G2 of his own. But then he was persuaded to appoint an officer who would go through the intelligence intake for him and select such material as was worthy of his attention. Krummacher desperately wished now he had never been given the job. He would have given anything to be back in China. At 1140 hours the staff car would be calling to take him up to the Berghof where those lackeys—like others of his kind Krummacher was apt to refer disrespectfully to his superiors behind their backs—would be assembled in the war room expecting him to give them a verbal rundown on the latest intelligence.

Not that he envied any of them their jobs. The Führer was up against the hell of a problem, the colonel grimly conceded. The Anglo-Americans were pouring more and more troops and material into the bridge-head. Rommel was clamouring for reinforcements. He wanted the Führer to send him armour and infantry now being held by the 15th Army north of the Seine in order to defend the Calais area against the expected main assault. And it looked as though the Führer was going to let Rommel have his way. If he did so, Krummacher confided to Borchers, it was a certain bet that, once Eisenhower discovered the armour had disappeared from the Calais sector, he would immediately launch the main assault across the Channel. All the best intelligence from England agreed on that.

And what else were all those airborne divisions and bombers for that were massed in East Anglia? Or that Anglo-American army group under General Patton? If only there were some illuminating piece of intelligence that he could place before the Führer. After all, it had been the Führer's own belief—supported by intelligence reports of the highest grade—that the landing in Normandy was a diversion in force intended to distract attention from what would shortly be revealed to be the target of the enemy's main thrust: Calais and the Belgian coast.

With a grimace of distaste the colonel turned back to his papers.

He was still reading when one of his telephones began to buzz. It was the direct line which connected him with the Department of Foreign Armies West, the intelligence branch of the High Command whose special task it was to collect and evaluate all information received about the British and American forces, most particularly about their landing in Normandy. The head of the department was on the line, Colonel the Baron Alexis von Roenne.

Roenne was in a state of high excitement. He had just received intelligence, he said in his high staccato voice, which made it seem extremely probable that the enemy was about to launch a large-scale operation from the East of England. A radio code message for the Belgian Resistance had just been intercepted. It indicated an enemy landing planned for June 10, probably in Belgium.

'To choose this moment, therefore,' said Roenne, 'to move our infantry and armour from the Pas de Calais area and Belgium in order to reinforce the front in Normandy would be suicidal madness.'

Not very tactful of the young staff officer, seeing that the move of the 15th Army's infantry and armour across the Seine to the Normandy bridge-head had after long hesitation been sanctioned only the previous evening by the supreme war-lord himself. But then Roenne, a confirmed unbeliever in Hitler's infallibility, had never made a great secret of his feelings.

Roenne added another piece of heresy. In his department's opinion, he said, it was high time that the Cherbourg Garrison got on with the job of blowing up the port installations. One could hardly expect Cherbourg to hold out indefinitely. (Hitler had sent a message to the troops there telling them he expected just that.) Total destruction of the docks and the other harbour facilities,

Roenne went on, could deny the use of Cherbourg as a supply base to the enemy for months to come.

'During the approximately eight days that we have left,' said von Roenne, 'every hour must be used for the destruction of Cherbourg's installations.'

Krummacher assured Roenne that he was in full agreement with him. 'I am off to the Berghof now for the noon conference and I shall put your points forward with all the emphasis at my command.'

Colonel the Baron Alexis von Roenne was a competent and highly methodical staff officer. Hardly had he put down the receiver than he wrote a minute of his conversation with the Wehrmacht-führungsstab's G2. Which is how we come to know about it. For the minute of their conversation, headed 'June 9, 1944. Chief of Department Foreign Armies West conducts telephone conversation with Colonel Krummacher', was filed in the records of the department. Towards the end of the war the records were hidden in a cave in the Thuringian Forest. There they were discovered by the advancing Americans and thus preserved for posterity.

When he arrived at the Berghof, Krummacher just had time to report the news of the impending second landing to Colonel-General Alfred Jodl, chief of the Wehrmachtführungsstab, while the two of them waited with the other officers for Hitler to join them in the Berghof's enormous hotel lobby of a living room. The living room served Hitler as his war room when the Führer headquarters was up here in his alpine retreat. As they waited, Jodl, Krummacher, Keitel and the rest of the staff—young officers mostly of the rank of colonel and lieutenant-colonel—stood gathered around the vast table in front of the plate-glass window which looked out on the Berghof's special attraction, a panorama of snow-topped mountain peaks.

Then Hitler came in and sat down at the table, a pair of metal-rimmed spectacles on his broad nose. (No pictures were ever published during the time of the Third Reich of Hitler wearing those spectacles. In his public image Germany's demi-god was allowed no human frailties.) Hitler, as usual, took his seat in a rush-bottomed rustic armchair and gazed at the maps which covered the table. They had been marked in accordance with the latest order of battle reports. No one else sat down.

Jodl then began his report on the military situation. He left the
report on the threatened landing in Belgium to the last, for a very
good reason. Hitler had been most scathing about the reports of
the various intelligence agencies concerning the invasion and Jodl
did not wish to provoke his irascible war-lord's wrath at the outset
of the discussion.

For the same reason his staff had been unwilling to wake Hitler
when the first reports of the Allied landing in Normandy came
through on the morning of June 6. Hitler had been so firmly
convinced that the first landing would only be a diversion intended
to trick him into engaging his forces prematurely and in the wrong
place that no one dared report anything to him at all for fear of
being accused of having fallen for an enemy deception.*

'Remember?' he said at the noon conference that day, 'there was
one report which predicted the invasion absolutely correctly. It
gave the date, the hour, and the place of the landing. Got them
exactly right. And that report confirms my belief that this is not
the main invasion but only a diversion to distract my attention
from the real thing. The report was deliberately planted on me by
the enemy.† Jodl,' he went on, addressing himself to his Chief of
Staff. 'How many of these agents sending us their reports do you
imagine are in the pay of the enemy? They are just sending us
reports intended to confuse us. I am not going to permit that to
happen. I'll refuse to allow these reports to be passed on. They'll
only make our people nervous. We'll take care of them here—in
the waste-paper shredder.' (Zerreiss-Wolf.)

All the same, a couple of days later, on June 8, he had yielded to
Field Marshal Rommel's appeal for reinforcements to help him
meet the Anglo-American assault in the Normandy bridge-head. He
had agreed to transfer to him infantry and armour intended for the
defence of Calais and the Belgian hinterland, where in his own
estimation the enemy's main landing was to be expected.

Now Jodl, greatly daring, put forward Roenne's report suggesting
that the Führer's first hunch had been right, that the order to
transfer the armour to Normandy should be revoked.

---

* Albert Speer, *Erinnerungen*, Propyläen Verlag, Berlin, 1969.
† The report in question almost certainly came from an Austro-Czech free-
lance agent in Lisbon named Jan Jindric. See page 224.

But with characteristic indecision Adolf Hitler, though impressed, did not act on the report. Not at that noon conference.

But at the midnight conference which followed he did. He gave orders to halt the move across the Seine to Normandy of the 15th Army's armour and infantry. He sent them back to their old positions guarding the Calais area to meet the threatened second landing and ordered a top-grade alert for the whole coast from the Seine to the Scheldt.

Hitler's mind had been finally made up for him by the arrival at 2220 hours of a wireless signal from Germany's most trusted spy in Britain, an agent whom even the suspicious Hitler believed. A *précis* of it had been teleprinted simultaneously to the Wehr-machtführungsstab and the Commander-in-Chief in France.

What was the message that so impressed the sceptical Hitler? Fortunately it too was in the file retrieved by the Americans from the cache in the Thuringian mountains.

Here it is:

*V-Cato, operation Ganelon, reports on June 9 from England: After a personal exchange of views in London with my agents, Freddy, Dick, and Desmond, whose reports transmitted today, and after considering the massive concentration of troops in eastern and south-eastern England which are taking no part in the present operations I have come to the conclusion that these operations are a diversionary manœuvre. Its purpose is to entice our reserves into the bridge-head in order that the decisive assault can then be launched at another point. Considering the continuous aerial bombardment of the area best suited strategically for an assault by troops from eastern and south-eastern England it seems that the objective could very well be in the region of the Pas de Calais, more particularly because in the event of an attack there the closeness of the air bases in south-east England would ensure strong air support for such an operation.

Krummacher submitted this message to Colonel-General Jodl, who, in turn, showed it to Hitler himself with a comment that it might be well to read it in conjunction with the previous report of an impending landing in Belgium.

---

* V-man = Vertrauensmann = confidential agent. For 'Cato', 'Ganelon', 'Freddy', 'Dick', and 'Desmond' see footnote on page 104.

For months it had been Hitler's belief that the main enemy thrust
would be delivered against the Calais area or Belgium. He had
forecast that it would come after diversionary attacks on the
Atlantic coast, on Normandy, Brittany, or even the South of
France. His military advisers in the Wehrmachtführungsstab
likewise believed that the Anglo-Americans would strike against
Calais, if only because this area was close to the ramps from which
the V-1 Flying Bombs were due to be launched against London
and that Calais, in the words of the railway posters, was the
'shortest and fastest route' from Britain to the industrial Ruhr
area and to Berlin.

Now 'Cato', Hitler's master spy in Britain, had confirmed that
the Führer's hunch was right, after all that the Normandy assault
was indeed only a cunning diversion, and that the main assault must
be expected elsewhere, most probably in the Pas de Calais. On the
strength of the spy's message, Hitler changed his mind about sending
help to the hard-pressed Rommel. As I have said, he recalled the
15th Army divisions from their move to Normandy and sent them
back to their old stations in the Pas de Calais area and Belgium.
He prevented them from helping the defenders of the bridge-head
at a time when their help might have been decisive.*

*   *   *

---

* When Field Marshal Lord Montgomery was CIGS after the war he told
Colonel Noël Wild, who had been in charge of the SHAEF deception
operation, that had there been an immediate move of the 15th Army into the
Normandy bridge-head after D-day, this coming on top of the loss of one
of the artificial ('Mulberry') harbours could have made it very doubtful
whether he could have gone on holding the original bridge-head.

It is sometimes argued that the success of deception in keeping the 15th
Army out of the Normandy bridge-head was not as important as the deception team likes to make out, that even without the 15th Army the Germans
had formidable resources facing the invaders. Certainly they did. But how
much more formidable they would have been had Hitler not recalled those
detachments of the 15th Army from their move into the bridge-head after
receiving the signal from 'Cato'!

Just before the invasion was launched there were three armoured divisions
with the 15th Army north of the Seine plus nineteen infantry and parachute
divisions. A month later (on July 8) 15th Army had twenty-two infantry
divisions and two armoured divisions. In fact the forces of the 15th Army
were stronger on July 8 than they had been on D-day. Those of the 7th
Army, reduced by heavy casualties despite some reinforcements, were still
considerably inferior.

Only one of the generals who read the 'Cato' signal and was
present at the conference at which the Führer stopped his Panzers
from going to Rommel's aid is alive today: General Buttlar von
Brandenfels, the Wehrmachtführungsstab's Chief of Operations.
I visited him in Kassel where he is now putting his considerable
organisational talents to the service of commerce rather than of war.
He is still a general, as he told me with a genial twinkle. 'But I am
not a general in command of troops, I am a general manager in
charge of a firm of wholesale grocers!'

I asked him what in his opinion the effect of Hitler's order counter-
manding the move of his armour from Calais to Normandy had been.

'In the long run it made little difference,' said the general. 'We
should have lost the war anyhow. But those divisions in the Calais
area were our best troops. Had they been flung into the Normandy
battle right away, and not sent back to wait for the assault from
south-east England that never came, we might have repelled the
invasion. Don't forget the weather was making the delivery of
supplies and reinforcements somewhat precarious for you. You lost
one of your artificial harbours in a storm. A concentrated attack
with the 15th Army's SS Panzers and the other armour might
conceivably have hurled back the invasion—despite your immense
air superiority. But what the hell! Even if we had repelled the
Normandy invasion we'd have lost the war in the end. No doubt
about that!'*

As the general said that he grinned cheerfully. Then, with an
'Excuse me for a moment', he got up and marched across to his desk
to sign a bundle of cheques a clerk had just brought in.

Who was this V-man 'Cato' whose signal had such a decisive
effect on the invasion? I put that question to every old Abwehr
hand I met in Germany. No one could or would tell me. One man,
who had been the Abwehr chief in Bulgaria and had later served

---

* General Buttlar's view of the decisive nature of Hitler's recall of the armour
to the positions around Calais is shared by Major-General Sir Kenneth Strong,
Eisenhower's Chief of Intelligence at SHAEF. In *Intelligence at the Top* he
writes: 'Whatever mistakes Allied intelligence may have made in the war,
none can possibly equal this unparalleled blunder by the Germans and their
failure to realise it. Had they moved their divisions from the Pas de Calais
to Normandy in the early days when bad weather hampered the build-up
and the air support, the Allied invasion would have been in grave jeopardy.'

Himmler's Security Service in the same capacity, grimly said: 'I don't know. But even if I did I would not tell you! We don't give away our agents, not even in peacetime twenty-five years after the war!'

A Bonn diplomat who had been a young captain in the Luftwaffe intelligence in 1944 came closest to the truth. ' "Cato",' he said, 'never existed. He, like the other agents allegedly supplying us with intelligence from England, had been invented by the Abwehr so that they could pretend they were doing important work justifying their comfortable jobs in neutral "listening posts" far from the fighting fronts and the bombs and hardship of war at home. The whole thing was a fake. Neither the Abwehr nor the Security Service ever had so much as one genuine agent in Britain.'

'Cato', however, did in fact exist. He did indeed operate in Britain and transmit intelligence about the British and American invasion preparations and much else to his German Abwehr controllers in Madrid, who then relayed it to Berlin after deciphering and re-enciphering it.

But genuine though he was, and genuine as much of the information was which he transmitted to his Abwehr controllers, 'Cato', holder of the Iron Cross and Hitler's favourite and most trusted spy, was in fact an operative of the top-secret Anglo-American unit entrusted with the task of misleading Hitler and his generals about the invasion. 'Cato' was a Spaniard who pretended a fanatical devotion to Hitler as leader of the 'new National Socialist Europe'. Together with two other V-men, a Dutchman and a Pole, whom the Abwehr believed it had successfully planted as spies in Britain, he spearheaded the ingenious and complex apparatus which conned Hitler's intelligence men into accepting plausible but disastrously false information. Not the least important item being that about a further Anglo-American army group, allegedly waiting with bombers, fighters and airborne divisions in south-east England for the cross-Channel assault on Calais. That army group and its ancillary airborne divisions were pure invention. But such was the skill of the fake V-men led by 'Cato' and of the British and American officers controlling them that the truth about the phantom army did not dawn on the German generals until long after the war.

I do not blame the German intelligence men overmuch for swallowing this Anglo-American 'poison'. They had little choice. Apart from the German agents working for the British, no others were active in Britain after 1941*—as we now know. The rest had all been rounded up. And, secondly, the Allied deception bosses, with sinister psychological understanding of an intelligence officer's mind, had provided 'independent corroboration' for the reports of 'Cato' and his colleagues. Mostly this was visual or acoustic.

If 'Talleyrand', the Abwehr code-names for the Pole, reported preparations in Scotland for a landing in Norway, Luftwaffe reconnaissance would be able to report a concentration of transports in northern ports. Dummy tanks and dummy landing craft in the East Anglian estuaries backed up reports of the presence of a vast Anglo-American Armada assembling there for the assault on Calais.

Fake signals traffic intercepted by the German radio interception units provided evidence for troop movements. Often these confirmed and amplified intelligence concerning the order of battle which one or other of the pseudo V-men had supplied.

'To see is to believe,' says an old Roman saw. The Anglo-American deception team provided a feast for their German customers' senses of perception. The one trouble was that the Luftwaffe had fewer and fewer aircraft available for reconnaissance as D-day drew nearer. In the estimation of the deception officers the role of the fake signallers increased correspondingly in importance.

---

* This was not realised in Britain at the time. During the war the German espionage services were held in great respect.

2

'A' Force—or Ex Oriente Lux

'It is often possible by adopting all kinds of measures of deception to drive the enemy into making erroneous judgments and taking erroneous actions, thus depriving him of his superiority and initiative.' Mao Tse-tung on the 'Protracted War', 1938.

In all their essentials the deception techniques which defeated Hitler's intelligence staff during the spring and summer of 1944 had been invented and perfected between 1940 and 1943 at the Cairo headquarters of General Sir Archibald Wavell and his successors.

The dummies of tanks and guns, the fake signals traffic, the double agents like 'Cato' and the many other devices of bluff and counterfeit which prepared the way for the establishment of the Allied bridge-head in Normandy had all previously played their part in Rommel's defeat in the North African desert. Nor was this coincidence. At the behest of General Sir Frederick Morgan, who was in charge of the preliminary planning of the invasion, the second-in-command of the Cairo deception unit was posted to London from the Middle East at the end of 1943. His task was to build up a joint Anglo-American deception team for the Allied Supreme Commander and to take command of it himself, applying the experience he had gained in Africa to the European theatre.

This officer was Colonel Noël Wild of Britain's crack 11th Hussars. He was an ideal choice for the job. Wild combined the dash, quickness of decision, and flexibility of a cavalryman with the attention to detail of a trained staff officer. In addition he was blessed with a creative imagination and an accessibility to fresh

ideas inherited from his father, a distinguished artist and cari-
caturist.

The father of deception as a special arm of the British fighting
services was General Sir Archibald Wavell. With Wavell it was
axiomatic that one of the most important factors in winning battles
was to surprise the enemy. Not that this thought was exactly
original, or exclusive to Wavell. What was new was Wavell's
insistence that the task of achieving surprise could not be left to
military diversions alone. Tactical moves in the field, he laid down,
must be supported by strategic deception, planned and imple-
mented by a special deception unit.

The trouble was that deception of the enemy with bogus information and evidence—except in so far as it was practised by the
counter-espionage services seeking to infiltrate foreign spy networks—formed no part of the responsibilities of the British armed
services. They wanted to have nothing to do with it and said so.

This being the case, Wavell decided that it was up to him to
create a deception unit under his own control. And that is how in
the autumn of 1940 the unit subsequently known as 'A' Force
came to be born in a house behind Cairo's famous confectionery,
Groppi's, which before it was requisitioned had been a brothel.
'A' Force quickly proved its worth and long after Wavell had left
the Middle East his successors continued to employ 'A' Force,
assigning to it tasks of ever-increasing importance and scope.

The Chiefs of Staff were so impressed by its achievements that
in 1941 they set up deception units for all other commands from
Europe to South-East Asia. Every deception operation in every part
of the world, they had decided, however distant, could have its
effect on every other operation. Therefore, the Chiefs of Staff
argued, if it was possible to deceive the enemy in one theatre, that
deception, especially on the strategic plane, must be controlled
from the centre to avoid its effects endangering operations in other
theatres.

So the Chiefs of Staff set up the London Controlling Section
Offices alongside those of the planners in the catacombs at Storey's
Gate and made Colonel J. H. Bevan the section's head. Bevan was
successful. His job was to produce an overall deception strategy
with which every theatre commander had to conform. Not only

did the commanders have to produce deception plans for their theatres from now on and submit them to London, but Bevan had to see to it that their deception plans received the approval of the Combined Chiefs of Staff in Washington. The London Controlling Section gave advice about any modifications that might be necessary. How valuable this was became clear when from the middle of 1942 the Middle East Command, based on Cairo, was mounting an offensive against the eastern flank of the Axis in North Africa, while a Command based on Britain and the United States was simultaneously staging an assault against its western flank. The plans became even more interwoven when the assaults on Europe from both Africa and England were under preparation, each with its own deception plan.

In addition to this onerous task of co-ordinating the deception plans of the various theatres Colonel Bevan and his LCS were at the same time made responsible for initiating deception in Northern and Western Europe. He also had the tricky task of co-ordinating Allied cover plans with the none-too-co-operative Russians. For this purpose he had to travel to Moscow, a journey which at that time could be hazardous.

To organise and command his Cairo unit Wavell did not pick an officer already on his staff. Instead he sent to London for an old friend of his, Lieutentant-Colonel Dudley Wrangel Clarke. Wavell had known Clarke for a long time. They shared the same military philosophy. While they were in Palestine in 1938 fighting the Arab rebellion against Britain's alleged championship of the Zionist cause, they had frequently discussed the role of surprise and deception in modern warfare. Wavell and Clarke were in full agreement on the need for a special unit which would conduct deception as a part of military operations.

Wavell's call to join him in Cairo delighted Clarke, who after helping to launch the embryo Combined Operations Unit in June 1940 and giving its troops the name of 'Commandos'—Dudley Clarke had spent his boyhood in the Transvaal during the South African War and had been inspired by the adventures of the Boer guerillas—was now bored by what had become a routine planning job in the Military Operations Directorate of the War Office. The speed with which he got himself posted and flown out to Cairo constituted a record. Even Wavell, however, was astonished at the sureness of touch with which Clarke picked his staff one by one and set them to work in this field for which there were no manuals of instruction, no service regulations, no precedents barring Chinese strategy and the Trojan Horse.

When a year later, in October 1941, Wild was shanghaied by Clarke into 'A' Force—he had come out to Egypt to join the 11th Hussars in the desert but discovered to his chagrin that there was no squadron left for him—he found himself second-in-command of a most unusual assortment of combatants. Along with a sprinkling of professional officers, most of them Staff College trained like himself, he found a motley array of civilians in uniform. They included an expert chemist, a merchant banker, a music-hall illusionist, a writer of film scenarios, and a number of artists and draftsmen. They had been selected by Dudley Clarke partly for their specialised knowledge but also for general qualities such as inventiveness and practical realism. He had picked well, as could be seen from the enthusiasm with which the team made up of so many different talents and drawn from so many different walks of life became a smooth-working and highly efficient machine.

The work of the deception unit involved a painstaking study of all intelligence concerning the enemy and most particularly the enemy's own intelligence on the British forces in Africa and the Middle East. For experience had shown 'A' Force that even the most plausible information would be rejected by the enemy if it did not fit in with his own previously conceived intelligence picture.* Before drawing up a deception plan, therefore, 'A' Force would make an 'enemy appreciation' of the situation as it would appear to a German or an Italian staff officer. Accordingly they looked for guidance to any enemy intelligence reports that had come into their hands about their own forces, their own dispositions, and their own intentions.

---

* How justified this 'A' Force doctrine was is proved not only by the subsequent successes of 'A' Force in North Africa and of SHAEF in Normandy, it finds confirmation from the German Abwehr itself. Thus Dr Will Grosse, a wartime captain in the Abwehr, writing after the war says not without a certain smug satisfaction: 'On the German side we only attached importance to the reports of agents in so far as they fitted in with our own conception of the situation.' (Lageauffassung.)

And, of course, in drawing up the actual deception plan there was in addition to all this the most meticulous attention to detail. Even the smallest minutiae were attended to with perfectionist respect. When it came to planting information on the enemy intelligence, through a double agent, for instance, the unit had to show immense care and ingenuity. For not only did the information have to be skilfully designed to prompt the enemy into the moves desired but it had to contain an inbuilt escape line.

'A' Force took great trouble to preserve an agent's credibility with the Germans. They wanted him to have a plausible 'out' in the event of the enemy discovering the information he had been giving was wrong. They did not want their man to lose his rating as an 'A1 source' on the Germans' list of V-men.

⋆ ⋆ ⋆

The new unit's first efforts at deception in the autumn of 1940 concentrated on the purely visual. They were enough, however, to provide the Italians with pretexts for not carrying out their orders or even for stampeding into flight.

There were, for instance, the telegraph poles slung between two or four oil drums with camouflage netting stretched over them. These deceived the Italians into reporting gun emplacements at the points where their aerial reconnaissance had made them out. Major Jasper Maskelyne,⋆ the celebrated stage magician, joined 'A' Force and, adapting the conjurer's art to tactical deception, made dummy tanks out of three-ton trucks and dummy trucks out of tanks.† The Italians did not know which was worse, to have a line of harmless-looking trucks suddenly open up with a vicious barrage of gunfire or to be chased across the desert by tanks which later turned out to be trucks camouflaged by a skilful use of canvas and wire to look like tanks. ('Atlees', an unkind wag christened them, adapting Churchill's famous gibe when the PM had described his Labour deputy as 'a sheep in wolf's clothing'.)

⋆ Jasper Maskelyne, *Magic-Top Secret*, Stanley Paul, London.
† The Germans adopted a similar ruse. They camouflaged Volkswagen cars to look like tanks, thus giving the British an exaggerated impression of Rommel's resources in the way of armour.

Later, when the Germans came on the scene the crews in the bogus tanks sustained heavy casualties. The Germans refused to be alarmed by the mere sight of a British tank. They attacked them—and quickly discovered the truth. Later still, however, genuine tanks were mingled with the dummies. The Germans, who had expected dummies, were awakened to a cruel shock when genuine armour attacked them with genuine guns. Jasper Maskelyne made dummies of everything under the North African sun: dummy submarines, dummy airfields, even dummy bomb damage. He literally got 'A' Force to fight the desert war with mirrors.

Typical of deception in this period of its beginnings was the occasion when 'A' Force learned that the Long Range Desert Group, the marauder squadron which cruised over thousands of miles of trackless desert attacking and destroying enemy forts and airfields, was planning a raid on the Italian Blackshirt garrison holding the Siwa oasis. Colonel Dudley Clarke offered to 'soften up' the garrison in advance of the raid. Wavell welcomed the plan.

In a secret workshop at Abbassya the group of sappers and decorators who had built the dummy tanks were now put on to the job of fabricating dummy paratroopers made of sacking and straw. Weights were inserted in their legs and firecrackers in their arms. The firecrackers were designed to bang away like Tommy guns. The dummies were then attached to parachutes so that they could be dropped from aircraft and make the Blackshirts believe they were being attacked by British commandos.

On Siwa's D-day a flight of Hudson bombers from 216 squadron took off for the oasis. To gain maximum effect the raid was staged just as night was falling. First they dropped flares and pencil-shaped percussion cartridges which on striking the ground fired Very lights into the sky. Then the dummy commando troop was dropped. They drifted down all around the periphery of the oasis, banging away with their 'guns' as they descended.

The raid was 100 per cent effective. The Blackshirts, believing that they were surrounded by a particularly ferocious and determined enemy, stampeded out of the fort in a panic. When the Long Range Desert Group followed up the next morning they found Siwa deserted by the Italians. Only the Senussi tribesmen remained.

Sir Archibald Wavell was duly gratified by this confirmation of what deception could accomplish. For Siwa, captured without a genuine shot being fired or a military formation being engaged, was of strategic importance. Not only did it provide an admirable base for the Long Range Desert Group, but it was linked by desert tracks with such important points as Matruh and Sidi Barrani on the Mediterranean coast road.

*   *   *

It was not, however, until Rommel and his Panzers arrived in North Africa that the war in the desert became truly sophisticated over its methods of reconnaissance, and intelligence and, as an inevitable corollary, of deception.

Rommel had brought with him to Africa a mobile signals interception unit ('Fernmeldeaufklärungskompanie') commanded by a certain Captain Seebohm. The captain was an ace in the arts of interception, radio location, and cipher breaking. Seebohm's unit, fitted out with the latest and most sensitive electronic equipment, listened in to the British army's signal traffic, uncovered troop and tank movements, deciphered messages, and generally provided Rommel with the material needed to anticipate the moves of his British adversaries. For all his dash and intuition Rommel would never have accomplished half of what he did without the help of the superb intelligence supplied by Seebohm. When on July 10, 1942, Seebohm's unit was overrun by British armour and destroyed and he himself was killed, his loss was for Rommel the equivalent of a major defeat.

The British however were aghast, when from the records captured with Seebohm's unit they discovered the extent to which their signals and ciphers had been penetrated. Drastic countermeasures were immediately taken to repair the leak. They were effective, and the Germans were never again able to rule the British ether waves, at any rate not over North Africa.

'A' Force, however, realising the extent to which Rommel must have come to depend on Seebohm's signals interception and radio location for his intelligence, turned what until the loss of Seebohm had been a strength of the Afrika Korps into a weakness. By laying on bogus wireless signals traffic to trick Seebohm's successors they misled Rommel about the British Army's movements as completely as Seebohm's brilliance had previously kept him informed.

'A' Force would have liked to supply Rommel with a further service which Seebohm had provided before his demise. From an entirely uncalled-for deference to imagined American sensitivities—from my personal acquaintance with the Americans I am sure they would have enjoyed the scheme and given it their chuckling approval—the idea was never allowed to be carried out. A pity. It could have been a most effective piece of deception.

This is how it went. Among the records that fell into British hands when the Seebohm unit was overrun were deciphered intercepts of the reports which Colonel Frank Fellers, the military attaché at the US Embassy in Cairo, had been sending to his masters at MILID WASH (the Military Intelligence Division in Washington). Unfortunately the colonel had been using an American diplomatic code which had for some time been in the hands of the German Abwehr. Within at most an hour of its leaving the Cairo transmitter the American colonel's invaluable dispatch had been intercepted and deciphered by Seebohm and was being eagerly read by Rommel, As the American historian David Kahn* was later to comment. Fellers provided Rommel with 'undoubtedly the broadest and clearest picture of the enemy forces and intentions available to any Axis commander throughout the whole war'.

The American colonel supplied not only his own acute first-hand observation of the British army units, their strengths and weaknesses, and their order of battle. He also gave Washington—and Rommel —British plans into which he had been initiated. For instance, the plan for the commando raids on nine axis airfields during the night of June 12–13, 1942, were signalled to Washington by the colonel twenty-four hours in advance of their taking place. Rommel was able to arrange an appropriate welcome, and what was to have been a major sea and air operation for the relief of Malta was condemned to costly failure.

When 'A' Force learned of the interception of the American colonel's dispatches they hailed this as an heaven-sent opportunity

---

* David Kahn, *The Code-Breakers*, Weidenfeld & Nicholson, London, 1966.

for deception. Fellers was already accepted by the Germans as an 'unconscious source of proven accuracy'. If 'A' Force could have continued his service to Washington they could have interlarded it with made-to-order information fitting whatever deception they wanted to put over on the Germans intercepting the messages. Of course, Washington would have to be let into the secret. So far the Americans knew nothing about 'A' Force. Not even the omniscient Fellers was in the picture.

'A' Force themselves saw one snag: Washington would have to be warned that their diplomatic code had been broken and must be changed. Wouldn't the Germans smell a rat, if Fellers alone among American diplomats continued to use this code, while the others all changed over to new and stronger ciphers? There was no need, however, for 'A' Force to concern themselves. The political high-ups who had to be consulted in a diplomatically sensitive problem of this kind refused to take the risk of offending MILID WASH by using the attaché as a stooge.

So reluctantly and regretfully the Fellers scheme was abandoned and the colonel himself was recalled to Washington. There in due course Colonel B. F. Fellers was tactfully rewarded with a high decoration and made a general.* One good thing did come out of the incident. General Sir Hastings Ismay† decided that it was high time the Americans were informed about deception so that they might play their part in it as well. He instructed Dudley Clarke to fly to Washington with Colonel Bevan of the London Controlling Section. The outcome of their visit was the close liaison in deception between the British and Americans which was to bring such valuable dividends during the subsequent Allied landings in French North Africa, Sicily and France.

Colonel Dudley Clarke's mission to Washington had yet one other consequence. His absence from Cairo meant that he himself could not be in charge when 'A' Force put over its most ambitious and most successful deception campaign to date, the campaign which enabled General Bernard Montgomery to surprise Rommel both with the timing and the direction of his offensive at El Alamein.

---

* General Fellers reappeared later in charge of Psychological Warfare on General MacArthur's staff in the Pacific.
† Chief of Staff to Churchill in his capacity as Minister of Defence.

Dudley Clarke had left a detailed plan for Wild to follow. Shortly after Clarke had taken off, however, Montgomery changed his battle plan, and the deception plan had to be re-written. But so well had Dudley Clarke indoctrinated his deputy and the rest of the staff that even with the new plan the operation went off as smoothly as if Clarke himself had been in command. It had gone off smoothly, what was more, although it was the first time ever that 'A' Force had followed the method of deception employed on this occasion. Noël Wild had done what Dudley Clarke had been longing to do himself, but for which he had not so far had an opportunity. He had combined all three main methods of deception—visual, fake signals, and double agents—and used all three to put over different aspects of the same deception plan.

Double agents were the most recent addition to the 'A' Force arsenal of deception weapons. Since the end of 1941 Dudley Clarke's organisation had been building up a small group of axis agents whom SIME (Security Intelligence Middle East) had captured and then 'turned round'. The agents ostensibly worked for the Axis. But the messages they sent they sent under British control. 'A' Force supplied their texts. They were transmitted on behalf of the agents in the ciphers supplied by the Axis, at the prearranged times and with the secret check signs the Axis controllers had provided to ensure the message was genuine.

The double agent 'A' Force now proposed to use was not a member of the 'A' Force pool of doubles but a new arrival. Although the man was still untried as far as the British were concerned, it was decided to have him put over the main deception story, while visual deception and fake signals were used in a supporting role. Their task was to back the spy's report with concrete evidence and provided his delighted chiefs with the confirmation that their V-man was telling the truth. Wild was so much impressed with the success and logical rightness of this system that later, when he was in charge of the deception campaign covering the invasion of France, he based his entire operation on it.

It is remarkable that the Germans should have been so naive as to select this particular V-man for such a tricky and important mission. For 'Orlando', as they had code-named him, was not as he pretended, an Italo-Croat from the Dalmatian port of Fiume, but a Jew from the Austrian Burgenland. What was worse from the point of view of his masters in Admiral Canaris's Abwehr, he was a member of the Hagana, the Zionist underground. But what the Abwehr did not know did not bother them. Apart from German, 'Orlando' could speak Arabic, Greek, Italian, and English. (He could also speak Hebrew, but he kept that quiet.) He claimed to have resided in Egypt as a businessman and to possess valuable contacts in Alexandria and Cairo, particularly among anti-British elements in the Egyptian officer corps. What he proposed to the Germans was that he should travel to Egypt ostensibly on business, set up his espionage unit there, then turn round and travel back to Italy before the British had time to suspect what he had been up to. His Egyptian officer friends, he was confident, could supply a transmitter and an operator as well as valuable intelligence.

The Abwehr men jumped at his offer. They provided him with ciphers, call and check-signs, a timetable for sending and receiving. They also provided money for 'Orlando's' Egyptian operatives— £1500 in crisp new five-pound Bank of England notes specially counterfeited for the Abwehr paymasters by the Reich banknote printers and papermakers.

'Orlando' travelled from Italy to Turkey, and thence, with the help of comrades in the Hagana, through Palestine to Cairo. There the Hagana had told him to report immediately to SIME head-quarters. He did so. The chief of the SIME, who had been working closely with Colonel Dudley Clarke, thought 'Orlando' just the man for 'A' Force. And so indeed he turned out to be.

'Orlando' had been quite right in assuring the Abwehr that he would have no difficulty in recruiting first-rate agents and a reliable radio operator. 'A' Force supplied the lot. A corporal of the Royal Signals took charge of the transmissions. The messages, written in the kind of English favoured by a Sandhurst-trained Egyptian officer, were full of most valuable information.

'A' Force would like to have kept 'Orlando' in Cairo until the new service had got well under way. But 'Orlando' persuaded them that it would be more convincing if he stuck to his plans as out-lined to the Abwehr. He was back in Italy by the time his 'Egyptian friends' went into action.

Despite the misgivings of 'A' Force everything went without a hitch. The Germans lived up to their reputation for efficiency. Within a minute of the signals corporal having made his first call at the time and on the date and the frequency arranged with the Germans the answering signal was received from the Abwehr unit in Bari. Whereupon the first message of 'Orlando's' new service was transmitted. 'A' Force was happy. The Abwehr was happy. And 'Orlando' too had every reason to be happy. He had done a splendid job for both his masters.

As everyone knows now, General Montgomery's plan was to stage his main attack in the north while the enemy were to expect it in the centre and the south. As his D-day he had decided on October 23. 'A' Force were to mislead Rommel into assuming that the British attack would be coming some time in November.

They did all that. So completely was Rommel misled over the timing of the British offensive that when the battle began he was at home in Germany on leave. As for its direction, Panzer-General Georg Stumme, who had taken over from Rommel, told his corps and divisional commanders that the British offensive should be expected in the southern sector. In the German intelligence summaries captured after the battle with much other material the reports received from 'Orlando's' V-men were described as coming from a 'reliable source'.

Highlights in the execution of their deception plan by 'A' Force were:

1. The skill with which the armour destined to carry the main thrust in the north was moved by night from its concentration points in the east to the jump-off area. There it took the place of dummy armour which in its turn moved to where the genuine armour had come from. Thus on the reconnaissance pictures of the Axis air force the British dispositions appeared to be unchanged.

2. To confirm the impression already given by 'Orlando's' signals that the main British blow would fall in the south, dummy dumps and dummy camps were built in the southern sector. They even had fake tracks leading to them through the desert. To make enemy observers believe that the water supply for the southern sector was being enlarged in preparation for the offensive a new pipeline was built. It was completely bogus but convincing, if viewed from the air or by untutored Arab eyes from the ground.

To underline that D-day was still a long way off, the pipeline was built at a pace which suggested it would not be ready before mid-November.

3. Bogus signals traffic was laid on to suggest to the radio-location units that the armoured divisions (which had in fact replaced the dummies in the north) were still in their camps in the south.

Not even once the victory was won did 'A' Force let up. The reliable 'Orlando' unit warned the Germans of British plans for a series of landings behind their front. Short as they were of petrol, munitions, and food it must have been a most uncomfortable feeling for Rommel's men that they now had to look over their shoulders for new enemy attacks from their rear.

*   *   *

After their joint mission to Washington, Dudley Clarke and Johnny Bevan saw quite a lot of each other—if you allow for the hundreds of flying miles that lay between Storey's Gate and the Sharya Kasr el Nil in Cairo. Sometimes Dudley Clarke flew to London. More often Bevan flew to Cairo and climbed up the stairs to Dudley Clarke's sanctum in the one-time house of pleasure. There was plenty for them to discuss. Bevan was co-ordinating the deception plans for the landings in French North Africa with the Americans. And, of course, 'A' Force played its part both in the making and the implementation of those plans.

In its elements the scheme—completely successful—was to mislead the Germans about the destination of the Allied convoys. They were tricked into believing that the convoy from the United States, which in fact was making for Casablanca, was destined for Dakar in French West Africa. Almost at the same time the Germans watched the huge Armada from Britain sail through the Straits of Gibraltar into the Mediterranean. Confidently they expected it to head for either the Peloponnese, as their intelligence had been encouraged to believe by 'A' Force, or Sardinia, as LCS had leaked to them. The Führerhauptquartier was completely taken aback when the convey which had been demurely steaming east suddenly changed course for Oran and Algiers.

As 1943 wore on, the impending invasion of France began to

loom larger and larger. Bevan was engaged on designing the deception strategy for the invasion of north-western Europe. In December he appeared once more in Cairo. This time he was appealing for help. General Sir Frederick Morgan, who as Chief of Staff to the Supreme Allied Commander (COSSAC) was in charge of the preliminary planning for the invasion, was clamouring for an officer who could build up a special Anglo-American deception organisation to provide 'cover' for the invasion of Normandy, just as 'A' Force had done for the El Alamein offensive. Could Dudley Clarke recommend someone from his team?

'Your fellows have the experience,' said Bevan. ' "Freddy" Morgan would like you to let him have the man whom you think best fitted for the job.'

Dudley Clarke recommended Noël Wild. Bevan enthusiastically agreed. Together they signalled London. Sir Frederick Morgan was delighted. General Bedell Smith, Eisenhower's Chief of Staff to be, also approved. He had met Wild when Wild visited 'A' Force's advanced headquarters in Algiers and had discussed deception plans with him. He had seen how well Wild worked with his American opposition numbers.

But when Wild set out from Cairo a week before Christmas 1943, he had not been told he was leaving 'A' Force and Egypt for good. He understood he was being sent to London on a routine liaison mission. As he climbed on board the flying boat at Cairo's Nile Airport, Rod el Farag, all he thought of was Christmas in England and seeing his wife again after an absence of two and a half years. He did not learn the truth for another week, not until he was summoned to SHAEF headquarters in Norfolk House a day after his arrival in London.

It was Bedell Smith who broke the news to him there.

'What are your plans, Noël?' asked the General after they had greeted each other.

'I have one or two bits of official business to attend to. After that I hope to take a few days' leave. I expect to be returning to Cairo in about three weeks' time.'

This was the cue Bedell Smith seemed to have been waiting for. 'Well now, Noël,' he said, his voice pitched low, his words coming slowly and impressively, 'I'm afraid you won't be. You see, Dudley

Clarke has very generously agreed to let us keep you here at this headquarters in order that you may organise and take charge of an Anglo-American Deception Unit for Overlord. I hope that is all right with you. I am sorry we had to get you here on false pretences . . . ', and now he grinned again, 'by deception, as it were!'

At this moment Major-General Charles West entered the room. In the absence of 'Freddy' Morgan (who was in hospital) he was the senior British officer at the Norfolk House headquarters. Bedell Smith now announced that he had, as Morgan had previously agreed, asked Wild to take over deception at SHAEF. He turned to Wild. 'It *is* okay by you, Noël, isn't it?'

'Of course, General. Delighted to be given the opportunity of serving under you.'

The three men sat down, Bedell Smith at his desk which had been placed on a dais with his back to the window so that he looked down on his mildly dazzled visitors, Wild and General West opposite him in two easy chairs.

Bedell Smith told Wild that he was giving him *carte blanche*. Anything he needed would be supplied and anyone he asked for would be assigned to his staff. 'There is only one favour I would ask. I would like you to include as many Americans in your team as you possibly can, so that your unit is truly Anglo-American in composition.' Wild immediately agreed to this. 'If you had not offered Americans of your own accord, General, I'd have insisted on having them just the same. Part of that *carte blanche*! We must have new blood and new ideas. Awfully easy to go stale in a game of this kind.'

Wild asked with some anxiety how much time he had to build the machine and get it working on the Germans.

'Very little, I am afraid,' said Bedell Smith. 'We are presently planning D-day for May 5th.'

West suggested that Wild should study the draft plans for the invasion and also the draft deception plan which had already been prepared. 'It is as yet only a draft, but you might find it useful.'

That was how the Anglo-American Deception Unit was born. As Bedell Smith had requested and Colonel Wild had promised— the lieutenant-colonel had been promoted to full colonel on assumption of his SHAEF duties—Americans were introduced

into the new unit at all levels. Wild himself was immediately
responsible to an American officer, Brigadier General Arthur S.
Nevins of SHAEF's G3 Plans Division. (Wild had direct access to
Bedell Smith whenever he needed it and equally to Eisenhower
himself.) His second-in-command was another American, Lieutenant-Colonel 'Freddy' Barnes. Two other Americans serving with
the small SHAEF Deception Unit were Major 'Al' Moody, of the
US Marines, and Major Jack Deane, son of General John R.
Deane, the head of the United States Military Mission in Moscow.*

As with 'A' Force in Cairo, the new deception unit, despite its
differences of nationality, social background, and professional
experience, quickly became an integrated team. British and
American officers thought out their problems, discussed, analysed,
and solved them, not as separate individuals but as a family. An
Anglo-American family.

Nursing the family along during these earliest and most critical
weeks of its existence was Colonel Bevan. They could not have had
a better godfather than this staff officer who in Churchill's underground dungeon at Storey's Gate had founded and masterminded
the London Controlling Section, the first unit to conduct deception
from the British Isles during the Second World War. Bevan advised
Wild on what contacts he should seek and what paths he should
follow in the dangerous jungle of Whitehall. Whenever he thought
it advisable, Bevan escorted Wild and personally introduced him to
the great men. He did so even though he and his LCS were working
full out planning, co-ordinating, and conducting such deception
campaigns as did not come within the scope of the SHAEF Unit.

He assigned to Wild a desk in his own underground office so that
he could be present at the planning conferences of the LCS. He even
made available to him the services of his own intelligence officer on
the staff of the joint planners who edited a daily intelligence digest
for the use of the two colonels. This officer was Wing Commander
Dennis Wheatley, the best-selling thriller writer.

Wild made no secret of the immense help the new Anglo-
American unit was getting from Colonel Bevan.

---

* Major Deane worked with the SHAEF Deception Unit as representative of
6th U.S. Army Group. Colonel W. Harris represented 12th Army Group.

3
20 = XX = Double-cross

During the war, so tradition has it, a certain Spanish diplomat who was a member of Boodle's Club in London's St James's Street used to sit in the club's venerable bay window pretending to read his newspaper. In reality, so the story alleges, he was watching the comings and goings in and out of the big building across the street in order to report on them to the Abwehr. For during the war that building, which after the war housed nothing more sinister than the London offices of Hollywood's Metro Goldwyn Mayer Corporation, was the hush and hush again headquarters of M.I.5, the Counter Intelligence and Security Department of the British Secret Service.

I would love to think that some pro-Nazi Hidalgo was watching from Boodle's on the crisp and frosty morning of Tuesday, January 3, 1944, as the two deception colonels stalked up the steps into the well-screened entrance lobby of M.I.5. For if he had been watching, then he was witnessing an historic occasion. Nothing less than the 'coming of age' of his distinguished fellow countryman 'Cato'.

Wild, who in the meantime had been given an office in Eisenhower's headquarters at Norfolk House as well as that desk in Bevan's dungeon at Storey's Gate, had, in accordance with Bevan's advice, spent most of his time during these first days of his new job calling on the British and American chiefs of the various services and service departments with whom he would be collaborating.

One of his visits had been to Major-General F. de Guingand, Montgomery's Chief of Staff. In the provisional deception plan for the invasion the main emphasis had been put on visual deception and deception by bogus signals traffic. Wild wanted 21st Army Group to take charge of both. They had the equipment. And in Colonel David Strangeways they had an officer on their headquarters staff who had plenty of experience in handling both. He had worked with 'A' Force on the staff of 8th Army at El Alamein.

After this meeting with de Guingand, Wild lunched with Bevan at Brook's Club and it was out of that lunch that the deception colonel's present visit to M.I.5 was born. For over lunch Wild had expounded his conviction that to gain their maximum effect visual and signals deception should be concerted with specially doctored intelligence planted on the enemy by double agents. Bevan listened, while Wild told him of the 'Orlando' outfit's contribution to the deception in the Western Desert.

'Do you happen to know whether M.I.5 have any tame agents in this country?' Wild asked somewhat ingenuously. Bevan grinned mischievously and nodded. 'Think they might let us use one or two of them?'

'They have some very fine ones,' said Bevan pleasantly, 'and I feel sure they would be happy to let you use them. You would, of course, first have to clear everything you want the agents to say or do with M.I.5. As a matter of fact, we at LCS have been conducting a few first tentative exercises with controlled agents, though as yet nothing integrated with signals and dummies. There has been no call for anything on that scale. But I believe M.I.5 will be delighted to have their doubles work for you. You can help them quite a bit, you know. I must arrange for you to meet the chaps whose business it is. Can you manage to be at 58 St James's Street at 11.15 tomorrow morning if I can fix it up?'

What Bevan had not told Wild—and this was why he had smiled at Wild's questions—was that he himself had been a member of this authority, sometimes known as the 'Double-cross Committee' or alternatively as the 'Twenty Club', ever since it was formed early in 1941. He could not tell Wild about it or its functions without first being authorised to do so by M.I.5. When the committee was formed neither Bevan nor the 'Double-cross Committee' had any connection with strategic deception. The committee then was solely concerned with security—the defence of the British Isles against German attempts to infiltrate them with spies.

The round-up of enemy agents in Britain during 1939 and 1940 had revealed that there was a substantial number of them who were only too ready to be 'turned round' and set to work against their Abwehr masters. M.I.5 were eager to have them continue to report home under British control with the text of their messages being supplied by M.I.5. The hope behind this procedure—routine with all counter-intelligence agencies after the capture of a spy—was that if the Germans could be induced to communicate with their men in England, believing them still to be active on their behalf, this would lead M.I.5 to other German operatives as yet undiscovered. Also that the queries put by the Abwehr to its agents would provide a key to enemy intentions.

Clearly, however, the decision to allow messages to reach the enemy could only be taken by an authority with a comprehensive knowledge of the security risks involved. And that is how at the beginning of January 1941 the 'XX' or 'Twenty' Club came to be founded by the Directors of Intelligence. Its members had been delegated from M.I.5 itself, its brother department M.I.6 (whose task was espionage in foreign countries), from the Foreign Office, the Home Defence Executive, and the intelligence departments of the fighting services. Regularly once a week the 'Double-cross Committee' met to consider the agents' messages submitted to it, co-ordinate them, and redraft them where necessary. At the same time the committee interviewed the so-called 'case-officers'. These were the officials of M.I.5 who had been put in charge of the 'reformed' agents. They had the job of looking after them, seeing that they were happy in their work—some of them were still behind prison bars—and not attempting a triple-cross of their new masters. In addition it was the 'case-officers'' duty to provide their charges with the material for their communications to the enemy and see that they sent their messages in the form agreed by the committee.

The 'Twenty Club' had been in session for about twenty minutes when Bevan and Wild were ushered into the third-floor room looking out on to St James's Street where they were holding their weekly meeting that Tuesday. Wild found about a dozen men, all of them in uniform except one, sitting around a large board-room table which took up most of the room. At its head sat a lieutenant-colonel of the Seaforth Highlanders. Next to him an elderly major of the Intelligence Corps who had spent the First War interned as a civilian in Germany. A rotund little man who had been on the staff of the British Consulate in Berlin from 1919 to 1939 sat opposite them. And so too did a shrewd-eyed financier with a bald round head who was a leader of the British insurance world. The

American OSS, forerunner of today's CIA, was represented by a New York newspaper publisher, a man of wide-reaching experience. Wild was impressed.

Fortunately the same was true of the committee, when Bevan had introduced him, and Wild was called on to explain how it could help with what Churchill called the task of 'mystifying and misleading the enemy'* as regards the coming invasion. The 'Twenty Club' members, far from treating Wild as an interloper about to trespass on their preserves, welcomed him. It was as Bevan had correctly anticipated: the defensive phase of the 'Twenty Club's' operations against the enemy was to all intents over. They now wanted to put the V-men they controlled to a more aggressive use. But how? Wild with his deception plan was the answer. He could provide an overall objective, a thematic framework for their reports to the Abwehr, and the material to include in them. The committee almost broke into applause when they learned of Wild's scheme to integrate visual and wireless deception with that of double agents, the three being blended and harmonised to corroborate and support each other and add up together to a picture which would trap Hitler and his intelligence into a catastrophically mistaken reading of the Allied intentions.

Right there and then Bevan, Wild, and the members of the committee got down to the task of reviewing the 'cases' of the almost embarrassingly rich choice of double agents M.I.5 had to offer. There were more than a dozen of them, all trusted V-men well established in the confidence of their German clients.

Wild pointed out that it would require superman feats of jugglery to keep even four or five deception agents in play simultaneously in the same campaign. More than that and there would be a risk of losing control and the whole team being blown. For, of course, the stories told by the agents had to be carefully co-ordinated so that they were not identified as being inspired by the same source.

One factor, however, quickly narrowed down the field: only three of the operatives had radio transmitters at their disposal.†

---

* Winston Churchill, *The Second World War*, Vol. V, page 358.
† It would, of course, have been easy for M.I.5 to supply transmitters, but unless this was agreed with the Abwehr in advance it would have aroused German suspicions.

The rest were scathingly dismissed as 'letter-writers'—correspondents who communicated with the Abwehr by writing letters in secret ink to cover addresses in neutral countries. This was a slow cumbrous method of communication, not really suited to the urgency of the task which lay ahead. Wild decided to concentrate on the agents with transmitters. He would use the letter-writers to fill in the occasional convincing detail.

The three agents with radio sets were the Spaniard, identified by his Abwehr controlling officer in Madrid as 'Cato', a Polish military attaché whose Abwehr code-name was 'Talleyrand', and a Dutch staff officer known to the Germans as 'Paul'. The 'Double-cross Committee' had been hesitating whether to allow 'Paul', a recent arrival, to be used for deception operations. But at the end of February they agreed to his inclusion in the SHAEF team. By doing so they made available a most redoubtable performer, the equal, and, in the belief of some of Colonel Wild's British and American colleagues, perhaps even the superior of 'Cato'.

The reason for the committee's hesitation was understandable. 'Paul' had only arrived in England from Holland late in 1943 and under circumstances which were bound to arouse suspicion, even though Dr J. M. Somer, the chief of the Dutch intelligence service in London, had known 'Paul' for many years before the war and guaranteed him to be a loyal and patriotic Dutchman.

The trouble was that 'Paul's' own story revealed that the Germans had sent him to Britain to spy for them 'Paul' under the auspices of SOE* had been operating a spy ring against the Germans since the earliest days of Holland's occupation. By the end of 1942 it had extended over most of Holland, Belgium, and Luxembourg. But the poor security arrangements which characterised so many SOE operations at this time allowed his network to be infiltrated by German agents. 'Paul' himself and thirty-six of his associates were arrested. Fortunately for him, his captor, Sturmbannführer (SS-Major) J. Schreieder, was jealous of the kudos won by the military Abwehr†

---

* SOE = The Special Operations Executive.

† The SIPO (Sicherheitspolizei = Security Police) came under the RSHA (Reichs Sicherheits Hauptamt = Chief Reich Security Office), which in turn came under Heinrich Himmler and was fighting a bitter war against the Abwehr (= Defence), a military organisation responsible for espionage and counter-espionage. Himmler was trying to take over the Abwehr and put it under the authority of the RSHA.

service in capturing and 'turning round' radio operators parachuted into Holland by the Dutch section of SOE. Schreieder, who represented the SIPO security police organisation, was anxious to beat the Abwehr at their own game by recruiting a captured Dutch agent to spy on the Allies in England and report on Allied invasion preparations. He picked on 'Paul' because he knew him to be not only an experienced staff officer but one who was intimately connected with Prince Bernhard and the Dutch royal family. If he could nobble 'Paul', decided Schreieder, he would have a prize indeed.

Schreieder's first move was to order 'Paul' to be transferred to the former theological college at Haaren which SIPO used to accommodate its most important prisoners. 'Paul', of course, guessed what Schreieder was up to the very first time Schreieder went to work on him. If nothing else would have given him away, it was the air of 'comradely sympathy' as one officer to another which this rotund little man with the bald bullet head adopted towards him. That and his false joviality.

Schreieder offered 'Paul' cigarettes, Dutch gin, and Amstel beer, luxuries normally reserved for the German occupiers. He began to talk of his deep personal concern over the tragedy of finding Germany at war with the Dutch 'brother-people', the need to end that war as quickly as possible and his anxiety to keep human suffering at a minimum.

'Paul' played the tough Hollander who had no illusions about the feelings of the SIPO towards their Dutch 'brothers'. All he was interested in, he told Schreieder, was the fate of his captured associates. That was exactly the opening Schreieder wanted. He rose to the bait with the eagerness of a pike snapping at an artificial mouse with a hook inside it.

'I am afraid things look very black for them,' said Schreieder with the expression of a pious pawnbroker dropping a penny in the collection box for the heathen. 'I was discussing their case only this morning with my superior, Brigadeführer Naumann. Not only do all thirty-six of them appear to be guilty of espionage, but many of them have also been helping to distribute guerilla arms dropped by the British. I do not need to tell you what the punishment would be should they come up for trial.'

And then Schreieder made his offer. He could arrange to let 'Paul'

escape and make his way to England, if he in turn would undertake
to send the Germans reports as good as those he had been sending the
Dutch intelligence in England from Holland and Belgium.

'We have read your reports,' he told 'Paul', 'with the greatest
admiration. They were magnificent, if you will permit an enemy
officer to say so. Quite magnificent!'

'Paul' pretended to be flattered, but he still held out. He held out
until Schreieder came across with an offer to spare the lives of
all the captured members of his group. In the end 'Paul' agreed on
condition that their lives were spared and that he would not be
expected to spy against the Dutch.

'I'll help you fight the others,' he said, 'but not my own people.'

Schreieder agreed to that. A regular contract was now drawn up
between the Dutch officer and the SS major. In return for 'Paul's'
services the lives of his captured comrades would be spared. Allegedly with the approval of Himmler himself the Germans
promised that in the event of 'Paul' performing some signal service
which hastened Germany's final victory the Netherlands would be
rewarded for this in the peace treaty. Schreieder for his part added a
clause to the contract to the effect that the SIPO would not be
bound by its promise to spare the lives of the Dutchman's comrades, if 'Paul' revealed to the Allies that he had undertaken to work
for the Germans.

The agreement duly signed and sealed, 'Paul' was instructed in
what was required of him, even though espionage at this time was
strictly outside the SIPO's sphere of responsibilities. He was even
shown how to build a wireless transmitter out of parts on sale to the
public in London. The next step came on August 31, the holiday
which the Dutch even during the occupation celebrated as 'Queen's
Day'.

On the pretext that he was being taken to the RSHA headquarters
in the Binnenhof at The Hague, a SIPO car collected 'Paul' from
Haaren. As the German car was slowly passing through a narrow
street crowded with people, 'Paul' suddenly flung open a doo.,
plunged out into the street, and vanished into the crowd. It was a
thoroughly convincing escape.

As agreed with Schreieder, 'Paul' then made his way through
Belgium, France, and Spain to Portugal, and eventually to Britain.

Once in Britain, he immediately revealed his mission to the authorities, Dutch and British.

Misgivings about 'Paul' were increased when he revealed that among the inmates of the Haaren College were a number of Dutch radio operators captured by the Abwehr. 'Everything that is being dropped to them, arms and agents alike,' said 'Paul', 'is going straight into the hands of the Germans. The captured operators have done their best in their signals to warn London. But no one has taken any notice.'

Alas for 'Paul'! The SOE Dutch section just would not believe him. They thought the Germans had either deceived 'Paul' or persuaded him to give this 'false' information in order to stop what was considered the most successful parachutist operation in any of the occupied countries.

So when 'Paul' was first allowed to transmit messages to his masters at Hamburg (to show them he had arrived and was ready for action) he was given only the tamest of material, a fact that did not go unremarked at the receiving end. 'The first signals with which it had been arranged he should report reached the RSHA at the end of December 1943', says one German report on 'Paul'.

The officers of the General Staff who received his signals were well pleased with them. There were no signs that his reports were intended to mislead. It is almost certain however that he had informed British intelligence of his arrangements and that the British thereupon formulated messages which arrived at RSHA headquarters as messages from the Dutchman. That the British refrained from including deception material in the Dutchman's messages must have been out of consideration for his comrades in German captivity. From a British point of view his messages were no doubt without importance. But for Germany they were by no means uninteresting.

To be sure they were not! There is plenty of evidence (which I shall present in due course) that from March 1944 onwards, when 'Paul's' messages were fully loaded with deception material, they had precisely the effect which the Anglo-American team helping 'Paul' to devise them intended.

What had removed the 'Double-cross Committee's' doubts about 'Paul' was the arrival in England of two of the captured Dutch radio operators from Haaren. They had managed to break out of the 'Theological college' by lowering themselves from a window with ropes made of strips from their mattresses. The sentries guarding the outside of the prison were members of the Dutch SS who were only too anxious to redeem themselves in the eyes of the Dutch underground by helping the escapers.

Apart from their own stories, the fugitives had been able to learn enough from their fellow captives to put an end to Operation 'North Pole', a brilliant hoax with which the Abwehr had duped the Dutch section of SOE for close on two years. Their reports removed the last vestiges of mistrust from 'Paul' who was now able to play his part in what turned out to be an even more successful hoax than 'North Pole' had been, and a very much more important one.

In a category all of his own among the Abwehr's British controlled agents was the Pole, number three in Colonel Wild's team. Like the two others, 'Talleyrand' had his own clandestine transmitter. (That is to say, the Germans accepted that he had one. In fact like the two other agents' transmitters it was supplied by M.I.5 and operated by the Royal Corps' of Signals.) He was, however, unique in that the 'Double-cross Committee' permitted him to commute between Britain and Lisbon and meet his German controller there.

He used to meet him at a secret rendezvous. There he was given elaborate intelligence questionnaires which he took back to London to answer. Like all intelligence agencies, M.I.5 liked to know what the other fellows wanted to find out and the questionnaires were much appreciated in St James's Street. 'Talleyrand' had many cosy chats with his German controller in Lisbon during which he mixed him an appetising cocktail of true and false information.

Clearly this was a most hazardous undertaking. Noël Wild was sick with worry every time his man went to face his Abwehr interlocutor. Not that Wild was excessively disturbed about the personal fate of 'Talleyrand'. The chance of abduction or assassination was something every agent had to face in wartime. That was implicit in his job when he took it on. What troubled Wild was that 'Talleyrand' might give himself away and thus break a vital link in the SHAEF chain of deception. Wild's confidence was fortified however by the cover story which 'Talleyrand' had been given to explain the amazing British willingness to allow him to travel to Lisbon.

'I am working for a secret department in the British War Office,' 'Talleyrand' told his German masters with disarming frankness. 'My job is to organise the escapes of RAF men from Poland and Germany, get them to Lisbon, and from there to Britain. If you could allow the occasional prisoner of war to escape to me it will be much easier to convince the British that my little trips are worth while. And it will keep them from suspecting the truth.'

Is it that the Germans are essentially more trusting than the British? Or was it that the Nazi superman complex had inspired in the Abwehr and their colleagues of Himmler's Security Service a rash contempt for the cunning of their adversaries? The British, if anything, erred in the other direction, holding the prowess of the German intelligence service in far greater awe than it deserved.

When 'Talleyrand' had his first tête-à-tête with his Abwehr controller in Lisbon at the beginning of March—until then he had been sending his messages by radio—he had the impression that he was suspected of passing planted material. His reception was distinctly frigid. At his next meeting, however, the climate was one of warmth and friendly trust. Presumably Colonel Rohleder, the chief of Department III F in Berlin, had examined his report in the meantime and found it to his liking. Indeed, evidence came to hand later that at first Department III F had suspected that 'Talleyrand' might be duped by the British. His dispatches, they thought, confined themselves to the trivialities which the British might well have been prepared to leak to diplomats. 'Talleyrand' had been warned by the Germans that his reports were not worth the money he was being paid for them. Under this threat, so Rohleder and Department III F congratulated themselves, 'Talleyrand' had begun to scout around for himself. His latest excellent report was the result. Department III F and their colleagues in the Foreign Armies West Department of the General Staff ruled that it was inconceivable that the British could have fed anything like it for deception purposes.*

---

* Colonel Rohleder is one of the many old hands of the Abwehr and SD who is still active in the Intelligence Service of Bonn's new Federal Republic. Rohleder joined General Reinhard Gehlen, the war-time opposite number of

Whatever the explanation, the Abwehr accepted 'Talleyrand's' story that his mission to Lisbon was authorised by the British only because he hoped to lay on an escape route for RAF men who had crashed in Germany or were being held in prisoner-of-war camps in Poland. They arranged for a few airmen to get away to Lisbon so that 'Talleyrand' could take the credit. The information he gave them in exchange they regarded as a very good bargain.

That information was indeed heady stuff—priceless for a body so starved of genuine intelligence as were the Germans about the preparations in Britain for 'Overlord'.*

Tragically, 'Talleyrand' did not stay the course to the final phase of the Great Deception. An intimate associate of his in Lisbon who knew the secret of his double game and was playing it himself was abducted to Germany by the Himmler Security Service. It looked as though 'Talleyrand' must be blown. Colonel Wild and Colonel Bevan for an unhappy few days considered the possibility that the whole of their deception enterprise was in ruins. They thought of closing down 'Paul' and 'Cato' as well as 'Talleyrand'. But within a few days evidence was received which convinced them and their friends in the 'Double-cross Committee' that both 'Paul' and 'Cato' were being received, read, and believed, as before. Probably 'Talleyrand' also could have continued.

The colonels, however, did not take the risk of letting 'Talleyrand' rejoin the team. For German consumption the story was put out that M.I.5 had come to suspect the Polish military attaché of being a German agent. All was well, however. Even with only two top agents the SHAEF deception team was still more than a match for the Germans.

I have outlined what I have been able to establish of 'Paul's' background. But what of 'Cato', for whom the decision of the 'Double-cross Committee' on this morning of January 3, 1944, to

---

von Roenne, as chief of the Department Foreign Armies East, when the Americans invited Gehlen to rebuild his service under their auspices (and financed by them). Rohleder did so in his old capacity as head of counter-espionage, Department III F.

* 'Overlord' was the Allied code-name for the invasion—known to the Abwehr since December 1943, when the Albanian valet of the British ambassador in Ankara had passed to them photographs of the dispatches in his master's safe.

put their troupe of double agents into the service of SHAEF's deception unit meant that he had 'come of age' as an agent, that his most important work was now about to begin? For me, as I study his history, he is the epitome of all the brave men who pretended to enter the service of the Third Reich with the intention of destroying it from within.

His story is full of the unexpected, not the least paradox being the fact that he might never have been recruited by the professionals of the British Secret Service but for the hunch of a young American who up to that time had little more than a student's interest in the international world of cloaks and daggers—and no practical experience of it.

4

A Spaniard Goes to War

Jorge Antonio—I am no more prepared to reveal 'Cato's' full name than are his former 'colleagues' of the Abwehr and SD,* I will confine myself to his two Christian names†—was a slim young Spaniard of medium height whose main features were a high forehead, a face of ascetic, almost El Grecoish, angularity, and eyes which impressed you with the burning sincerity of the man behind them.

He had just turned twenty-nine in the late summer of 1940. Hitler was at the height of his triumph. Denmark, Norway, the Low Countries and France had been overrun almost as easily as Poland the year before. On the frontier bridge across the Bidasoa river, between Spanish Irun and French Hendaye, Hitler's Feldpolizei were fraternising with Generalissimo Franco's carabineros. Rumours were strong that Franco contemplated following the example of Mussolini in the hope of picking up a share of the victor's loot. He had his eye in particular on Gibraltar and French North Africa. Britain alone in Europe was still defying Hitler.

And though the Battle of Britain between the Luftwaffe and the Royal Air Force appeared to be going in Britain's favour, Jorge Antonio was a very unhappy young man. He feared Hitler was going to win the war and he did not want him to win it.

A German victory would mean the perpetuation of Franco's

---

* SD= Sicherheits Dienst= Security Service. RSHA—Reichs Sicherheits Hauptamt= Chief Reich Security Office. Both were names for the Himmler intelligence service which took over from the Abwehr of Admiral Canaris in 1944.

† I do not identify 'Cato' because, although he himself is now dead, his family lives in a part of the world where there are organisations of unregenerate and militant Nazis who might be tempted to avenge 'Cato's' double-cross of the Führer on his widow and their children. A kind of belated 'Sippenhaft', as the system was called under which the family of a man who worked against the Nazi régime was punished as well as the man himself.

police state. The only hope for Spain, he believed, lay in the defeat of Hitler by the British.

In a way this attitude of Jorge Antonio's was surprising. For when the Civil War broke out which was to put Franco and the Falangists in power Jorge Antonio had every opportunity to join the anti-Fascists. But he did not do so. He was in Madrid studying electrical engineering to qualify for a career he had been offered with an electrical concern not far from his home town of Alsasua. As a student—and an engineering student at that—he might well have been expected to join the students and workers who had over-powered the Madrid garrison when it rose in rebellion against the left-wing Republican Government and who were now fighting the insurgent armies marching on Madrid. But Jorge Antonio had a mind of his own. He was outraged by the brutality and lawlessness with which even before the Army's rebellion the so-called 'demo-crats' had burned and sacked churches and convents, murdered nuns and priests, and with which at the start of the Civil War they stood anyone against the wall whom they believed to be a member of the hated bourgeoisie.

Everywhere in Madrid at that time men and women of the upper and middle classes were either trying to escape to the parts of Spain held by the insurgents or going into hiding. Preferably they tried to find refuge in one of the foreign embassies, or, if they could not manage that, in one of the many houses protected by a foreign power which the Republican Government was anxious not to offend. That was what Jorge Antonio did. He hid in the house of a Madrid doctor who was an old friend of his family.

By virtue of being married to an Englishwoman and himself being appointed to the British Embassy as a physician this doctor had acquired a Union Jack which he flew over his house in the outskirts of Madrid and a letter signed and sealed by the British Consul General. This was prominently displayed on his front door. The letter proclaimed that the house, its contents and occupants (duly identified by name), were under British protection. An endorsement by the Chief of Police declared the doctor's house to be the Spanish equivalent of 'off limits'.

Despite the Union Jack, despite the letter of protection and its imposing seals, agents of the SIM (the Service of Military Investigation, as Republican Spain's Security Service was called), paid no fewer than eight visits to the doctor's home between September 1936 and October 1937.

'You will excuse us, Doctor, I am sure,' the captain in charge of the search party would say, 'we know how wholeheartedly you support the cause of democracy. But we have reason to believe that without your knowledge or that of the señora members of the Fifth Column have been using your house as a base for their nefarious activities.'

Eight times the doctor's home was raided and searched without the SIM finding Jorge Antonio or the two other men hidden there. On the ninth occasion, however, they found them. Jorge Antonio, the doctor, his wife, and the two other 'guests' were driven away under arrest. In the early days of the Civil War they would undoubtedly have been taken to the bullring and shot without more ado. By November 1937, however, the revolutionary ardour of the 'Loyalists' had cooled somewhat. The doctor and his wife were released that same day after a perfunctory interrogation. Only Jorge Antonio and the two other 'Fifth Columists' were kept in gaol.

And even then Jorge Antonio did not remain a prisoner for more than five months. When he had satisfied the police that he had no connection with Franco or the 'Fifth Column', and even expressed an eagerness to join the Republican Army, the SIM officer conducting his examination supported his application. With his technical knowledge of electronics and electrical engineering, the man from the SIM argued, Jorge Antonio could be useful to the Army. He was released from gaol and posted to a signals unit where he was trained in radio telegraphy.

Jorge Antonio did not, however, remain with General Rojo's signals unit for long. By 1938 the Spanish War had become a fast-moving war. Soon Jorge Antonio had an opportunity to escape. He took it, and deserted to the forces of Generalissimo Franco. The Spanish Nationalists accepted him as they had accepted so many other deserters from the Republican Army. And, of course, his record of incarceration by the Spanish 'Reds' and his subsequent escape and service with Franco stood him in good stead not only in Franco's army but when he became 'Cato' and went to work for

Franco's German ally and benefactor. In fact, however, his experiences in the Franco army were the finishing touch in turning this young Spaniard against the Caudillo and his régime.

I don't know what psychological factor it was that made this young engineer such a determined enemy of whichever side in the Civil War to which he happened to find himself attached. I suspect it was the Basque in him. For though Jorge Antonio's father was a Castilian from Burgos, his mother was a Basque and he was brought up in the little town of Alsasua near which his father owned and managed a flourishing textile mill. His father died when Jorge Antonio was only eleven years old, and his mother never lost an opportunity of impressing on her son the ancient liberal traditions of the once independent Basque people. It seems probable that his devotion to Basque tradition put him against both Franco and the 'Reds', for neither the Nationalists nor the Communist-dominated Republicans were prepared to recognise the aspirations of the Basques to autonomy.

After the Civil War his Basque patriotism was reinforced by his sense of outraged Spanish pride and resentment of what he considered Franco's craven appeasement of Hitler in even contemplating the possibility that Spain might join the Axis and go to war on the side of the arrogant Teuton aggressors. It was this sense of outraged Hispanidad that caused him to take a stroll one day towards the end of September and call in at the British Embassy in Madrid's Calle Fernando el Santo. Somehow he managed to persuade the doorkeeper to let him see George Young, who presided over the ambassador's ante-chamber. 'Jerry', as his friends called him, was his usual gay and friendly self when Jorge Antonio came out with his proposal that he should serve Britain as a spy against the Axis powers. Jerry brought out a bottle and a couple of glasses from his desk and offered the would-be secret agent a drink. Then he broke the disillusioning news to him.

'I am afraid His Britannic Majesty's Embassy has nothing to do with espionage and that sort of thing. The Foreign Office would never approve, you know.' Which was pretty cool of Jerry, who as Duncan Sandys's successor as Third Secretary in the Berlin Embassy had himself pulled off some remarkable intelligence coups against the Third Reich.

'Well, if you don't have anything to do with such things,' Jorge Antonio persisted, 'who does?'

'I have no idea, my dear fellow, no idea,' said Jerry. 'Have another drink.'

Jorge Antonio went on trying. He tried the British Council, which all Spaniards regarded as a branch of the intelligence service. But Walter Starkie was as bland as Jerry Young. He tried the British Information Service, and the Commercial Secretariat. All to no avail. Eventually he landed up with the inevitable 'Major Thompson' —no such name figured in the diplomatic list—who, after asking him all sorts of questions about himself and how he proposed to set about the job, sent him packing with a flea in his ear. What Jorge Antonio had proposed to the 'Major' was nothing less than what 'Cato' was eventually to put into practice. He would get himself recruited as a spy by the Germans and then in that capacity find out what they wanted to know and plant false information on them. 'Major Thompson' dismissed the idea as old hat—which it certainly was—and Jorge Antonio himself as an agent provocateur set on him by either the German Abwehr or the Spanish Police. The next few times that Jorge Antonio called the 'Major' was unavailable. He had gone on leave, Jorge was told. No one else would see him.

Undaunted, Jorge Antonio decided to try the Germans instead. If he could prove to the British that the Germans had taken him on and believed in him, then perhaps they would change their minds. So off he went to call on the Germans in their embassy in the Castellana, a building which held none too pleasant memories for him from the time of the Civil War, when the SIM had used it as a prison and interrogation centre.

The Germans were much more forthcoming than the British. As Franco's allies they could afford to be. They did not have to watch their step as carefully as their British counterparts found politic in the Madrid of 1940, which, though officially non-belligerent, was in some ways almost Axis territory. Jorge Antonio was passed on to an official who took down his particulars and listened to his proposition.

This was that he should use the business connections of his family's textile firm to get himself sent to Britain as a buyer of spare parts for their textile machinery. With his representation of the family firm he proposed to combine the representation of a firm of Valencia fruit exporters. 'The British cannot do without our oranges,' he chuckled. 'War or no war, they must have their orange marmalade!'

The correspondence his commercial activities would involve, he suggested, would give him good opportunities for sending valuable information to the Germans in Madrid. 'I am not after money,' he declared. 'I want to help you because you and your glorious Condor Legion helped us during the Civil War. Also, because my personal experiences during the Civil War have convinced me that the only man who can unite Europe and give it the new order it needs is the Führer, Adolfo Hitler. Britain, the eternal obstacle to the unification of Europe, must be eliminated and the sooner the better. Anything I can do to bring that about I am ready to do. If necessary I will give my life.'

The Germans must have checked up on Jorge Antonio's past record and found it satisfactory. And why not? Arrest by the SIM after more than a year in hiding, his desertion to the army of Generalissimo Franco at the first opportunity—everything spoke in his favour. His proposition to go to England as a businessman representing his family firm—they checked on that as well, and found it in good standing—was most promising.

Berlin thought so too and instructed the KO Madrid (an Abwehr station in a neutral country was referred to in Abwehr jargon as a K.O.—Kriegs-Organisation to contact Jorge Antonio again and, if they still thought him suitable material, to provide him with the necessary equipment and speed him on his way to Britain.

Apart from Jorge Antonio's record, there was yet another and most imperative reason why the Abwehr should accept Jorge Antonio's tempting offer. In the spring of 1940, when Hitler had begun his offensive against the West with the attack on Norway, the code-breakers of Goering's Forshungsamt★ and the German Navy's B-Service† had been intercepting, deciphering, and reading British signals with the greatest of ease. But in August the British ciphers had been fundamentally changed. The code-breakers' job had become more difficult—much more difficult.

★ Forschungsamt = Research Office.
† B-Dienst = Beobachtungsdienst = Observation Service.

The intelligence reports of the code-breakers which kept the U-boat service and the German battle fleet informed of every movement made by the British Navy and the Merchant Marine had suddenly dried up. Admiral Canaris, head of the German intelligence service, was clamouring for agents to be sent to England who would supply from observation on the ground the information which the code-breakers were at least temporarily unable to provide and Luftwaffe reconnaissance patrols owing to increased RAF opposition and their own inefficiency did not seem able to obtain either. For a terrible thing had happened.

Almost at the same time as the Germans overran France the last German agents in Britain were rounded up by Scotland Yard's 'Special Branch' working in close co-operation with M.I.5. The agents' reports had dried up as dramatically as those of the code-breakers. Only a trickle still came through. It was essential to send in new under-cover men unknown to the British to carry out visual reconnaissance, particularly in the ports.

As a result of this urgency, Jorge Antonio had two further meetings with the Germans within a fortnight of his first visit to them. This time he did not meet them at the embassy but at a flat in the Calle Velazquez. The first time a young man received him who spoke perfect Spanish. He invited Jorge Antonio to call him Jaime and never to refer to him by any other name. Not that Jorge Antonio could have done so, because at that time he did not know Fritz Knappe-Ratey under his real name. Jaime suggested that at their next meeting Jorge Antonio should bring along the letter of invitation from the firm in Britain which had proposed that he should visit their works in Lancashire, and inspect the textile machinery they were offering for sale.

Fortunately Jorge Antonio had already prepared such a letter. It was an exact copy of one his family firm had received early in 1939. It was a perfect forgery complete with engraved letter-head and carefully forged signature. Even type and the size and shape of the note-paper was correct. The only thing changed was that he had substituted a more recent date of dispatch.

Two Germans were present in the flat in the Calle Velazquez at his next visit—Jaime and an elderly military character whom Jaime introduced as his boss Alfonso. Alfonso was General Erich Kühlenthal, a former military attaché of the German peacetime embassy in Paris, who was now the second-in-command of the Madrid KO. The two of them inspected the letter and seemed quite satisfied with it. 'Alfonso' asked whether Jorge Antonio had kept the envelope. But it did not seem to upset him when Jorge Antonio said he had destroyed it. 'Alfonso', alias Kühlenthal, then asked Jorge Antonio how he proposed to get to England.

'I think it would be best if I travel to Lisbon first and apply for my English visa there. It will look better to the British, if I approach them in Portugal, which is a country friendly to them, rather than in Spain which is not. Besides, there is an air service from Lisbon to England and none from here.'

'Better look out that you don't get yourself shot down by the Luftwaffe!' said 'Alfonso' with a jovial chuckle.

So that was it. 'Alfonso' Kühlenthal agreed that Jorge Antonio should travel to England via Portugal, and even undertook to fix him up with the necessary facilities in the way of a Spanish exit visa and a Portuguese transit permit. He also provided some foreign currency—Portuguese escudos, pounds sterling, and US dollars.

'If you find yourself running out of funds to finance your operations when you are in England just let us know. We can send you more. Your status as a businessman will allow you to receive transfers from abroad without arousing suspicion.'

Then he asked Jorge Antonio to allow himself to be measured for a new suit. 'Jaime' did the measuring himself with all the expertise of a Savile Row cutter. 'We have some special wadding,' he explained, 'which can be sewn in as stuffing under the lining. You can remove a little of it at a time, soak it in water with a solution of quinine hydrochloride which you can get from any chemist's shop and you'll find it provides you with an absolutely secure form of invisible ink. A little invention of our German chemists!'

He produced a sample of saffron-coloured wadding, soaked it in water, added the quinine solution and dipped a pen in it. He wrote a few words on a piece of paper without leaving the slightest trace. But when he brushed it with a solution of iodine and calcium chloride it became visible and legible, just like a photographic print in a developer.

With a noble gesture of sacrifice Jorge Antonio immediately

volunteered to leave the gabardine raincoat he was wearing with 'Jaime' to have it stuffed with the wadding as well. 'No,' ruled 'Jaime', 'a raincoat is not really suitable. It might get wet, and then the ink would be used up to no purpose. It's very precious stuff, our yellow wadding!'

The most important items of his espionage equipment, however, were not handed to Jorge Antonio until his third and last meeting with the Abwehr men. In addition to the new suit he was then provided with a Spanish dictionary, the 1928 edition of the Pequeño Larousse, a mini camera capable of reducing either his own dispatches or any documents that might come his way to microdots which with the aid of a kind of syringe he could insert as harmless punctuation marks into any typewritten document he might be sending to his German masters.

For one moment of ecstatic anticipation Jorge Antonio thought he was going to be handed a radio transmitter. 'You were trained as a radio operator during the Civil War, weren't you?' 'Jaime' asked him. 'Do you think you could operate one again?'

Jorge Antonio said he felt sure he could. But all he got were instructions on how to build himself a transmitter with spare parts, obtainable, said 'Jaime' knowledgeably, in any London radio shop. 'Jaime' assumed that Jorge Antonio's technical experience made it unnecessary for him to be given the usual lesson on how to assemble the apparatus.

The Larousse he was told would provide him with a cipher. 'You take the day of the month and add or subtract a number from it which we will give you. The number produced is the number of the page. The first word in the first column is your code-word.'

For the time being, however, he would confine himself to messages written in secret ink in between the lines of harmless-looking business letters which he would send by courier. And by courier he would be sent a radio cipher when he could report that he had built a transmitter.

'We shall give you a key to a safe-deposit box at the Espiritu Santo Bank in Lisbon,' 'Jaime' went on. 'A duplicate will be in our possession. Your courier—and selecting a courier is going to be your first really testing task—will deliver your package to the safe-deposit box. We will collect it from there, and at the same time leave our mail to you in the same box for the courier to pick up and deliver to you in England. Think you can work that all right?' Jorge Antonio said he would do his best.

General Kühlenthal, alias 'Alfonso', had been listening to his subordinate instructing Jorge Antonio in the technical side of his communication methods without saying a word. Now it was his turn to brief the Abwehr's new Spanish recruit as to what kind of intelligence he should concentrate on getting.

Not unnaturally it was intelligence of interest mainly to the Navy, particularly the U-boats and to the Luftwaffe—the two services most actively engaged in fighting the war against Britain at this time.

Kühlenthal wanted Jorge Antonio to report the extent of damage from the Luftwaffe bombing raids. He wanted to hear of the effects of bombing on British civilian morale. How much absenteeism was it causing among British workers? Were they failing to clock in at their factories, and, if so, was it because they were afraid the place might be bombed, or because of transport chaos, or because their homes had been destroyed? He would be grateful for information about British aircraft production, what new factories were being built and where. He would welcome any technical details of new types of aircraft or electronic equipment which Jorge Antonio's engineering experience might enable him to collect.

He was thirsting for information, too, about the times of arrival, departure and expected arrival in British waters, of Atlantic convoys. He wanted anything that would indicate the routes followed, for instance their points of assembly. And he wanted any information Jorge Antonio could pick up about independently routed ships. It was a tall order, this long catalogue of questions, for a lone civilian travelling to a country he had never visited before and whose language he did not speak. But Kühlenthal had no misgivings on that score. He had a solution to offer.

'Don't hesitate to take on sub-agents to help with your work,' he urged. 'But be careful not to compromise yourself when doing so. Before you recruit a sub-agent I suggest you had better consult us. Describe him or her, so that we can advise you whether in our opinion the candidate is suitable. The British are good at planting stoolpigeons. If they suspect you, their police might do just that!

You have never done this sort of work before, have you?' Kühlenthal added, giving Jorge Antonio one of those theatrical X-ray stares beloved of spy-masters in all the best espionage fiction.

'No,' said Jorge Antonio. 'But I will tread carefully and try to learn the trade as I tread!'

'That is the spirit,' said Kühlenthal with a smile of fatherly approval. 'And remember we are here to help you all we can!'

That system of sub-agents recommended by General Kühlenthal was to prove an invaluable asset to Jorge Antonio once he had become 'Cato' and Operation 'Ganelon' had got under way. For not only did it enable him to cover a vast terrain, but in the event of any of his deception stories being proved false by his German customers he could always blame one of his sub-agents for the error. Before the war was over, 'Cato' employed a whole 'orchestra' of them, as German Abwehr jargon described an espionage group. 'Cato' conducted no fewer than twenty-five 'instrumentalists', all of them—including that distinguished trio, 'Freddy', 'Dick', and 'Desmond'*—approved by Kühlenthal prior to their engagement, all of them paid for by him, and all of them completely fictitious. Jorge Antonio never revealed their identities to his German masters, however much they might badger him for this information.

'That would endanger the security of our operations,' was his invariable answer. 'Wait until the final victory is won. I will tell you then.' All that he did was to describe the agent and his potential usefulness. Fortunately Kühlenthal was so pleased with the information 'Cato' was providing that he left well alone and did not press him any further.

As soon as he received his marching orders from Kühlenthal, Jorge Antonio called once more at the office of 'Major Thompson'. Once more the British turned him down. But this time they did at least make a note of the 'Poste restante' address in Cascais near Lisbon where Jorge Antonio said he would establish his secret headquarters. 'If you change your minds you'll be able to find me there,' were Jorge Antonio's last words—evidence of the immense trust he placed in the British.

On November 26, 1940, Jorge Antonio travelled from Spain to

---

* Mentioned in 'Cato's' report, Chapter 1.

Portugal on the passport and visas obligingly supplied to him by the Abwehr and promptly went into hiding.

Only three months later, on February 27, 1941, he delivered his first message to Kühlenthal. He himself placed it in the safe-deposit box at the Espiritu Santo Bank in Lisbon which Kühlenthal had proposed should serve as his post-box.

The letter was dated February 15, 1941, and stated that he had established himself without difficulty in Britain. He gave a harrowing picture of the demoralisation and defeatism he had found both in London and in Manchester, the seat of the textile-machinery firm with which he was negotiating.

'Both are cities,' he said, 'where you can go for days without seeing a smile.' The population was in abject fear of the Luftwaffe raids and furious with Churchill for turning down Hitler's 'generous offer of peace'. He said he was sending the letter by a venal steward of the BOAC flying boat which plied between England and Lisbon. He had made friends with him during his flight from Lisbon. For a fee of a dollar a letter the steward undertook both to deliver his letters to Lisbon and to collect any mail that might be awaiting him in the box at the bank. He had told him that it was confidential business correspondence which he did not want to be delayed by postal censorship or betrayed by censors to his business rivals. Jorge Antonio signed his dispatch with the pseudonym Dionisio Hernandez which Kühlenthal had given him and requested that 'Alfonso' or 'Jaime' should acknowledge receipt of the letter without delay. 'My courier is anxious to earn as many dollars as possible,' he commented sardonically, 'and I am anxious to be assured you are receiving my messages.'

What amazes me is that the Germans did not keep a watch over the safe-deposit box to find out who was acting as Jorge Antonio's courier and check up on him. Nor apparently did their agent's blatant ignorance of the geography and customs of the country which he claimed to be visiting arouse their suspicion. In submitting his expenses he said he had arrived at Southampton and charged fifteen shillings and sixpence for his trip from there to London's *Liverpool Street* Station! In fact, of course, the port of arrival was Poole in Dorset and the London station would have been Waterloo or Victoria, not Liverpool Street. He charged only thirty-five shillings for his fare from London's *Paddington* Station to Liverpool. From Liverpool he reported that the dock workers were a drunken lot, that if you stood them a litre of wine in one of the innumerable bodegas they would tell you practically anything—a most intriguing piece of information about the revolution in Liverpudlian drinking habits. And a most impressive anticipation of decimalisation! Kühlenthal, however, was so relieved to be able to report he had established an agent in England that he simply would not allow himself to suspect that he was being hoaxed—even though Lisbon at this time was a veritable hive of forgers and fakers inventing news to sell to Allied and German intelligence men.

Jorge Antonio to the best of my knowledge was unique among the Lisbon operators in one respect. This was that he convinced the credulous Abwehr men that he had penetrated the British security net himself and was actually sending the messages from Britain, while in fact at that time he was dreaming up his reports in Portugal, like the rest of his competitors.

Kühlenthal must have been much gratified by Jorge Antonio's success when he compared the ease with which he had established himself in Britain with the failure of another Spanish agent sent to Britain from Spain by a rival section of the Abwehr about the same time. He did not last even a month. Then the special branch of M.I.5 which dealt with German agents posing as neutral newspaper men was on to him. He spent the rest of war in Parkhurst Prison.

But there it was. Jorge Antonio got away with his fake because Kühlenthal and the Abwehr and later Himmler's Security Service *wanted* to believe him.

5

Sea Voyage

Jorge Antonio had already sent his masters several reports and received appreciative replies when 'Major Thompson's' office in Madrid received information that caused them to revise drastically their attitude to the young Spaniard whom they had dismissed in such cavalier fashion.

Naval intelligence in London had discovered a series of orders from Admiral Doenitz's U-boat command directing one of his submarine flotillas to ambush a convoy which the Admiralty knew did not exist and had never existed. Further investigation revealed that the false information about the convoy had come to Doenitz through the Abwehr in Madrid. British intelligence in Madrid was instructed to look into the matter.

The British naval attaché in Madrid was a forceful young officer who spoke Spanish not only fluently and idiomatically but with an accuracy which pleased and flattered his many influential Spanish friends. Captain Alan Hillgarth, RN, had been well prepared for his important assignment by serving for some years before the war as HM Consul in Mallorca, an island in which he himself owned a centuries-old *finca* (farmhouse), with its own ancient oil press and a carefully cultivated grove of olive trees. To him among others now fell the task of trying to trace the Abwehr source that was misleading Doenitz into sending his submarines on wasteful and dangerous expeditions against non-existent convoys. The flash of inspiration which led to Jorge Antonio in his hide at Cascais did not, however, come from Alan Hillgarth but from a young man who had no official connection with British Naval Intelligence, the Secret Intelligence Service, or any other British service.

It came from a young American who before being sent to

Madrid had been a lawyer attached to the FBI in Washington. Because of the increasing involvement of the United States in the Battle of the Atlantic he had recently been attached to the United States Embassy in Madrid as an assistant naval attaché. Lieutenant M. W. Williams, USNR, had developed a habit of dropping in on Alan Hillgarth to pass the time of day and discuss any little problems which Alan felt he could confidentially talk over with the young American. (It was a habit they were to continue with beneficial results for both the United States and Britain right up to the last stages of the war when the young American had become one of the executives of the OSS on General MacArthur's staff and Hillgarth had been appointed chief of British Naval Intelligence for the Pacific theatre.)

Alan Hillgarth was telling Williams of his problem with the phantom convoy when the American suddenly interrupted: 'I wonder whether by any chance it could be that young Spaniard who was hanging around your SIS chaps a little while back. It sounds the kind of thing he would be up to, if he got the chance. . . .'

After that it was less than a week before Jorge Antonio found himself on the way to being enrolled for the job which he had waited and worked for with such patient perseverance. Hillgarth had two extremely knowledgeable and experienced assistant naval attachés, one of whom, Commander Salvador Gomez-Beare, RNVR,* he now deputed to travel to Lisbon and look up Jorge Antonio. Gomez-Beare, who was bilingual in English and Spanish, had previously handled quite a number of 'peculiar cases' for Hillgarth. The captain decided he was just the man to handle this one.

It took Gomez-Beare very little time to persuade Jorge Antonio to produce his carbons of the dispatches he had been sending the

* Commander Gomez-Beare, a Gibraltarian of Spanish and English descent, had the unusual distinction of having served in all three services. In 1914, when he was a medical student in Philadelphia, he immediately volunteered for the British Army. After two years in the trenches he transferred to the Royal Flying Corps and then to the RAF. In 1939 Hillgarth suggested he should join him as an assistant naval attaché but proposed he be given the rank of a captain in the Royal Marines because of his enormous RAF moustache. Back came a signal from the Admiralty approving the appointment on one condition: 'He must shave!'

Germans. And there, sure enough, was the report about the phantom convoy.

Gomez-Beare was impressed.

'You want to go to England and join us in the fight against the Germans?'

Jorge Antonio's eyes shone with enthusiasm.

'Well, keep all this to yourself and keep out of circulation for the next four days. Can you do that?'

'Of course!'

'Then do it. Within the next four days you will hear from me.'

Captain Alan Hillgarth had greater influence with the authorities of the intelligence world in London than was warranted by his rank or his embassy post as naval attaché. He was listened to with respect by the head of the Secret Intelligence Service, General Sir Stewart Menzies, and his own immediate bosses, Rear-Admiral John Godfrey, the Director of Naval Intelligence, and Sir Samuel Hoare, the ambassador to Spain. Even 'the former naval person', Prime Minister Winston Churchill, took a lively interest in the activities and the dispatches of the naval attaché. The result was that when Hillgarth sent a signal recommending certain action that action was apt to be taken without being subjected to the usual delays and questions of Whitehall bureaucracy. Jorge Antonio was lucky in having such a man as his sponsor.

Gomez-Beare had visited Jorge Antonio at Cascais on the evening of April 30. On May 2, 1941, he was back again, this time accompanied by another man whom he introduced as 'Mr Shaw'.

'It is all fixed up for you to go to England,' Commander Gomez-Beare told Jorge Antonio, 'but I had rather you did not travel by air. We know the Germans keep tabs on the passengers using those flying boats. They even have them secretly photographed. As they are under the impression that you are already safely installed in hated Albion, I think it would be unkind to disillusion them. In fact it would be positively inhuman, if we allowed them to discover that you are on your way there only now. So I think it would be best for you to travel to Gibraltar first, and then on to England from there.'

Jorge Antonio chuckled. This certainly was the way to handle things. These men really were professionals.

'There is just one snag. Are you a good sailor? I ask because the best way to send you to Gibraltar is by fishing smack. That way your departure will not attract the attention of the International Police.* They rarely inspect the sardine boats. The one trouble is that the weather might be unfriendly. In which case your journey might be a trifle rough.'

Jorge Antonio was willing to face anything, even sea-sickness, and said so.

'Mr Shaw' now spoke up. He would come for Jorge Antonio at seven the following evening and pick him up in his car.

'It will be as well if you take only essentials with you—just a toothbrush, a razor, a comb, and the sort of stuff you can cram in your overcoat pockets. I would rather you did not take a bag or a suitcase. We don't want people to get the idea you are off on a journey. And please be ready to start punctually and without delay. The car must not be kept hanging around where it will attract attention.'

And that is how it was. On the dot of 7 pm the next evening the Englishman who went by the name by 'Shaw' knocked on the door of Jorge Antonio's lodgings. Jorge Antonio was waiting for him in his new suit with the German 'lining', and the two of them immediately climbed into the car and drove out of Cascais. Soon they left the main road and drove on to a rough and narrow coast track. They drove along it for about half an hour until they reached a tumbledown fisherman's shack overlooking the wide Tagus estuary. A gnarled old mariner came out and welcomed 'Shaw' as though he was his long-lost son. He invited him and Jorge Antonio— whom he took to be one of the escaped prisoners of war for whom it was 'Shaw's' normal business to arrange transport—into the dark and smoky interior of the shack, sat them down at a table and produced a pitcher of rough country wine. The old man's wife came over from behind the stove and served up a delicious fish stew with chunks of bread rubbed in garlic floating among the saffron-flavoured slabs of fish, crab, and mussels. 'Shaw' chatted away with the old couple in rapid Portuguese. He then turned to Jorge

---

* The Portuguese Government had organised a special corps of International Police whose duty was to watch the large numbers of foreigners who had flocked into Portugal during the war.

Antonio. 'High tide,' he said in Spanish, 'is at half past midnight. So if you can get away in the boat soon after, you'll get the benefit of the ebb.'

At midnight the three of them, Jorge Antonio, 'Shaw', and the old man, crept out of the shack and walked cautiously between lines of drying trawling nets to a shaky landing-stage where a skiff had been tied up. They got into the skiff and the old man skulled it out to the sardine boat which Jorge Antonio noticed was just beginning to swing round on its anchor with the changing tide. The old man introduced Jorge Antonio to two young men who made up the crew. 'My sons,' he said, pointing to them in turn, 'Simoes and José.' They shook hands and Simoes politely invited the passenger to regard the galley as his state-room for the journey.

'I must bid you farewell now,' said 'Shaw'. 'I trust your voyage will not be too uncomfortable. Gibraltar has been warned to expect you. When you arrive there—that should be in thirty-six hours or so—please ask for the Port Intelligence Officer and give him this letter. Good luck!' He handed Jorge Antonio a buff envelope embossed with a vermilion seal. Then he stepped back into the skiff and the old man skulled him back to the shore.

Simoes and his brother noiselessly upped anchor, brought out their oars and rowed the boat out to sea. They rowed for about ten miles. Helped by the tide and a friendly following breeze the boat slipped quickly and silently down the Tagus and out into the Atlantic. Only when they had gained the ocean and the coast was out of sight did Simoes and his brother hoist the boat's solitary sail and start up the auxiliary engine.

With only his grey-green gabardine raincoat to keep him warm Jorge Antonio soon began to feel the chill Atlantic winds. He withdrew to the shelter of the galley where he found his hosts had thoughtfully stacked two straw palliasses covered with some rugs as a couch for him to rest on. 'In a week's time,' he said to himself as he dropped off to sleep, 'I shall be in England.' In fact it was to take him almost a week to get to Gibraltar and many weeks more after that before he stepped ashore in Britain.

At 5 am on May 9, 1941, the Bay of Gibraltar seemed fast asleep. Simoes, having carefully avoided Spanish waters and the German watchers established in their Algeciras observation posts, drifted past two British naval patrol boats. The brothers had furled the sail and had once more taken to rowing their small craft. But although the Portuguese fishing smack flew no flag and carried neither identifying number nor name, the patrol boats did not bother to stop it or even give it a hail. In the harbour they found the aircraft carrier *Ark Royal* and three destroyers. Still there was no sign of life on the ships, nor even of any lighters or labourers as they approached the jetty. They tied up the little boat at a suitable-looking quay and Simoes and Jorge Antonio clambered ashore looking for someone to report to. At last they found a Gibraltar policeman. To Jorge Antonio's gratification he looked in his blue uniform and helmet exactly like those London policemen he had seen pictured on the walls of the British Council's office in Madrid.

'I am looking for the Port Intelligence Officer,' Jorge Antonio told the constable in Spanish. 'I have a letter for him.' Being a Gibraltarian, the constable spoke Spanish. 'Just come with me to that telephone box over there and I'll give him a call.'

Jorge Antonio listened to the conversation. But this time he could not understand. It was in English. 'Is the duty IO around?' and then when the IO was on the line: 'Constable Jesus Hassan speaking, sir. There's a couple of chaps just arrived in a fishing boat from Lisbon, sir. One of them says he has a letter for the Port Intelligence Officer. What shall I do with them, sir? . . . Yes, sir.'

Constable Hassan turned to Jorge Antonio. 'We are to go to the mess and wait there. The IO will be over in a jiffy. Would you care for a cup of tea?'

Both Simoes and Jorge Antonio accepted the constable's invitation. It was the first of many unwonted cups of tea Jorge Antonio was to drink between now and the end of the war.

The IO on arrival turned out to be an alert young sergeant of the Intelligence Corps in battledress, who seemed to be able to speak any language you chose. He read the letter 'Shaw' had given Jorge Antonio, examined his passport, paid off Simoes and José, and made arrangements for them to leave again at nightfall. Then he took Jorge Antonio to a place called the 'Officers' Transit Mess' and fixed up for him to have a room, a bath and breakfast.

The sergeant stayed with Jorge Antonio all day. He took him for a drive around the almost empty streets of Gibraltar and suggested,

'If there's anything you need you could not do better than buy it here. Prices in Gib are about a third of what they are in the UK.' Jorge Antonio bought himself a pair of silk pyjamas made in Hong Kong with huge green dragons on them. He also bought an overnight bag in which to store his few odds and ends now that he was on British territory and no longer under the necessity of disguising the fact that he was a traveller.

Jorge Antonio stayed at the Transit Mess for a day and a night. The following morning, while he was breakfasting, the sergeant came in and announced to him: 'You're sailing for England, señor, sometime today.'

During the night the cruiser *London* had put into Gibraltar, accompanied by five destroyers and an auxiliary cruiser. She was to escort a convoy of merchantmen to Britain and then go for a refit herself. There were about twenty passengers already on board her, most of them officers travelling home to Britain from the Middle East. Jorge Antonio was invited to share the chaplain's cabin.

It was a slow and monotonous journey. *London*, with her destroyers, kept circling and zigzagging around the ships in the convoy, guarding them against lurking U-boats, signalling changes of course. Jorge Antonio thought with irony of his German boss in Madrid and how much he would have given to hear all about these manœuvres his spy was watching.

Jorge Antonio's conversation with the chaplain who spoke a little Spanish was confined to the weather and speculation about the motives of Hitler's deputy, Rudolf Hess, whose parachute landing in Scotland the BBC had just announced. It was just polite chitchat and meaningless.

And then quite suddenly the whole atmosphere on board changed. While *London* and her charges had been zigzagging through the Atlantic, news came through that they would not only have to cope with U-boats now. *Bismarck*, the most modern and most powerful battleship of the German Navy, accompanied by the cruiser *Prinz Eugen*, had left Norwegian waters near Bergen, on May 21, with the manifest purpose of breaking through to the Atlantic and destroying British merchant shipping there. The British battle fleet had been alerted and was closing on the German warships. The crew and passengers of *London*, though their ship was not yet involved in the chase, were following its progress with breathless interest. From *London*'s commanding officer speaking over the intercom they had learned of the sinking of the British battle fleet's flagship *Hood* after she and *Repulse* had intercepted *Bismarck* on May 24, while the two German warships were racing through the Denmark Strait between Greenland and Iceland.

Blow by blow they followed the drama as the British fleet hunted the two German raiders. It reached the climax for them on Monday, May 26, when *London* herself received orders to abandon the convoy she was escorting and steam northward with two of her accompanying destroyers to head off *Bismarck* as she tried to make for the French coast and the protective cover of the land-based Luftwaffe.

For Jorge Antonio, who had persuaded the chaplain to translate the half-hourly announcements with which the bridge kept everyone informed, it was a highly emotional experience. He was what Spandiards call an afficionado, an ardent fan of the bullfight, and this battle had for him all the drama of the corrida.

As the British ships bore down on the wounded *Bismarck* sending in Catalinas and Swordfish aircraft to soften her up with their torpedoes and bombs he saw them as banderilleros and picadors planting their darts and pikes in a weakening bull to prepare it for the matador's final sword-thrust. It was a superb demonstration of the power of the British Navy and the skill of its intelligence service which had so quickly located and brought the German ship to bay. In this sea battle Jorge Antonio saw more than just the present struggle. He saw in it the pattern of things to come, the pattern of how Nazi Germany, after first having tasted victory, would be harried to final helplessness and defeat. He was burning to get to England and play his part in the battle against the allies of the dictator that ruled over his own country.

But alas for him! The sinking of *Bismarck* set a train of events in motion which was to delay his arrival in England for many weeks. For hardly had the commanding officer of *London* announced to the cheering ship's company that the rudderless *Bismarck* had been set on fire and sunk when he received a signal ordering him to turn about and land Jorge Antonio and the twenty other passengers at Bathurst on the coast of then British West Africa. After that

London and her destroyers were to join in the ocean-wide hunt
for the supply ships which had been sent out ahead of *Bismarck*
and *Prinz Eugen* to keep them fuelled, watered, and fed while they
preyed on the British Merchant Navy. Now it was to be the supply
ships' turn to be hunted and harried as *Bismarck* had been.

Jorge Antonio stayed in Bathurst for a week. The Port Intelligence
Officer to whom he showed a new letter, this time issued by the
IO in Gibraltar, was anxious to help, but apologetic.

'I had wanted to put you on board an aircraft for London. Unfortunately for you, the son of President Roosevelt turned up. He
had to be given the VIP passage I thought I had safely in the bag for
you. So I am afraid we must send you to Freetown now, señor.
There is a convoy assembling there in which you can sail to
England.'

In the corvette which took him to Freetown, Jorge Antonio
shared the captain's cabin. He never met the captain, however. That
officer seemed to be permanently on the bridge. For Jorge Antonio
it was not a restful voyage either. At night the inevitable order
would come over the ship's intercom: 'Everyone on deck.' And
Jorge Antonio, his raincoat over his green dragon pyjamas, would
climb the narrow companionway to the deck to watch while the
ship's crew lobbed depth-charges into the sea to destroy the U-
boats they suspected in the waters around them. Whether the depth-
charges destroyed any U-boats he never learned, but they most
certainly shook the corvette—and Jorge Antonio.

Freetown he liked better than Bathurst. He liked the green conical
hills of the wooded Sierra Leone peninsula, the bay in which he
watched the corvettes scurrying to and fro among the ships of the
convoy as they gradually gathered in this vast natural harbour.
He liked the gay giggling Negresses who walked about the streets
of the town, topless and all but naked. He even liked the cacophony
of the gramophones screaming shrill, stomping Bantu music from
every hut. He enjoyed the friendliness of the Syrian-owned hotel
where he was given a room and a bed.

Nevertheless, he was relieved when at the end of ten days the
convoy in which he was to sail—mostly ships from Cape Town—
was at last ready to depart. Even in ten days the diet of lamb chops,
sweet potatoes, bananas, melons, and oranges—as he later told his

envious friends in England—was beginning to prove nauseatingly
monotonous to his Spanish palate.

They assigned him to an Elder Dempster liner, the ship of the
commodore commanding the convoy. In it he was given the
commodore's own state-room. The liner was the fastest and most
modern ship in the convoy, which was escorted by two destroyers
and an armed merchantman.

On the third day out, Jorge Antonio went down with malaria.
The kindly steward who looked after him insisted it was blackwater
fever and that he must have picked up the bug in West Africa while
waiting for his passage. Jorge Antonio, however, knew it was
malaria. For he had been stricken with malaria once before towards
the end of the Civil War when he was serving with the Franco army.

Nor did it help him shake off his malaria that the U-boats were
in full cry after the convoy and that the depth-charges were louder
and more frequent than ever. Every night they seemed to lose a
ship or two. When at last the ships reassembled off the coast of
Northern Ireland, Jorge Antonio discovered that eight of the
twenty-five merchantmen which had formed the original convoy
were missing. On June 17, 1941, he stepped ashore at Liverpool
after a journey which had lasted more than a month instead of the
week he had expected.

The liner had tied up near the Royal Liverpool Building. Jorge
Antonio kept out of the way until the Customs and Immigration
men who had come aboard had attended to all the other passengers.
Then he presented his Spanish passport to the Immigration Officer,
as well as the letters of introduction he had been given in Lisbon,
Gibraltar, Bathurst and Freetown.

The officer did not speak Spanish, and Jorge Antonio feared the
worst when he tore a slip out of his book and handed it to him.
'Permission to land refused', it said. But the Immigration man was
not as bureaucratically inhuman as he appeared. He called up a
Spanish-speaking steward and explained through him that he was
compelled to give Jorge Antonio this order because he had no
British entry visa in his passport.

'Of course, you cannot stay alone here on this ship,' he added.
'Come ashore with me and I will take you to an hotel where you
will stay until I have received instructions from London what to do

with you. Have your meals in the hotel and it will be best if you don't go out. It may take until tomorrow evening to find someone who knows about you. I am afraid it is Sunday today!' And the Immigration Officer smiled a self-deprecatory smile, as though to say, 'You see we British never keep our offices open on Sundays, not even in wartime!'

'Shaw' had warned Jorge Antonio before he set out from Cascais that he might find the authorities a little sticky when he arrived in England. 'Just make sure that they call this telephone number,' he said, handing it to him on a piece of paper, and announce your arrival. Then one of our chaps will come and pick you up.'

In fact, all things considered, he had expected a much tougher welcome. He had not even been searched. No one had examined the special lining of his suit, or the micro camera. No one had asked any questions about the syringe-like instrument in his sponge bag. The Customs man had confiscated only one thing—the Pequeño Larousse dictionary. 'Sorry, but I have to take that from you temporarily. Defence Regulations, you know. It will be forwarded to you in due course at your address.'

As it turned out, Jorge Antonio did not have to spend the night at the hotel, after all. For when they went ashore the Immigration Officer took him first to his office. And there, as soon as his identity had been revealed, another officer said, 'Would you mind stepping in here, sir? There is someone waiting for you.'

As he entered this second office, a plump, elderly man stepped forward to welcome him. Lieutenant Angus MacMillan had dressed in ordinary mufti so that his meeting with Jorge Antonio should not attract attention.

'Ah, there you are at last,' he said in reasonably good Spanish, and warmly shook Jorge Antonio by the hand. 'We've been expecting you for weeks. Hope they made you as comfortable as they could on your long journey. I expect you will want a bite to eat. And then we must be off. I have a car waiting.'

Jorge Antonio would have loved to have a look around Liverpool and said so. He would have liked to see what this port was really like whose drunken and talkative citizens he had described in such detail to his German masters in Madrid.

'No time for that now, I am afraid, old chap,' said Lieutenant MacMillan in his breezy way, 'though I expect they'll show you the place later, if you really must see it—I could think of pleasanter spots myself. My orders are to give you a meal and then drive you to your headquarters without delay.'

They had a snack and a drink at the Adelphi and then with Jorge Antonio's few belongings, minus the Pequeño Larousse, stowed away in his Gibraltar bag, they set out in the official Humber which was waiting for them with a good-looking khaki-uniformed girl driver at the wheel.

The hotel, the meal in its restaurant—to Jorge Antonio's surprise no ration coupons were required for it—the drive through the streets of Liverpool and then the motor roads to the south from which all signposts had been carefully removed, all of it was completely new and fascinating to Jorge Antonio. Eagerly he drank it in, especially the attractive and competent young woman driving the car.

6

Case Officer Meets Case

Carlos Reid, a youngish man, neither short nor tall, with fierce black eyes and a hawk-like nose, thick well-oiled black hair slicked back from a low forehead, looked a casting director's ideal choice for a desert sheikh or a slinky tango lizard. In other words as un-British as they come.

In fact he was the son of a Scottish laird and an Andalusian mother. (His mother had insisted on his being called Carlos.) He had been educated first in Spain and then at Stonyhurst, a Jesuit public school in England, to which many Spanish aristocrats sent their sons. As a result, he not only spoke and wrote Spanish but he had that special ability to project himself into the mind of a Spaniard —they called it 'empathy'—invaluable to him as a key man in the Spanish section of M.I.5.

Hillgarth knew 'Charlie' Reid well. Reid also had a house in Majorca and they had met frequently before the war, while Hillgarth ran the British Consulate in Palma. So it was entirely natural for Hillgarth to write to Reid and ask him to keep an eye on his young Spaniard and protect him from the more flat-footed and unimaginative of his colleagues in M.I.5 who were not gifted with his own intuitive understanding of Spanish psychology.

Which is why when Jorge Antonio and Lieutenant MacMillan drove up the rhododendron-lined chase to the isolated but comfortable house outside Markyate in Hertfordshire which the department had assigned to Jorge Antonio as his home, they found 'Charlie' Reid already installed there and waiting to welcome the the Spanish newcomer. He had got himself appointed as Jorge Antonio's case officer.

In the ordinary way an alien arriving in England under Jorge Antonio's circumstances would have found himself quarantined at

the Royal Patriotic Schools in London's Wandsworth and submitted to a period of intensive questioning by the spy-catchers of
M.I.19, as the special department was known which screened the
refugees arriving from occupied Europe. Reid had wanted to spare
Jorge Antonio this ordeal for fear that it might sour him.

'I will screen him myself at Markyate while we discuss the job,'
he had told the 'Double-cross Committee'. They had readily
agreed, especially in view of the fact that during the weeks of his
voyage to Britain there had already been a thorough check-up
on Jorge Antonio's background by British intelligence men both in
Spain and Portugal and the reports had all been favourable. They
had confirmed Jorge Antonio's own story in all checkable details.

Reid had done a first-rate job in preparing for Jorge Antonio's
arrival. He had arranged an identity card for him, an alien's
registration certificate, ration books, clothing coupons, and all the
other bureaucratic accessories essential to existence in wartime
Britain. He had even obtained a work permit for him and a job with
a firm of Covent Garden fruit importers whose director was in the
confidence of M.I.5.

Jorge Antonio was assigned a desk in the firm's head office in
Bow Street. Conscientiously he made a point of spending several
hours at work there most weeks, so that if any German agent were
to check on him he would find that he was indeed employed there.
Quite plausibly, too, in view of the difficulty firms like fruit
importers had in finding staff in a Britain all of whose available
manpower was mobilised for war work or the fighting services.

It was magnificent cover for Jorge Antonio, that job in Covent
Garden. It gave him the perfect pretext for staying in England well
beyond the period his negotiations with the firm in Manchester
could have been expected to last and also served to allay any
suspicions Kühlenthal might otherwise have felt concerning the
freedom with which his V-man travelled all over Britain. His
journeys, Kühlenthal could tell himself, if he had any misgivings,
were an essential and indispensable part of his job in the fruit
business. The Anwehr general, however, never did have any
misgivings.

Not so Carlos Reid. With all his instinctive liking for Jorge
Antonio he was not prepared to rule out as utterly impossible that

he might in fact be working for the Abwehr while pretending to the British that he was double-crossing it. Unbeknown to Jorge Antonio, therefore, Reid provided him with yet another appurtenance: a tail. If Jorge Antonio left the house at Markyate, unaccompanied by Reid or some other member of the small staff, the tail would follow him. It was done so carefully and so skilfully that Jorge Antonio never suspected. Nor did he spot the occasional test questions with which Reid tried to trap him. He passed them all. Soon the tail was only instructed to make spot checks on him at irregular intervals. Later still, the main function of the tail was to make sure that no German agents were following Jorge Antonio on his unlawful occasions. For although M.I.5 had in fact eliminated all German agents operating in Britain—as was proved after the war—they were still far from sure of having done so.

Soon after his arrival at Markyate, Jorge Antonio himself suggested it would be wise to send a message to his Abwehr employers giving them the good news that he had got a job which with luck would permit him to stay in England indefinitely.

'Perhaps I should also include a dispatch about the popular reaction here to Hitler's invasion of the Soviet Union. Something that they would like to hear. You know the sort of thing: that most people here are sure that Hitler will be in Moscow by Christmas, that on the one hand they are glad to see the world being freed of the Bolshevik enemy, on the other they are sorry that Britain is not allied with Germany in this great crusade. I might quote someone as saying that by next year with Russia overrun, her grain, her oil wells, and her iron ore in German hands, Hitler will be free to invade this country—if Churchill is not overthrown before that date by the Peace Party which is getting stronger all the time. The Peace Party, I suggest, wants to negotiate with Hitler through Rudolf Hess.'

He grinned as though it was all a prank. 'And maybe I could put in a bit that the Americans, as I learned in Liverpool or some other port, are causing dismay in the government by cutting down their supplies to Britain because they are sending everything to Russia.'

One other suggestion made by Jorge Antonio in these first weeks of his work with him showed Reid that his Spanish colleague had a natural aptitude for the game. 'Would I be right in thinking that our operations at this stage have two overriding objectives—firstly to build up my credibility as a source of accurate and valuable information, secondly to make the Germans anxious to get my reports more quickly than by courier? Would that be right?'

Reid agreed that this was exactly right.

'How would it be, then, if in order to account for my silence over the last few weeks I told them I had been having some difficulty in contacting my courier, the BOAC steward? That owing to the irregularity of the flights he has twice failed to turn up at our appointed rendezvous and has had to fly to Lisbon without being able to collect a message from me? Also might it perhaps help if I were able to give them a piece of news occasionally which was secret at the time I had allegedly sent it but has been overtaken by events and confirmed by an official release by the time it reaches them?'

Jorge Antonio looked at Reid rather diffidently. He was still cautiously feeling his way and did not want to seem brash or over-confident. He was essentially rather shy. But he was immensely eager to plunge into his new job—as far as he understood it. Reid grinned his encouragement and approval. In a mixture of English gestures and Spanish words he gave him a smiling thumbs up and cried '*Olé!*'

There was no time, however, to include the nugget of accurate news in this first dispatch. And so Jorge Antonio, having prepared a measure of invisible ink from the stuffing of his suit, carefully wrote out his message, closely watched by Reid, whose first experience this was of ink made from wadding. He wanted, moreover, to make quite sure that the message written was exactly what had been agreed. Then, when the ink had dried, Jorge Antonio typed out a letter over it, ostensibly dealing with the business affairs of his family firm. He handed it to Reid for him to have it forwarded to Lisbon and delivered to the safe deposit in the bank.

The letter was not, of course, entrusted to a BOAC steward but travelled by diplomatic bag to the British Embassy at Lisbon. There it was handed to the local SIS officer, who in his turn sent a British agent to the Espiritu Santo Bank and the box. With realistic attention to detail the British saw to it that Jorge Antonio's messages were only delivered to the box after the arrival in Lisbon of one particular steward (who needless to say was unconscious of the treasonable role which had been notionally assigned to him). This was a precaution in case 'Don Alfonso' and his friends should get hold of the roster of the stewards on the Poole–Lisbon run and use it to check who was carrying their agent's messages. As things turned out the precaution was unnecessary. The Abwehr never checked, never doubted. Incredibly careless and unprofessional!

As has been seen, the double agents controlled by M.I.5 in Britain at this time were not being used for strategic or tactical deception of the enemy but defensively for the infiltration and confusion of the Abwehr's espionage against Britain. This was also the function of Jorge Antonio, when he first went to work with Reid in the house outside Markyate. But the style in which they performed their task showed all the calculating subtlety with which three years later they set about the serious business of deceiving Hitler about the Allied invasion of Normandy and keeping him deceived.

Two specimens of the 'intelligence' Jorge Antonio passed to the Abwehr bosses in Madrid provide excellent examples of his technique. The first was intended to stimulate Kühlenthal's anxiety to speed up his spy's news service.

On June 21, 1941, Churchill had ordered General Sir Archibald Wavell, who had been in command of the British Forces in the Middle East, to swap places with General Sir Claude Auchinleck, the Commander-in-Chief in India. At the same time Oliver Lyttelton was being sent out to Cairo as Minister of State to represent the War Cabinet and take the political decisions which the military were in the habit of referring to London and thereby causing delay which would now be avoided.

These appointments were top secret at the time, though in due course they were bound to be made public. The thing now was to give Jorge Antonio a scoop and let him reveal just enough knowledge to impress his German masters with his value as a source.

It was up to Reid to work out how Jorge Antonio could have found out about the story, how much he could plausibly know, and when and what he was to communicate to Madrid. His solution of the problem was ingenious. Jorge Antonio, he decided, could have heard something that put him on the trail at the Brevet Club. This was a club in London's Mayfair district much patronised at this time by Polish, French, and Czech officers as well as British officers and civilians. It was a thoroughly cosmopolitan sort of meeting place to which Jorge Antonio might easily have been introduced by one of his business contacts.

On July 17, 1941, 'Alfonso' Kühlenthal received a dispatch from his Spanish V-man in England. It had been picked up for him the previous day from the safe-deposit box in Lisbon's Espiritu Santo Bank. Jorge Antonio had dated it June 22.

'In the Brevet Club', the Abwehr general read after the invisible ink had been put through the developer, 'I picked up a bit of news which may possibly be of interest. I thought it useful to join this London club because it is much frequented by British and Allied officers and their friends of the opposite sex. Drink is plentiful and this leads to conversational indiscretions. Thus I overheard a Polish pilot of the RAF Transport Command cancel an assignation with his English inamorata. He spoke French with her. So I was able to understand quite clearly what he said. The Pole informed the lady that he would not be able to dine with her on June 23 as promised because he had been given orders to fly on an important mission that day with a cabinet minister and his staff as well as a group of officers of the Indian Army General Staff. I gathered that he would be flying via Gibraltar and Takoradi to Khartoum. He did not say what his final destination was to be. Cairo would seem the most likely one. On the other hand, why should officers of the Indian Army General Staff be going to Cairo? New Delhi would seem indicated for them. . . . I am taking English lessons at the Berlitz School so that I can talk more easily with the natives. That will be useful both in my work for you and that with the fruit importers.'

Kühlenthal looked up the reports from his agents watching Gibraltar. With interest he noted that they had reported the arrival and departure after refuelling of an RAF Liberator. Its passengers had been observed to include a number of male and female civilians as well as officers wearing red tabs on their tropical uniforms suggesting high rank.

Jorge Antonio's report from the Brevet Club had exactly the effect on the Abwehr general its authors had intended: Kühlenthal cursed the delays which meant that he did not receive a despatch of June 22 until July 17. His impatience for more rapid communication with his new V-man grew even more intense when in due course its explanation was revealed: the exchange of posts between Wavell and Auchinleck was announced, together with the appointment of Oliver Lyttelton to Cairo. Nor did Reid and Jorge Antonio have too long to wait for Kühlenthal's reaction. In an encouraging note—transmitted through the Lisbon bank's safe-deposit box—Kühlenthal enquired what progress Jorge Antonio was making with the assembly of his transmitter.

In September 1941 Jorge Antonio reported another mouth-watering piece of intelligence to Madrid. He had picked it up in Coventry, he said, while on a visit to that much bombed industrial centre with his friends from the Manchester textile machinery firm which he said was now concentrating on the manufacture of components for long-distance bombers. A Coventry town councillor, hearing that he came from Spain, had engaged him in a long discussion of his experiences of German bombing during the Civil War. In the course of this conversation the councillor had told him that the Air Ministry and the Home Office had been making a special study of the effect of the German attack on Coventry of November 14, 1940. Analysis had revealed that the weight of the raid had amounted to approximately one ton of bombs to every eight hundred of the population. The reduction in the index of industrial activity had been calculated at about 73 per cent on the morning of the 15th November. Despite the most intense efforts, recovery to normal productivity had taken forty-five days.

Jorge Antonio commented that it seemed the British were much impressed by the effectiveness of the German attack and were planning to raid a series of German industrial centres with even greater bomb loads and many times more aircraft than the Germans had used during their attacks on Britain. They calculated that by doing so they would effect a proportionately greater dislocation of the German industrial effort.

The Coventry dispatch had been submitted not only to the 'Twenty Club' but also to Colonel Bevan's newly founded London Controlling Section which had approved it. It fitted in with a campaign which the LCS had just launched to stampede the Germans with the threat of vastly increased RAF bombing raids on

Germany's industrial heartland into withdrawing fighters from the Russian front.

But its beauty was that while the statistics of damage to production in Coventry were only slightly exaggerated, Jorge Antonio's conclusions as to Bomber Command's plans would soon prove to be well founded. The fulfilment of his predictions would help to build up Kühlenthal's V-man in Britain as a valuable and reliable source not only in Kühlenthal's eyes but in those of Kühlenthal's masters in Berlin.

And to kill two birds with one stone was always a favourite sport for masters of the double-cross like Reid and his Spanish acolyte.

★   ★   ★

For the rest of 1941 and most of 1942 Jorge Antonio's operations were routine, concentrating in the main on building up his reputation as a reliable source of information. It was not until the year after this that Jorge Antonio began to venture more frequently into the realm of strategic deception.

7

'*Cato's*' '*Orchestra*'*

Kurt Georg Kiesinger† was a man of ambition. He was also a man
of courage.

As he sat down in his seat at the big horse-shoe table in Goebbels's
conference room on this morning of Saturday, November 27,
1942, he was determined to prove both. He was going to make a
scene at the Propaganda Minister's daily eleven o'clock conference.
The kind of scene he hoped would appeal to Goebbels, mark him
out as a fearless critic of inefficiency, and point to him as a go-getter
deserving promotion to the top echelon of the leadership cadre. He
had a subject that was bound to appeal to Goebbels: intelligence from
Britain. Or, more accurately, the lack of intelligence from Britain.

Punctually at eleven o'clock the curtains at the far end of the room
parted and Goebbels made his entrance. The 'Propaganda Dwarf',
as they called him behind his back, carefully ensconced himself in
his high-backed armchair and the conference began. For about
half an hour it ranged over the multiplicity of subjects which the
power-hungry minister claimed affected morale and therefore came
under his jurisdiction. Then Kiesinger boldly caught the minister's
eye and asked whether he might be allowed to bring a matter of
some importance to his attention. Goebbels frowned. Kiesinger was
a member of Ribbentrop's Foreign Office and only present as a
liaison officer to help co-ordinate foreign broadcasting policy
between the Foreign Office and the Propaganda Ministry. But he
did not say no. With the eyes of the minister and his top advisers
fastened on him, Kiesinger made his scene. He made it very well, as
is borne out by a special minute recording his intervention which
still survives in the Potsdam archives of the Soviet-controlled
German Democratic Republic.

---

* See page 61.
† Chancellor of the German Federal Republic from 1966 to 1969.

The minute is dated 'Berlin, November 27, 1942' and is headlined 'Intelligence Contact with Britain'. It says:

The Liaison Officer of the Foreign Office to the Ministry of Propaganda, Dr Kiesinger, who has special responsibility for all questions concerning radio propaganda, had some highly critical remarks to make about the efficiency of the Economic Broadcasts. He was fully supported by Dr Hunke.*

Dr Kiesinger said it was almost unbelievable and presented an impossible state of affairs, that as good as no intelligence was being received in Germany from Britain. There was no kind of information about what things were really like there. In this matter, which after all was of decisive importance for the war, all departments concerned seemed to have fallen down. The situation was simply intolerable. Sweden had fairly regular communications with Britain. But apparently no department had as yet succeeded in exploiting this channel for procuring usable and accurate intelligence about conditions in Britain. No one in Germany was informed for instance what kind of meals could be obtained in British restaurants, what the size was of the portions that were being served there, what one could get without food coupons in the restaurants, and what the overall situation was in Britain with regard to supplies in general. In Germany one was almost forced to invent reports dealing with subjects such as these from the puniest crumbs of evidence. Surely it must be possible to find suitable persons, neutrals best of all, who could establish contacts with the British to find out things of this kind, perhaps even to fly to Britain themselves.

Dr Kiesinger asked that Professor Hunke should arrange a meeting for a more detailed discussion of this matter.

Professor Hunke and other officials of Department A pointed out that in the first place it must be the task of the diplomatic missions to arrange the necessary contacts. To this the representative of the Foreign Office made no reply.

Kurt Georg Kiesinger was not as ineffective as the last sentence of the Propaganda Ministry's minute suggested.† Goebbels himself

---

* Professor Heinrich Hunke was Chief of Department A, the Foreign Affairs Department of the Propaganda Ministry.
† Dr Kiesinger certainly made an impression on Goebbels. That was proved when Goebbels later tried to get Kiesinger transferred to a top job in the Propaganda Ministry. But Ribbentrop would not let Kiesinger go.

must have entered the battle. One can imagine the glee with which the Propaganda Dwarf called Hitler's attention to the egregious shortcomings of the diplomats and the Abwehr, both of them bodies disliked for their 'snooty stand-offishness' by Hitler and his proletarian paladins. The Abwehr was put on the carpet.

That they tried to defend themselves by demonstating their efficiency is shown by the fact that in the last week of December 1942 the ball served with such vigour by Kiesinger in Berlin landed in Kühlenthal's court in Madrid and was promptly bashed on by him to his faithful V-man in London. The general sent a special New Year's greeting to Jorge Antonio, in which he thanked him for his mangificent services during 1942 and expressed his confidence that he would do even better in 1943 which would be the year of final victory. Almost as an afterthought he requested that Jorge Antonio should let him have an end-of-the-year round-up report on the general economic situation in Britain. The report should include a word picture of what life in besieged, bombed, and blockaded Britain was like for the average citizen. 'What sort of meals does he get in restaurants and canteens?' asked the general. 'What is the size of the portions served? What are the food rations for the family? What is the size of rations for clothing, petrol, consumer goods, and so forth? Which shortages do people complain of most? What are their biggest grumbles?'

Jorge Antonio, his case officer Carlos Reid, and Colonel Bevan's LSC all had fun with Kühlenthal's gastronomic questionnaire. When it was completed the reply was a masterpiece of descriptive reporting devoid of any deception material and spiced with some highly apropos culinary experiences on the part of Jorge Antonio and his friends.

Berlin liked the report so much that Kühlenthal was asked for more like it. None was sent, however. For already Hitler, badly shaken by the military disasters in Russia and North Africa, and the catastrophic U-boat losses in the Atlantic, was becoming more and more apprehensive of Allied landings and invasions along the coastline of his 'Fortress Europe'. Kühlenthal kept plying his man in London with questions. There was little time for 'feature articles'.

Jorge Antonio was instructed to keep eyes and ears open for any signs that the Allies were planning an occupation of the Iberian

Peninsula or the Mediterranean islands. Was there anything to suggest they were planning an invasion of northern Norway during the remaining period of Arctic darkness? What could he, with his specialist knowledge of electronics, find out about the new device by means of which the British were locating submerged U-boats from their aircraft? Could he discover on what frequencies this device worked? To help him answer these questions Kühlenthal suggested that Jorge Antonio should expand still further his network of sub-agents.

★　　　★　　　★

To Colonel Bevan and his team at Storey's Gate the Abwehr general's queries were sheer music. They showed how well their deception campaigns were getting across. Campaigns intended to suggest a variety of Allied operations aimed at targets in north-western Europe and the Mediterranean, at Norway, the Pas de Calais, the French Atlantic ports of Brest and Bordeaux, the Iberian Peninsula, Greece, and Sardinia.

To support the Calais threat it had been intended to mount a feint assault. But when its D-day arrived on September 8, 1943, shortage of troops and landing craft cut the operation down to a mere gesture. Minesweepers went out and cleared the Straits of mines. Destroyers escorted a convoy of what might have been troopships through them. Coastal guns started a cross-Channel bombardment. Squadrons of fighters and bombers from the RAF and the US Air Force roared into the sky over the Calais area. But the Germans did not rise. Not even the Luftwaffe. A German on the other side of the Channel was heard calling a comrade on his radio-telephone: 'What is all the fuss over there?' (*'Was ist denn da drüben los?'*)

These campaigns* had three main purposes. Firstly to aid the Russians by threatening Hitler on his inactive fronts so as to deter him from denuding them to reinforce the East, secondly to rivet

---

* The campaigns were each provided with a code-name. Thus 'Cockade' stood for the overall campaign to pin down the German forces outside Russia by encouraging the OKW to expect the Allied invasion in the West during 1943. 'Tindall' designated the threat against Norway, 'Starkey' that against the Pas de Calais, 'Wadham' that against the Atlantic ports of France.

German attention on the Pas de Calais as the intended number one invasion target, thirdly to mislead the Germans about the coming landing in Sicily as decisively as they had been misled about the landings in French North Africa and Morocco.

A glance at the intelligence reports which filled Colonel Krummacher's 'In-tray' at Hitler's headquarters during 1943 shows how persuasive these misinformation campaigns were. Not that all the reports were planted deception. To a substantial extent they originated in rumours spontaneously generated in the climate of opinion created by the Storey's Gate campaigns. But whatever their source they were lapped up eagerly by the German intelligence men, still punch-drunk from the surprise blow of the North African landings and the Führer's fury at not having been warned in time.

Young Walter Schellenberg, the ambitious chief of Himmler's foreign intelligence, is a good example of the German hysteria. Ever since the failure of his none-too-subtle attempt in 1940 to kidnap the Duke and Duchess of Windsor while they were in Portugal after the fall of France, Walter Schellenberg oddly enough had been considered to be a great expert on Iberian affairs. He was on another of his periodic visits to Spain when on November 14, 1942, he sent off a top-priority Blitz Teleprint to Himmler, sounding the alarm that the Anglo-Americans were about to seize the island of Minorca.

Schellenberg's Teleprint makes dramatic reading, and to judge from the initials and comments scribbled in its margins it created the desired stir in the Führerhauptquartier.

Secret

For immediate transmission to the Reichsführer SS.
Subject: Anglo-American operations in the Western Mediterranean.
Reichsführer!

As already reported, the Spanish government was requested by the Allies, to hand over to them for a few months the Balearic island of Minorca with its harbour Mahon. This presumptuous demand was turned down by the Spaniards. As has now been ascertained by a reliable V-man, the British on November 12, 1942, instructed a number of their agents to collect urgently all available information about the Balearic islands, Minorca in particular. Plans, maps, Baedekers etc. were to be collected and delivered to the British. In carrying out these instructions a British agent left a travel prospectus concerning Minorca on a café table. The V-man, whose reliability up to now has been beyond doubt, handed the prospectus which includes some hand written notes concerning fortifications, landing places, etc., to one of our own men who will fly to Berlin with it, arriving on November 16.

Attention is drawn to the danger that the Anglo-Americans may try to occupy the island of Minorca against the will of the Spanish government in the course of the next few days. It should be emphasised that experience during the Spanish Civil War has shown that because of its naturally steep coastline and favourable harbour conditions Minorca is easy to defend and difficult to attack. Its military protection by the Spaniards is exiguous. Nothing is known of any intention to reinforce the Spanish garrison on the island.

Chief Reich Security Office A VI
signed Schellenberg
SS-Standartenführer.*

The seriousness with which this Schellenberg canard was debated and analysed at the court of Adolf Hitler is shown by a note pencilled and initialled by Jodl: 'The Führer has ordered that this matter should be brought to the attention of the Spanish Government by the German military attaché with the comment that in the present situation the Balearics are of the greatest importance to the Anglo-Americans and that an improvement of their defences is highly desirable.'

Apparently it had occured neither to Schellenberg nor the military and naval experts surrounding Hitler that the British were intimately acquainted with the defence characteristics of Minorca since the eighteenth century, when they had been in occupation of the island themselves; that long-range naval guns had been installed there by the British firm of Vickers-Armstrong shortly before the outbreak of the Civil War; and that the British Consul in Mallorca during this period had been the lively Captain Alan Hillgarth, RN, now the British naval attaché in Madrid. Hillgarth was hardly the man to require a Baedeker or a hotel prospectus to inform him

---

* SS-Standartenführer = SS-Colonel.

about the Minorca defences. None the less when in 1944 the time came to dismiss Admiral Canaris, the head of the Abwehr, and integrate Abwehr with SD, it was the naive SS-Colonel Schellenberg who was picked for this top intelligence job.

Next exhibit is a dispatch to Ribbentrop from Baron von Hoyningen-Huene, the German minister in Lisbon, dated February 22, 1943. It carries a cornucopia overflowing with news of ill omen.

. . . Spanish tankers have been forbidden to enter US ports during next ten days. This suggests that a large fleet of American transports is about to leave the USA during this period.

. . . A British staff officer passing through Lisbon has told a V-man who is an old friend of his, that he is on his way to Gibraltar in order to join a big American convoy which left the United States on February 14 for Gibraltar with 280 vessels escorted by ten warships, among them two battleships. The staff officer did not know the destination of the convoy. But he did know that forty tankers already in Gibraltar are to join the convoy. As there was ample fuel available in North Africa he concluded that the convoy is not destined for North Africa but is intended for a mission which requires exceptional amounts of fuel.

Lisbon Abwehr has reports confirming this report about the convoy. But Abwehr considers Liverpool or Glasgow as likely destinations. The staff officer mentioned in this connection that Churchill had ordered a tightening up of security concerning military and political plans of the Allies.*

The British officer who was himself taking part in the execution of the secret plans knew only that among the officers of the General Staff in London three possibilities were being discussed for the convoy's employment:

1. Several landings to be made in Norway and France—including the French Mediterranean coast. Convoy could well be intended for this last. Operations of this kind are not, he said, intended to constitute the opening of the Second Front, although they would be carried out by contingents larger than those used on the Dieppe raid, but only as a diversion to cause the withdrawal of German troops from the Eastern Front.

2. A landing in Greece and Albania with the intention of joining up with the Jugoslav forces fighting there. Such an operation would

---

* Caustic marginal note in Jodl's handwriting signed with his initial: 'Presumably that is why he reveals all this! J.'

be preceded by an assault on southern Italy in order to secure bases in the Strait of Otranto.

3. An operation on the Iberian Peninsula.

The above information wins special importance from a conversation which the secretary of Lord Beaverbrook had in a very restricted circle. Lord Beaverbrook's secretary said that the Americans had declared against a large scale operation on the continent because in the light of the coming presidential election a failure of the assault would have catastrophic effects on Roosevelt's chances of being re-elected.*

'It was to be assumed therefore,' argued Lord Beaverbrook's secretary, 'that the Allies would not attempt a major assault at any central point, e.g. France, but would try to establish a bridge-head on the periphery of Europe in order to work their way gradually inwards towards Germany, this strategy involving less risk.'

This thought also suggests the question of an operation against the Iberian Peninsula. Lately alarming reports have been multiplying indicating an operation by the enemy to occupy a number of bases on the peninsula.

In Brazil two such possibilities are being considered. A Portuguese acquaintance of mine received a telegram from his brother in Brazil urging him to leave Portugal immediately and take all his money with him.

The British staff officer mentioned that shipping for 35,000 men would have been made available in Britain by the end of this month, as well as shipping for a further 120,000 in North America and for 40,000 in Canada.

Signed Huene

Received: 22.2.43.
16 Hours: Schröder.

Splendid stuff! It covered almost the whole range of the Colonel's deception campaign.

In March, April and May 1943 the Abwehr in Spain entertained the Führerhauptquartier with blood-curdling reports of Anglo-American plots to stage anti-Franco risings in Spain and follow these up with armed intervention by Allied forces in the peninsula. In April for instance the Abwehr reported that it had succeeded in

* Neither of Lord Beaverbrook's personal secretaries, both of them friends of mine, were at any time during the war in Lisbon. Nor do they know of any other member of Lord Beaverbrook's staff who was.

penetrating an anti-Franco organi.ation secretly set up by the British Embassy. The plan of the organisation was to seize the internment camp at Miranda del Ebro, arm the 6000 internees, and establish bridge-heads on the coast of northern Spain near Vigo for a clandestine landing of arms, agents, and commandos. Once this was accomplished, preparations were to be made for the reception of parachutists, airborne troops, and arms supplies. Twenty arrests, said the Abwehr, had been made, and the monarchist conspirators had given up their plans. Arms and equipment captured had been handed over to the Falange. In June the Abwehr claimed to have discovered in Spanish Morocco that Franco's High Commissioner, General Orgaz, an Anglophil monarchist, was planning a coup. There were to be simultaneous risings in Morocco and Malaga. The risings would give the Allies a pretext to occupy Spanish Morocco and later to land in Spain itself.

All this 'intelligence', recorded in Abwehr situation report 2980/43 of July 1943, was just so much routine compared with the spectacular deception coup by which the Storey's Gate team succeeded in diverting Hitler's attention to Sardinia and Greece when the Anglo-Americans were about to land in Sicily. This was the celebrated *Man Who Never Was* hoax, subject of two books, a novel, a film, and a TV series.

It consisted of the planting on the Abwehr—its Spanish section once more were the victims—of what purported to be the corpse of Major Martin, a British courier washed up near Huelva on the Atlantic coast of Spain. 'Major Martin' had apparently drowned in the Atlantic while on his way to Cairo with top-secret plans and letters for General Sir Maitland ('Jumbo') Wilson, the C-in-C Middle East. The letters and the plans indicated that the targets of the next Anglo-American operation were Sardinia and the Peloponnese, while Sicily was the subject of an elaborate deception by which the British hoped the Germans would be duped. The most scrupulous care had been taken to get every detail right—'Martin's' identity papers, his personal correspondence, the condition of the corpse, the plans, the covering letter from General Sir Alan Brooke to Wilson written by himself in his own hand ('My dear Jumbo'), the direction of the currents—all had been attended to and provided for with such skill and imagination that even less gullible intelligence

officers than the Germans would have been taken in. Hitler gobbled
it all up with the greed of a starving alligator. Even after the Allied
landings in Sicily had taken place he continued to await the planned
landing in Sardinia for another thirteen days. He sent an armoured
SS division under Sepp Dietrich to Greece and kept it there even
longer.*

The Storey's Gate deception campaign did not let up even after
the Sicilian triumph. Jorge Antonio, who up to now had only been
used most sparingly for strategic deception—his credibility and
authority with the Germans were still being built up—was allowed
a little practise canter. He was brought in to help with the bonus
preparations for an invasion of France. On June 8, 1943, the Abwehr
disclosed: 'A V-man of the KO Spain reports from England that on
May 22 he observed an unusually large number of ships at Milford
Haven. British seamen had told him that in the area of Plymouth
there were also substantial concentrations of shipping. They were
being got ready for landing operations.' Abwehr Telegram No. 669
from Tangiers takes up the story on the same date:

'. . . The Allies consider the French army in North Africa by no
means unsuitable for operations on the (European) continent,
once its formations have been re-armed and re-equipped. Preparations are in hand for a landing in France.'

German 'diplomat' in Tangiers quotes his Spanish colleague to
much the same effect in Telegram IM 2043/43 of June 1, 1943:

'Castillo, Spanish envoy in Tangiers, has reports from sure source
that large numbers of French officers and men are being embarked

---

* Needless to say, German writers today have endeavoured to pooh-pooh
the success of 'Operation Mincemeat', as the 'Man-Who-Never-Was' deception was somewhat ghoulishly code-named. Former Abwehr officer
Gert Buchheit, for instance, in his *Die Anonyme Macht* (Athenaion, Frankfurt,
1969) claims Hitler's insistence that Greece not Sicily was the Allied target
had nothing to do with 'Major Martin'. It was due to Hitler's unwillingness to
believe that his friend Mussolini's country was to be the victim of an Allied
attack. 'The deception with the corpse of the pretended British major,'
declares Colonel Buchheit, 'did not have the effect which is still being at-
tributed to it today.' As proof, the colonel cites the fact that more than fifty
Abwehr reports had correctly predicted Sicily would be the next allied
objective. No doubt. But General Brooke's letter to General Wilson had
asked that the deception campaign pinpointing Sicily as the target be stepped
up—just the argument that would impress Hitler who was always anxious to
show himself more perspicacious than the Abwehr and his generals.

from Casablanca to Britain, and that an assault on France from bases in England is being planned for immediate future. V-man reports from Oran that French soldiers are being sent to Casablanca where they are being partially trained, then shipped to Britain in readiness for an attempt at a landing which is to be made on the Atlantic coast. From Tunis and Algeria French troops are also being sent to Casablanca for training and subsequent transport to Britain in order to take part in landing operations on French Atlantic coast.'

On June 10, 1943, under Abwehr IMW/KO No. 31279 a 'hitherto untried V-man', who has managed to get into Government House in Gibraltar, reports that Churchill proposed at the conference in Washington that the assault on Europe should be begun by establishing bridge-heads on the Atlantic coast of France. But Churchill had also agreed to launch assaults against Ostend, Haarlem, and southern Norway. At Government House, however, says the new V-man, one is convinced that the main offensive will take place in the Mediterranean. Only secondary importance is given to the operations on the Atlantic coast. These plans had not been modified by the Washington decisions.

Just to prove how wide the Abwehr net was cast and how far the influence of Colonel Bevan's rumour machine extended Abwehr IM/West KO No. 62561/31 of June 10, 1943, reported: 'From a sure source in Budapest it is learned that the British will attack simultaneously in the night of June 12 to 13 in Portugal, Holland, Flanders and Norway. The Russians will support the British landings with a Big Offensive.'

The Pas de Calais was stressed as the target area for a cross-Channel assault in Abwehr Message No. 1129/43 of August 27, 1943: 'Extensive preparations for assault. Landing craft assembling in Dover and Folkestone. Big bombing attack is being prepared as well as cross-Channel artillery bombardment with destruction of defence works as objective thus giving cover to landing units in said sector.'

From Lisbon the Abwehr reported at the beginning of September: 'A Portuguese who has just returned to Lisbon from London reports that foreigners resident in London have been requested to move into the country. The same applies to diplomats living there. They are being asked to evacuate London and take up residence in the country outside the capital. Fresh instructions have been issued to the population. Prisoners of war confined in camps outside London are being transferred to London itself. The authorities are counting from day to day that the Germans will begin their promised Retribution attack on London.'

Then another message from Jorge Antonio. 'V-man of the KO Spain reports on September 3, from London: Shoreham, west of Brighton. Approximately 100 small ships have arrived here. Among them landing craft, MTBs, and gun-boats. At the landing stages mechanised guns and motor transport are being loaded every day on to landing craft which then depart with them for camouflaged embarkation points. Further Panda divisions arriving in Brighton.'

To keep up interest in the Iberian Peninsula a 'very reliable V-man' reports that 'the war materials being supplied to Portugal and Spain under Lease Lend are intended for use by Anglo-American forces in the event of a Second Front being launched from the Iberian Peninsula.' 'As similar messages have been received earlier and the V-man is regarded by his controller as being particularly reliable,' comments the Abwehr, 'the report deserves special consideration.'

My last exhibit in this cavalcade of alarmist fantasy comes from no less imposing a personage than General José Mosquardó, the valiant defender of Toledo's Alcazar during the early months of the Spanish Civil War. Now the old warrior commanded the Barcelona military district. He was a great admirer of Hitler and liked to visit General Petersen who commanded the 4th Luftwaffe Field Corps on the other side of the Pyrenees at Montpellier.

On April 3, 1944, Dr Hans Kroll, the German Consul General* in Barcelona, sent a top-secret and top-priority cipher telegram to his supreme war-lord, revealing the Allied invasion plan.

Telegram. Barcelona, 3.4.44. No. 126.

General Moscardó has passed to me information about the allied plan for the invasion of France. It comes from a reliable source. Main contents as follows:

1. With the help of parachutists, gliders, and artificial smoke

---

* Many years later Dr Kroll was to achieve fame as the West German ambassador to Moscow who won the special confidence of Nikita Khrushchev.

150,000 soldiers with full equipment will be landed over France and distributed along the following main lines: from north to south: Amiens–Orleans–Limoges–Montauban–Toulouse; as well as along the diagonal Bordeaux–Tarascon. These troops will have the mission of supplying French patriots with arms. The patriots are to join up with Allied troops in rear of German coastal defences and create serious unrest.

2. Should this plan succeed, as is expected, the coastal fortifications will be attacked from the sea and from the interior after the French communications network has been demolished. Appropriate instructions have been given in person by liaison officers. These instructions also provide for the creation of disturbances in Spain, thus giving the Allies a pretext for invading Spain in order to restore order.

Above order was passed on January 26 to the British bases.

3. No decisive operational value however is attached to this airborne landing. It has as its purpose the creation of maximum disorder in the French interior and the launching of individual attacks. Also to confront the German High Command with a serious problem of communications and supply.

4. As for the timing of the operation, it is pointed out that among the iron rations of the Allied soldiers are saveloy sausages which only remain edible for fifteen or twenty days. These saveloys were issued to British troops in England between March 20 and March 30. Also in Sardinia and Corsica.

5. So far as Spain is concerned an order exists to create internal disorders in the districts bordering on France in order to supply a pretext for invasion.

6. The report comes from a Russian named Nikolas Putiloff Budienni, a V-man of Stalin's, who was parachuted into France in order to start a Communist movement. He has had to escape from there. His information, it is stated by the V-man of the Spanish General Staff, is absolutely reliable. . . . It is further emphasised the Russian could have no knowledge that what he said would be passed on to collaborators of Spanish General Staff. General Staff observes that the Germans may already have corresponding suspicions. This is shown by recent concentration in the South of France.

Moscardó asked me to inform General Petersen urgently in Montpellier.

Identical text to Madrid.

                                                            Kroll

That is a representative cross-section of the reports pouring into the Führerhauptquartier day by day. But just in case anyone jumps to the conclusion that the officers of the German General Staff were all as credulous and gullible as Himmler's spy-master Walter Schellenberg, here is a pail of cold water from von Roeme, the officer analysing the reports for the Foreign Armies West Department of the General Staff in the steel and concrete underground headquarters at Zossen outside Berlin. His memorandum is dated October 2, 1943, by which time it was, of course, too late in the year for large-scale amphibious operations. Nevertheless, he must be congratulated for introducing a note of realism.

The multiplicity of the at times utterly fantastic reports about allegedly imminent operations on the North Sea littoral and the Channel coast as well as the French Atlantic coast reveal an intention to deceive and mislead. Among such deception material must be counted reports about alleged preparations along and behind the English coast which are alleged to be directed against the French coast immediately opposite. The Allies are under no illusion about the difficulties of a large scale assault against the by no means numerous coastal sectors suited for a landing. Also, that once they have launched an assault of this kind it will not be possible to call it off except at the cost of enormous losses.

The constant insistence of the Soviet Union that a second front must be established forthwith in the occupied Western Territories with a large-scale landing will meet with considerable resistance on the part of the Allies under existing circumstances.

The coming negotiations first at the Foreign Ministers Conference then at the meeting of Roosevelt and Churchill with Stalin provide a welcome opportunity to avoid binding obligations vis à vis the Soviet Union.

Military and above all political considerations therefore suggest that the big Allied assault in the West will be postponed for the time being and that we scarcely need expect it this year. On the other hand, operations with limited objectives may continue to be expected.

More and more pronounced is the Anglo-American anxiety to bring Spain and Portugal into the war on their side. The Iberian Peninsula however is no longer looked on as a bridge-head for operations in conjunction with a second front but is being treated rather as a base from which to penetrate Europe in the final stage of the war.

This dispassionate appraisal did not stop the Führerhaupt-quartier from being alarmed by sensational reports nourished by Colonel Bevan's team at Storey's Gate, who were anxious to keep as many German troops as possible in the mild climate of France and the debilitating uneventfulness of Holland, Denmark and Norway.

Fear of imminent landings by the Allies in Portugal caused Hitler to think twice whether he should not call off a planned U-boat attack in the North Atlantic for fear that the U-boats might not be able to get down south in time to prevent a landing in Portugal.* As a result of deception warnings of an Allied assault on the Biscay region the Führerhauptquartier and the C-in-C West had an anxious week at the end of January 1944. A Luftwaffe reconnaissance pilot on January 29 had reported sighting what he took for an Allied naval force about to attack the mouth of the Gironde. In all haste the SS Panzer Division 'Das Reich', which was in France for a refit, was rushed down to repel the enemy landing, only to discover that the enemy assault force was a group of harmless Sardine fishermen from northern Spain.†

The Führer, proud of his divinatory gifts, kept selecting new target areas in which to expect the Allied assault. Holland, Jutland, the Bay of Biscay, the Calais Straits were all picked by him. Even Normandy. At other times he prophesied that there would be no Allied invasion at all, that all the noise about it was 'just an impudent bluff'. These constant changes of mind by the Führer made it difficult for his generals to develop a coherent defence strategy.

Not that the German generals or Hitler can altogether be blamed for that. Up to the end of 1943 the Allies themselves had not evolved an agreed and coherent strategy. But the Teheran Conference put an end to all that. At Teheran it was at last decided that the long-threatened Second Front would be launched with a cross-Channel invasion in May 1944.

Along with that decision went another: to provide 'Overlord' with an inter-Allied cover plan which was to mislead the Germans about the place and time of the attack and to prevent them from

---

* Führer Conferences on Naval Affairs, January 24, 1944, page 382 (2j).
† Führer Conferences on Naval Affairs, January 24, 1944, page 386 (6g). Percy Schramm, *Kriegstagebuch des OKW*, IV-1, page 90.

bringing their full available forces to bear against the Allied armies landing in the beach-heads. Churchill, in pressing the conference to agree to a concerted Allied deception scheme, said with character-istic flamboyance: 'In wartime Truth is so precious that she should always be attended by a bodyguard of lies.' The phrase caught on, and when the task of drawing up the master deception plan was given to Colonel J. H. Bevan and his team at Storey's Gate its code-name was, almost inevitably, 'Bodyguard'.

The scares launched by the deception teams in Cairo, Algiers, and London, exploiting and increasing the confusion caused by the Allied forces in one part of Hitler-occupied territory after another, had already reduced the dictator to a paranoiac wreck increasingly dependent on the syringes of his pet quack Professor Theodor Morell. Now he was to be faced with the supreme show-down, the Anglo-American assault on Europe from the West and the simul-taneous drive by the Russians from the East. And leading the assault would be the phantoms conjured up by 'Bodyguard'. They would combine to produce in him a mental state where he could no longer distinguish what was real and what was illusion. (Symptomatic of his condition was an order he gave to his chief signals officer General Albert Praun, instructing him to check the Führerhaupt-quartier's telephone lines for bugging devices by which spies of the Allied radio 'Soldatensender West'—directed by me!— were able to listen to top secret conversations and then broadcast the information thus obtained!*)

*   *   *

General Kühlenthal had suggested to Jorge Antonio that he should expand still further his existing 'orchestra' of sub-agents.

Not that Jorge Antonio needed much prompting. He was always ready to take on new recruits if opportunity offered and occasion demanded. Reid and he invented new agents and wrote them into and out of the network with all the virtuosity of television drama-tists scripting a soap-opera. But before any new character was taken on the strength Jorge Antonio with exemplary obedience to the security procedure laid down by Kühlenthal always submitted

---

* Praun, *Soldat in der Telegraphen und Nachrichtentruppe.*

him or her to Madrid for approval. Only one sub-agent had been selected and appointed by Jorge Antonio without Madrid being consulted. This was the BOAC steward who (notionally) acted as courier.

Of the four original sub-agents only two were still active in 1943; the BOAC steward and a wealthy Venezuelan business man living in Glasgow whose job it was to report on what went on in Scotland. One of the two departed had dropped out because he had been called up and sent overseas. The second, poor fellow, had died after an illness described in harrowing detail by Jorge Antonio. (To make sure there were no inconsistencies in the clinical story of his illness Reid, careful as ever, consulted one of M.I.5's medical advisers.)

It had become necessary to write this sub-agent out of the script because he had been described as living in the Liverpool suburb of Bootle and was thus especially well placed to observe Liverpool shipping. He should therefore have been able to pick up valuable information about the troopships leaving for the landings in French North Africa. Which meant that he had the choice between disappointing Kühlenthal, and perhaps even arousing his suspicion—and death. Reid made the decision. The verdict was death.

In the course of 1943 Jorge Antonio took on a Gibraltarian waiter who—according to Jorge Antonio's story—worked in a NAAFI canteen attached to a big army depot near Chislehurst in Kent. The Gibraltarian—like the other civilian inhabitants of the Rock he had been forcibly evacuated to Britain and consequently hated both the British and their climate—was a useful fellow because he was able to pick up many odd scraps of information from the military personnel passing through the depot. The waiter in his turn introduced Jorge Antonio to a young conscientious objector who had been excused from joining the Army on condition that he worked on a farm for the duration of the war. This young Englishman had great sympathies with the cause of the Spanish Republicans and loved reminiscing to Jorge Antonio about his experiences in Spain during the Civil War. He had served there as a volunteer ambulance driver with a left-wing humanitarian organisation called 'The British Medical Aid to Spain'.

'His potential value to the network', Jorge Antonio reported to

Kühlenthal when asking permission to take him on, 'does not lie in the information he can provide. That should be infinitesimal because he lives in comparative isolation on a farm. His value to us is that he is a fanatical amateur radio operator and still has his own transmitter. He operated it freely before war broke out, sending and receiving messages to and from other radio amateurs all over the world.

'Although he is aware that it is illegal for him to operate his transmitter under present conditions, he is willing to do so for me. For I have convinced him that I am working for the Secret Service of Dr Negrin's* London Committee and that he could render the cause of Spanish democracy a valuable service by sending signals to the anti-fascist underground organisation in Spain. As a wireless operator the man is undoubtedly efficient. I have tested him myself. I see no dangers in this scheme. The man will have no knowledge of what he is transmitting as the messages will be in cipher. If the British should by chance blunder on to our signalling post it would lead them only to that degenerate Kremlinite ninny Negrin, not to us. If you approve, please advise me what frequencies to use and at what times.'

It was an historic message, for Kühlenthal gave the new recruit his blessing. And soon Kühlenthal's German station operating just outside Madrid under cover of the Spanish Army's Signal Corps was in regular communication with the bogus conchy's transmitter served by a very genuine M.I.5 operator. Kühlenthal never suspected. Not even when Jorge Antonio's operator, heroically defying all risks of discovery, remained on the air for an hour or more at a time.

That this was so is proved irrefutably by the records of the Foreign Armies West Department of Hitler's General Staff which were captured by the Americans at the end of the war. While Colonel Alexis von Roenne, the department's chief, astutely suspected other reports passed to him by Abwehr or SD of being 'deception material' planted by the enemy, he awarded 'Cato's' reports such descriptions as 'from a V-man of frequently proved reliability' (e.g. 'Appendix to short appreciation of enemy situation West of 9.4.44, Nr 2129/44 Top Secret'). Not once does von Roenne doubt

---

* Negrin at one period of the Civil War was premier of the Spanish Republic.

'Cato's' honesty and genuineness, although he sometimes disagrees with his conclusions and interpretations.

Reid and Jorge Antonio took immense trouble to make sure that the sub-agents 'Cato' recruited were of a type he could plausibly have met and made friends with. And that they were citizens such as the Germans would accept as friendly to themselves and hostile to the 'plutocratic régime' of the 'warmonger Churchill'. Jorge Antonio busily collected Welsh, Irish, and Scottish 'Nationalists'— the kind of Britons with whom Kiesinger peopled the English language 'Freedom Stations'* under his control. But occasionally he also took on agents who were frankly mercenary, helping him not from idealistic motives but selling him information for whatever they could get for it—as Jorge Antonio pointed out to Kühlenthal with commendable realism.

One such mercenary was a retired Merchant Navy seaman who lived in Swansea. Reid and Jorge Antonio had invented him in order that he should become the nucleus of a network of agents distributed along the south and south-east coasts who would be able to observe preparations for the coming invasion. (Wisely they wanted to have these men on the spot before the area was closed to outsiders as a security precaution.) In due course, so Jorge Antonio reported, the mercenary ex-seaman announced that he had met the leader of a militant organisation of Welsh nationalists whose members believed that their best hopes of liberating Wales from the Anglo-Saxon yoke lay in the defeat of Britain by the Third Reich. They had founded what they called the 'Aryan World Order' to collaborate with Aryans the world over and the Germans in particular. One of their leading members ironically was a fanatically anti-British Palestinian Arab—presumably what Hitler would have called an 'honorary Aryan'.

Jorge Antonio was inclined to scoff at the society whose members he said spent their time making lists of people—Communists and Jews mostly—who should be liquidated when Germany's victory gave the members of the 'Aryan World Order' theirs. Kühlenthal, however, no doubt aware of the danger of not showing himself

---

* Stations like 'Radio Caledonia' and 'The Workers' Challenge', which pretended to be operating from 'somewhere in Britain', but in reality were broadcasting from Berlin under German direction.

responsive to Aryan idealists—even when they included an anti-Semitic Semite—urged Jorge Antonio to make every possible use of the society. Which Jorge Antonio did with the well-paid assistance of the Swansea seaman who thus became head man of a ring of five agents—the Palestinian, his Welsh mistress (a pretty girl serving in the WRNS) and three Welshmen who were described to Kühlenthal as 'Welsh National Socialists'. (What fun Reid and Jorge Antonio had!)

The Swansea seaman's sub-agents knew nothing of his own existence, Jorge Antonio told Kühlenthal. And the seaman in turn was under the impression that he and the 'Aryans' were the total membership of Jorge Antonio's spy-ring.

Jorge Antonio also reported to Kühlenthal on what he called his 'unconscious' sub-agents. These were particularly important now that Madrid was not asking only for information that could be gathered from observation on the ground but was clamouring for inside news of a secret and confidential nature which could only be obtained from those treading the so-called corridors of power. But Jorge Antonio rose to the occasion. He made two first-class contacts.

The first was a 'he', an official at the Ministry of Information who seems to have been exceptionally well placed for political and strategic information. From what Jorge Antonio said about him Kühlenthal could have gussed that this official was nothing less than the top man of the Ministry's Iberian section.

The other was a 'she'. And ungallantly Jorge Antonio dropped broad hints that not only had he declared his love to the young woman—she was a secretary in what Jorge Antonio described to Kühlenthal as 'probably the War Cabinet'—but that he had been rewarded with a passion of which he had not suspected an English girl of being capable.

All this was good novelettish stuff calculated to appeal to the romantic in Kühlenthal. But Jorge Antonio added another touch which showed him as a shrewd professional. 'The señorita,' he said, 'is far from beautiful and rather dowdy in her dress. Although in her early thirties she is clearly unaccustomed to attentions from the opposite sex. This makes her all the more accessible to mine. Already she is delightfully indiscreet.' The American newspaper publisher who represented OSS in the 'Twenty Club' sardonically warned Reid not to overdo the secretary's sexual thraldom. 'Otherwise you'll have Kühlenthal expecting too much of her and the poor girl will have to be liquidated!'

By the beginning of 1944, when Wild was all set to begin his first campaign, Jorge Antonio had no fewer than twenty-five imaginary agents under his command, much to the gratification of Kühlenthal who saw in 'Cato's Orchestra' a successful German rival to Moscow's celebrated 'Red Orchestra' which Gestapo and SD had—as they believed—rounded up and destroyed in 1942.

Jorge Antonio was a model Commander-in-Chief. He personally reconnoitred the terrain on which new recruits had reported in order to check their facts and assess to what extent their powers of observation could be relied on. One of the 'Aryans' had, for instance, reported on the situation at Dover. Jorge Antonio forwarded the report to Kühlenthal with a warning that this source was as yet untried and that he would do his best to check the report himself. A week later he followed this up: 'I was able to confirm last Sunday the accuracy of the report sent by 18b* from Dover. I shall therefore be able to classify him in future as a good reporter.' Of another member of the Aryan team he said: 'I consider this first report fairly good as he tries to get details. These show the trouble he takes in explaining what he has seen.'

To spice the reports of Jorge Antonio's network with the kind of picturesque and intimate detail only a genuine on-the-spot observer could have discovered Wild laid on a special service with M.I.5. Field Security officers in civilian clothes were sent out to patrol the area in which the notional V-men were supposed to be operating. Their orders were: 'You will put yourself in the shoes of an enemy agent and report anything you see or hear which you think might be of interest to the enemy. Add your conclusions as to the meaning of what you have picked up.' The reports were sent to St James's Street once a fortnight and, after being carefully doctored by the

* Eighteen was the number under which the Swansea seaman's reports were passed on to Madrid. His sub-agents figured as 18a, 18b, 18c, 18d, 18e, and so forth. Madrid forwarding their reports to Berlin gave them and their network pseudonyms. For instance, the seamen's network was called 'Dagobert' and the three Welsh sub-agents 'Freddy, Dick, and Desmond'. In the same way Jorge Antonio's network as a whole was 'Operation Ganelon' and he himself was 'Cato'.

'Twenty Club', they were used in Jorge Antonio's reports to
Madrid. All that the unsuspecting Field Security men were told
about their exercise was that they were helping to check whether
there were any holes in Allied security.

Kühlenthal was delighted with the results. He was fulsome in his
praise for the new arrangements. 'I have taken note with great
interest of what you have told me about the amplification of your
network, and the messages you have sent have demonstrated that
you were absolutely right in nominating the old and tried collaborators as sub-agents of new networks. The network of Eighteen'
(the Swansea seaman) 'seems to be the one giving the best
results.'

By the beginning of 1944 'Cato's Orchestra' was at its battle stations ready to report on the invasion the moment the situation
required it. Also ready were the other agents Wild had obtained
from the 'Double-cross Committee'—'Paul', the Dutch staff officer,
'Talleyrand', the Polish military attaché, and a few minor actors
whom I shall only mention when they appear on the scene.

But not only were the agents ready. So too were the dummy
landing craft and the other devices of physical deception. The War
Office had supplied an entire Wireless Deception Group equipped
with an ingenious mechanism which enabled a single wireless
transmitter to simulate the traffic of six. Thus one wireless truck
could fake the traffic of an entire divisional headquarters. In
accordance with the arrangements made with General de Guingand
(see page 39) the group was immediately put under the command
of 21st Army Group.

The Americans for their part shipped a complete and fully trained
Wireless Deception Unit across the Atlantic which on arrival in
Britain first came under the command of ETOUSA,* later under
that of General Omar Bradley's 12th Army Group. The American
unit did not have the special equipment of the British. None the less
it was able to represent the traffic of no fewer than three army corps
and nine divisions as well as the headquarters of an army group and
an army. What is more the Americans were able to signal while
they were on the move around the country, just as they would do

---

* ETOUSA = European Theatre of Operations United States Army.

under actual field conditions—a most useful accomplishment, as will be seen.

By February 1944 everything was ready and waiting for SHAEF's new Anglo-American Deception Unit to launch its first major campaign.

8

Norway

In addition to the general objective of deceiving the enemy as to the timing, weight, and direction of the invasion (once it had become evident that the preparations for it could no longer be concealed), the newly created Anglo-American deception team had been set three tasks for their opening campaign.

They were to try to make the German High Command believe that:

1. The Channel assault had been postponed.

2. The Anglo-Americans did not intend for the time being to attempt a major landing on the Continent but would content themselves with reoccupying such territory as the Germans evacuated voluntarily.

3. A landing was to be mounted in Norway some time in May by an Anglo-American force based on Scotland and Northern Ireland.

At first sight the project for a landing in Norway seemed to contradict the display of tame inertia indicated in the postponement of the invasion and the limitation of military enterprise in Hitler-occupied Europe to a mere follow-up of German evacuation. As it turned out, however, the campaign suggesting the imminence of a landing in Norway was not launched until late in March, while the themes of 'postponement' and 'reoccupation' were taken up as early as January.

Jorge Antonio was given the honour of kicking off. To him fell the by-no-means-simple task of convicing the Abwehr that 'balanced forces are being held in readiness in England to occupy any part of north-west Europe against the contingency of a German withdrawal or collapse'.

He performed it with his customary skill, pouring scorn on the naïvéte and wishful thinking of the Anglo-American command in contemplating an eventuality so unlikely as a German withdrawal.* 'Amazing as is this underestimation of the Führer's determination to defend the Fortress Europe against the forces of the plutocrat reactionaries and the Bolshevik barbarians,' commented Jorge Antonio, 'it is none the less a fact. The British and the Americans genuinely delude themselves that under the combined menace of the Russian advance on the Reich frontiers from the East and their own bomber offensive against the Reich from the West the Führer will be compelled to give up outer positions in order to reinforce the defences of the Reich itself.' And Jorge Antonio went on to quote from genuine contingency plans which AMGOT (Allied Military Government of Occupied Territories) had drawn up for the emergency administration of occupied territories in the event of their being liberated following a German evacuation or surrender. As the source of his information he shyly mentioned the lady secretary in the War Cabinet.

But he did not let the matter rest there. His friend at the Ministry of Information was now brought on to the stage. About a fortnight after he sent his first message revealing the 'peaceful reoccupation' plan Jorge Antonio reported how while visiting his Spanish-speaking pal at the M of I he had noticed a leaflet lying on his desk.† It was in French and contained instructions for the French

---

* In fact such an Allied estimate of Hitler's possible strategy would have been by no means as ludicrous as Jorge Antonio sycophantically pretended. In August 1943, just before the collapse of Rumania, Hitler—as Allied intelligence had learned—was considering substantial withdrawals from northern and southern Europe so that he would be better able to meet the critical challenges from the east and west. He asked Albert Speer, his Minister of Armaments, to report on the economic consequences of such withdrawals.
† Jorge Antonio also reported his conversation with the man at the M of I in a further message. An extract from it appeared two months later in an Intelligence Summary of the Department Foreign Armies West: 'Appendix to short enemy assessment (kurze Feindbeurteilung) of 9.4.44 No. 2129/44. Below we reproduce the report on a conversation with an acquaintance in the British Ministry of Information from a frequently proven V-man. (Time: end of February.)'
'Two days ago I had another opportunity to talk at length with my acquaintance at the Ministry of Information. I expressed my doubts about the possibility of a voluntary German withdrawal from France. He replied that authoritative British circles took a different view. If the Germans had to choose between two evils, he said, then surely they would prefer the Western

population on what they were to do in the event of the Germans withdrawing. The leaflet promised that Allied troops were on their way and called on the French to give them their fullest co-operation. 'This leaflet,' said Jorge Antonio, 'has clearly been prepared for use in the event of a voluntary evacuation of France by the German Army. Would you like me to send it to you by our courier? I managed to lift a copy without my friend noticing. I think you would find it both instructive and diverting.'

Kühlenthal did indeed want to have the leaflet and said so in a radio message on the very next transmission. As luck had it, the 'BOAC steward' was departing for Lisbon within the next forty-eight hours. Thus Kühlenthal received his leaflet in record time. It had been specially written and printed for him by the French section of the Political Warfare Executive, one of whose duties was to prepare the 'Avis au Peuple Français' leaflets dropped by the RAF and the US Air Force over France. Kühlenthal's copy was unique. It had been produced for him alone in a special run of less than fifty copies the rest of which were incinerated once Kühlenthal had been sent his.

A variety of reasons was put forward to account for the post-ponement of the Channel assault. One of them was labour troubles in the United States which were delaying the production of landing craft. Without landing craft there could be no landing. The so-often-criticised Field Marshal Montgomery was another. It had already been made public that the field marshal was to command the invasion force during the landing and now Monty's notorious passion for 100 per cent perfection in any operation of which he had charge was blamed for the postponment. 'Paul', the Dutch officer on the staff commanding the Dutch invasion contingent, was thought to be the best channel to convey this information authoritatively. Said he in a message at the end of January to his control in Hamburg: '. . . There is an opinion among us, that, as in Egypt, Montgomery will insist on training the troops all over again.'

Allies to be the ones to occupy Berlin and dictate the peace terms. For this reason the Germans will be compelled to withdraw troops from the West in order to reinforce the Eastern front—should the Soviet advance continue at its present rate and the Germans want to prevent the Russians from crossing the frontier. "That will be the moment," he said, "when we can land without any difficulty." '

One of the Swansea seaman's Aryan sub-agents in a dispatch from the south coast said that roads in that area were being widened and improved but at a pace which did not suggest any urgency. Similar reports were being received from south-east England and were duly passed on by Jorge Antonio to the Madrid K.O. And 'Talleyrand', the Polish military attaché, visiting Lisbon about the same time, told his German control officer how he had checked a report that embarkation camps were being built in Kent. He found that at the sites mentioned to him the foundations for a considerable number of prefabricated huts had indeed been laid. Work, however, had now been halted. No builders were present on the sites, let alone at work. Only a few guards and caretakers were lounging around. Most significant of all, he thought, was the fact that derricks had been brought up to sink artesian wells. No crews, however, were on the sites and work appeared to have come to a complete stop. The British, he commented, did not seem to be in much of a hurry to launch the famous second front in France, despite all Churchill's promises to the Russians. In fact both they and the Americans seemed more than a little scared of the whole thing. Sometimes one got the impression, he said, that the British and the Americans wanted to leave the war in Western Europe to the bombers which were doing what everyone in London thought a highly effective job. 'The bombers could knock out Germany by themselves. No need for an invasion yet,' was the view among top people he met.

While Colonel Wild's double agents were reporting all this comforting news to the Germans direct, Colonel Bevan and his LCS were taking care of the indirect channels. Foreign diplomats at home and in the neutral capitals were the recipients of many a calculated 'leak' building up to much the same picture. I myself in my capacity as a Psychological Warrior did my best to help.

I persuaded my colleagues of the BBC and the Voice of America that in our output there should be no reference either direct or indirect to an invasion of France, no 'the-Yanks-are-coming' biceps-slapping. In the counterfeit of a German Forces Radio which I directed—its purpose was to 'soften up' the German troops in France in readiness for the invasion—we insisted that Russia was the all-important front where Germany's destiny would be decided, that France in the eyes of the OKW was no more than a training and recuperation area.

The 'Soldatensender Calais',* as we called the station in imitation of 'Soldatensender Belgrad' and other German Forces Radios in occupied territory, incessantly and quite truthfully reported the departure of units from France for the Eastern Front and Italy. The deception colonels approved. It fitted in nicely with what they and 'Cato' were putting across.

The Soldatensender's emphasis on the importance of Italy as a possible jumping-off point for an Anglo-American push into south-eastern Europe also harmonised with another deception campaign which Colonel Bevan's LCS had been conducting since November 1943. This exaggerated Anglo-American strength in the Mediter-ranean and played down the build-up in Britain. (The 'Postpone-ment' theme was intended to contribute to this.)

But although wireless silence had been imposed on the British and United States formations arriving in Britain this was not one of the most successful campaigns. For one thing General Kühlenthal's observers at Algeciras were quick to report the British and American transports sailing west through the Straits of Gibraltar, for another Field Marshal Kesselring's military intelligence in Italy soon became aware that such old friends as the 50th British Infantry Division and the 51st Highland Division were no longer opposite them in Italy. Had they been sent to North Africa for a rest and re-equipment? Or had they been sent to Britain to get ready for the invasion of France?

The Abwehr promptly sent out queries to its V-men in England. On January 11, 1944, Jorge Antonio received a first enquiry from Madrid: 'Which are the British divisions that have been with-drawn from Italy and have returned to Britain?'

The deception colonels and their staffs in London put their heads together to puzzle out what answer Jorge Antonio should give to that one. They decided that it would be difficult to keep the Germans from knowing that troops had in fact returned to Britain from the Mediterranean. There were too many Africa Stars being

---

* 'Soldiers' Radio Calais'.

worn around Piccadilly for foreign diplomats and others not to have noticed them. So it was decided to compromise.

'English troops wearing the Africa Star have been seen around London,' replied Jorge Antonio. 'It is believed that these men have returned from the Mediterranean to assist in training the less experienced units.' One of the letter-writing agents, a vivacious French lady who loved the London night spots, reported chattily: 'On New Year's Eve I met some officers of the 8th Army in the Four Hundred Club who were wearing the new yellow ribbon of the African campaign. They said they had been exchanged for officers from Britain in order that they should tour the camps instructing troops and lecturing to them.'

Though the 'Postponement' theme had scarcely got off the ground, it was becoming clear that it was going to be hard to keep up. By the middle of March there were so many complaints that the ban on the use of wireless was interfering with the training of signals' units that Wild and his SHAEF team recommended that it should be lifted. Colonel Dudley Clarke in Cairo however wanted to keep both the wireless silence and the 'Postponement' story alive. for he and his 'A' Force still had the task of exaggerating the Allied strength in the Mediterranean.

What finally killed 'Postponement' was the decision to hold an invasion rehearsal in the Channel early in May, with assault divisions and their attendant naval escorts taking part. Obviously it was going to be impossible to keep a movement on this scale hidden from the Germans. Nor would it be possible to fool them into believing that the Allied Supremo was going to take his troops for a Channel outing months before sending them into battle. An agent continuing to plug 'Postponement' to the Germans would therefore stand revealed as either a fool or, worse still, a fraud. 'Postponement' accordingly was quietly abandoned. After March it was forgotten.

*   *   *

The planning of the fake expedition to Norway had enjoyed top priority with the SHAEF deception artists since the end of January 1944. It was to be a truly substantial operation. Everything was being laid on for it—wireless deception, visual deception, double-

cross agents—everything. Even genuine British and American
infantry formations were involved in the plan—purely notionally
of course—as well as Polish, Dutch, and Norwegian units. Allied
naval forces were to stage mock sweeps in Norwegian waters, while
long-range fighters and reconnaissance planes would carry out
genuine sorties over targets in Norway.

Primary purpose of the enterprise was to deter the Germans from
moving to France any of the sixteen divisions they had stationed
in Norway and Denmark or their arms and ammunition. This was
important because the forces in Norway disposed not only of arms
that were badly needed in France by Rundstedt and Rommel but of
well-trained fighting divisions as well. In southern Norway, for
instance, there was one armoured division which Rommel was
anxious to have in France. Also one thousand four-inch guns
which would have come in most useful in strengthening defences.
It was the task of the deception unit to see that the armoured
division and the guns remained in Norway until it was too late
for them to play any part in preventing a landing. A secondary
purpose of the Norway deception was to educate Hitler's intelligence
officers to look to their SHAEF-controlled V-men for their main
information about the build-up and location of the Allied forces in
Britain.

Feeding a false order of battle to the enemy intelligence is a
process that takes time. The order of battle cannot be handed over in
one package with a simple 'Here you are, old boy. It's all yours!'
It has to be leaked gradually bit by bit so that the intelligence
officers have the satisfaction of fitting the information together on
their staff maps like pieces of a jigsaw puzzle. They must be encouraged to take pride in the astuteness with which they have
made their deductions despite the enemy's cloak of security.

This made it essential therefore to start the notional build-up of
the expeditionary force for Norway as early as possible. Further it
was advisable to have the assembly areas for the Norway force far
away from the genuine assembly areas and embarkation points in
southern and south-western England where the troops for the
Normandy landings would in fact be assembling and embarking.

Scotland was the area chosen. It was ideal for the purpose. Firstly
because it was the natural starting point for an expedition to Nor-

way. Further because there were a number of genuine formations in Scotland which were being trained for the Normandy landings. It would be fairly simple to adapt their training programmes in such a way that any outside observers would draw the conclusion that the troops' destination was Norway. Of course the SHAEF deception team had to make sure that none of these genuine units would be involved in the Normandy preparations so early that they could be discovered and identified by the Germans as Normandy divisions and thus give the hoax away.

Next most important consideration was the timing of the fake expedition so that it should have the maximum impact on Hitler's High Command. It was calculated that at the very least it would take the Germans a fortnight to transport a division from Norway to France. Most probably much longer in view of the bombing of road and rail communications.

To ensure therefore that the threat of an Allied landing in Norway would be holding down the German divisions in Denmark and Norway at the time of the Allied landings in Normandy it was necessary to persuade the Germans that the landing in Norway would be taking place on a date which was in fact a fortnight after the D-day—unknown to the Germans—planned by Eisenhower for Normandy.

When the original plan was made for the Norway deception, Eisenhower's D-day for Normandy had been fixed for May 5. The fictitious D-day for the first landing in Norway was accordingly put down as the end of May. When, however, Eisenhower postponed the Normandy landing to the beginning of June the deception planners followed suit and postposed their notional Norway D-day as well.

The tactical and strategic plan for the fake expedition was worked out as carefully as if it had been a genuine operation involving the lives of thousands of Allied soldiers. This was necessary so that the dispositions of the units—genuine and fictitious—taking part in it would be convincingly realistic at whatever point a part of them was uncovered for the Germans.

The plan accordingly provided for two main landings, one in the north, the other in the south. The northern landing was the first. It had the iron-ore port of Narvik as its primary objective and was to be carried out by two divisions. These, so the Germans were to be persuaded, expected to be joined by a Russian contingent after they had pushed up the railway line to Gällivare in Sweden. There the Russians would link up with them in a campaign to open up northern and central Sweden.

The southern landing by an assault division, supported by commandos and parachute troops and escorted by long-range fighter-bombers, was to seize Stavanger and its airfield. Within three months the southern force would be built up to three divisions. The assault was to capture Bergen and Trondheim and then fan out in a series of mutually supporting land and amphibious operations to strike at Oslo. Pressure would be brought to bear on Sweden in order to secure the use of Swedish airfields. With southern Norway under their control the Allies would then launch a campaign for the liberation of Denmark.

Quite an elaborate plan it was. And from a German point of view a menacing one. For with the liberation of Denmark as its objective it was clearly preliminary to a descent on Hamburg, Lübeck, and the North German plain, a poetic reversal of the strategy with which Hitler in 1940 had begun the subjugation of Western Europe. Possibly for that reason this prospect was particularly alarming to Hitler who throughout 1943 had been subjected by Colonel Bevan to a series of Norway scares. In his 'Führer Directive No. 51' of November 3, 1943, laying down his dispositions for meeting an Anglo-American attack in the West, Hitler referred specifically to the possibility of a large-scale assault against Denmark: 'A large-scale assault on Denmark is by no means excluded. From a naval point of view it is less feasible' (than a landing in the Pas de Calais area where Hitler expected the main assault) 'and it is less capable of being effectively supported from the air. In the event of success however its political and operational consequences would be the greatest.'*

To convince the German intelligence that the Norway expedition was really on after having been planned in 1943 and then cancelled meant that the SHAEF deception team would have to produce evidence for German consumption that an army command was in

---

* Percy Ernst Schramm, *Kriegstagebuch des OKW*, IV 2, page 1531.

charge of the party with at least three army corps under it, one for the north and the two others for the south. There had to be evidence of the presence of eight divisions.

In Scotland there were two genuine British divisions, the 52nd Lowland Division near Dundee and the 3rd Infantry Division which was undergoing assault training in the Moray Firth for the Normandy landing. In addition there was an impressive Polish force distributed over the Lowlands, a contingent of Norwegians and Dutch at Brahan Castle near Dingwall and the British 113th Brigade in the Orkneys. In Northern Ireland there was the 55th British Infantry Division and the American 15th Corps which had under its command the 2nd, 5th, and 8th US Infantry Divisions. The Americans were intended for use in Normandy, but not until about three weeks after the invasion had been launched. The British 55th Infantry Division was on garrison duty in Northern Ireland and could therefore be expected to remain there as long as the SHAEF deception required.

Of imaginary units invented for the previous Norway scare by Colonel Bevan's London Controlling Section there was the very convenient 4th Army which had been pictured as a branch of Scottish Command with headquarters a few miles from Edinburgh. In Iceland there was the fictitious 55th US Infantry Division which had first been reported by British-controlled agents and had since been kept alive by two young Norwegians whom the Germans had sent as V-men to Iceland but whom M.I.5 had promptly picked up and turned round.

Such was the genuine and fictitious skeleton around which the Deception Unit would now have to build the phantom Expeditionary Force. The first thing was to arrange for the signallers who would supply to the German radio-location and interception services the evidence for a resurgence of the Fourth Army with its ancillary British and American Corps and divisions.

*   *   *

Colonel Roderick MacLeod, an elderly (52) regular staff officer who had served with distinction in the first war and was unlucky not to have been given a division in the second, had never concerned himself with strategic deception. He had not taken any interest in it except as a student of military history and of General Allenby's deception of the Turks during the 1918 campaign in Palestine.

Now, at the beginning of March 1944, Colonel MacLeod had just finished umpiring army manœuvres in the bitter cold of the Yorkshire moors. He had then travelled south to Cambridge to spend a week's leave with his family. Hardly had he arrived in Cambridge, however, when a telephone message came through ordering him to report forthwith to Headquarters Home Forces in London. Brimful of excited anticipation, the old soldier packed his active-service kit ready for any desperate mission on which the Army might send him. The next morning he caught the first train to Liverpool Street, where a staff car met him and drove him to Hounslow Barracks, the home of Headquarters Home Forces. They were expecting him there, and without delay he was taken to the office of an old friend. This was Brigadier Barker, who had been Chief Signals Officer at Scottish Command when Colonel MacLeod had been training its divisions, setting them elaborate field exercises in preparation for the invasion of France. He and Barker had worked closely together. Now Brigadier Barker was Chief Signals Officer at Home Forces.

Barker had a mischievous sense of humour and he had looked forward to playing a little prank on his friend. 'Colonel MacLeod,' he had planned to say, 'you will travel to Edinburgh tonight to take command of an army, the 4th Army to be precise, whose task it will be to effect a landing in Norway and engage the German forces there.'

But when he was face to face with the colonel, and saw the eagerness with which his friend was hanging on his words, he thought better of it. All he said was 'Rory, old boy, you have been selected to run a deception operation for SHAEF from Scottish Command. You will travel to Edinburgh. And there you will represent an army which does not in fact exist. By means of fake signals traffic you will, however, fool the Germans into believing that it does exist and, what is more, that it is about to land in Norway and clear the Germans out of there. The whole thing is an important part of the coming invasion of France. You are to keep the Germans fully occupied in Norway so that they don't reinforce the units in

France from there. When I was asked whether I knew anyone who could direct this show I recommended you because I remembered those ingenious schemes for field exercises you had worked out, while we were at Scottish Command together. This is very much the same sort of thing. It is terrifically important that it should be a success.'

Brigadier Barker then filled in the colonel on essential technical details. In addition to the signals of the genuine British and American formations co-operating in the deception scheme he would have special British and American signals detachments attached to him which would represent the army headquarters and those of the three fictitious corps and any fictitious divisions created for the deception. 'The Germans,' said the brigadier, 'are damn good at interception and radio-location. They'll have your headquarters pinpointed with a maximum error margin of five miles. And it won't take them more than a few hours to do so. What is more, they'll be able to identify the grade of headquarters—whether army, division, corps, or what not—from the nature of the traffic and the sets being used.'

He handed the colonel a paper on which he had marked down the periods of normal wireless activity, intense activity, or of wireless silence with dates and times. 21st. Army group, the brigadier promised, would refrain from excessive use of the wireless so as to leave the ether clear for MacLeod and make sure the Germans did not overlook '4th Army' in a welter of other signals. 'Your signals campaign,' he added, 'will begin on March 17.'

Colonel MacLeod sighed. It was already March 4. He would have less than a fortnight to make his arrangements. There were fore-bodings in his heart as he left the Hounslow Barracks and had him-self driven to Norfolk House. There he received a further and more detailed briefing from the SHAEF deception planners. He felt reassured by what they told him, and by the time he fell asleep in his berth on the sleeper train to Edinburgh he was looking forward with pleasure to his new task. The next morning he reported to General Sir Andrew Thorne, the GOC Scottish Command, in his headquarters at Edinburgh Castle.

Sir Andrew was in the know about the scheme. In fact he was to play a part in it himself—as the notional commander of the phantom '4th Army'. 'Bulgy' Thorne was well known to the Germans from the time he had been military attaché at the Berlin Embassy during the early years of the Third Reich. That a general as experienced as Sir Andrew should be put in charge of the Norway expedition would, the psychologists of the SHAEF Deception Unit argued, be bound to add to the gravity of the Norway threat in German eyes.

Colonel MacLeod quickly showed that a good choice had been made in selecting him for his part in the Norway deception. He knew his way around both Scotland and Scottish Command. He understood what accommodation to request for his signals staff and where to place the headquarters of the units they were to represent. Moreover, his recollection of the 1940 campaign in Norway, in whose planning and direction he had shared as Military Assistant to General Sir Edmund Ironside, the then Chief of the Imperial General Staff, enabled him to fill in many details that had escaped even the meticulous planners in Norfolk House.

About twenty officers from a recently disbanded Corps Head-quarters of Scottish Command were now assigned to him by Sir Andrew Thorne, as well as an officer who was to serve as his second-in-command, Lieutenant-Colonel 'Nigger' Horn. He was also joined by Captain Ralph Ingersoll of the US Army who was to serve as his liaison officer with the American 15th Corps in Northern Ireland. Ingersoll in civilian life was a distinguished New York newspaper man. The 4th Army was his first experience of deception, but not his last, for with Ingersoll it was love at first sight, and he became one of the foremost American exponents of the art of deception. He later practised it with devotion and great success on behalf of General Omar Bradley's 12th Army Group.

Colonel MacLeod distributed his officers as if they were taking part in one of his set-piece exercises around the Staff College sand-box. Two majors took on the tasks of corps commanders. Major Rumsey with six junior officers assumed command of the imaginary 2nd Corps with headquarters near Stirling. Major Bowles, with six officers, became commander of the fictitious 7th Corps near Dundee. 4th Army headquarters itself was put in charge of Major Edwards, with Major Wheeler as 'A and Q',* Captain Coxhill in charge of signals, and Captain Skinner as cipher officer.

---

* The Adjutant General's and the Quartermaster General's departments.

Everything was coming along splendidly. Colonel MacLeod was well contented. Signals units representing fictitious formations were being set up all over Scotland and preparing to combine in their (fictitious) assault training with that of the three genuine infantry divisions and genuine naval and airforce units. But then suddenly the Admiralty stepped into the picture and blew an icy wind across the scheme, compelling its revision. Once more the trouble arose from that rehearsal in the Channel which had already forced the abandonment of the 'Postponement' theme.* Now it forced the withdrawal of the genuine 3rd Infantry Division from the list of formations taking part in the Norway expedition. For the Admiralty ruled that the 3rd Infantry could not be excused from the Channel exercise. Rather than run even the remotest risk of premature discovery it was decided to release the 3rd Infantry Division from the Norway expedition and substitute in its place a fake formation, the 58th Infantry Division.

The wireless resources at the disposal of Colonel MacLeod were, however, not equal to the creation of this new division. Fortunately, 21st Army Group were able to come to the rescue. Colonel Strange-ways† lent MacLeod a detachment of his No. 5 Wireless Group to represent the 58th Division on the air. Hastily a cover story was improvised to account for this new division which no one, least of all the Germans, had ever heard of before.‡ The 58th, said this legend, had made its first appearance at Aberlour not far from Inverness. It had been built round a cadre of battle-trained officers and NCOs withdrawn from Scottish regiments that were still in the Mediterranean theatre. As a special touch of whimsy it was decreed that the newly born division should be given a divisional emblem. To be suitably suggestive of the Highlands a stag's antlers were chosen.§

---

* See page 112.
† See page 39.
‡ When the German intelligence officers learned about it, they pretended they had followed it for years, but had recently lost it.
§ It will be recalled that around this time the SHAEF deception unit and 'A' Force in Cairo were still trying to hide from the Germans the return of British formations from the Mediterranean. To account for officers and men of, for instance, the 51st Highland Division being encountered in London by foreign diplomats, the SHAEF unit had been putting it around that these were from drafts sent home to provide cadres for new divisions. See page 112.

Much to the relief of Colonel MacLeod the opening date of the wireless campaign had been postponed from the 17th to the 24th of March. But on March 24th it opened up in full blast. Operational and routine messages flew up and down Scotland from army to corps, and corps to divisions and brigades. The genuine 52nd and the fake 58th as well as some of the wireless divisions held brigade exercises. They staged artillery exercises and even an artillery practice camp with shooting on the range, and all of it was conducted in wireless messages. After a few days of this it became evident that 4th Army headquarters could not cope with all the administrative and routine traffic required to simulate a busy headquarters. So Scottish Command sent MacLeod another officer to deal with this extra work. Captain Johnson turned out to be a born deception artist. Although his main task was to simulate radio traffic which by its density would suggest the presence of important and substantial forces to the Germans, Johnson interlarded this with unciphered messages and radio telephony which would fascinate the Germans. He sent out messages which hinted at amazing new weapons of mountain warfare being issued to the troops and others dealing with such mundane events as court martials. One calculated indiscretion pointing at Norway was a hurry-up order for skis. Methodically he kept files recording all open messages sent, so that there should be no contradictions to attract the suspicions of a wary intelligence officer. Most of the traffic however was a meaningless mumbo jumbo of indecipherable cipher messages whose only purpose, as I have said, was to provide the Germans with evidence that the Allies were assembling an expeditionary force in Scotland.

By the end of the first week in April the whole of MacLeod's network in Scotland and Northern Ireland was alive with messages exchanged in cipher, clear text, or radio telephony. Two Admiralty wireless units took up an elaborate imitation of naval assault forces training in the Clyde, one manifestly intended for a landing in northern Norway, the other for the south. The RAF also joined in. To a cunning accompaniment of radio signals it went through the motions of transferring medium bomber squadrons from airfields in Suffolk to north-eastern Scotland. To back up the signals eight genuine Spitfires were sent up to Peterhead in north-east Scotland and stationed there along with eight dummies.

In the meantime Jorge Antonio and the other bogus V-men lent by M.I.5's 'Double-cross' Committee had been busy—to the considerable satisfaction of their Abwehr clients who showed their appreciation with numerous messages of congratulation. The congratulations were deserved. A great deal of trouble had been taken by the SHAEF Unit, not only to supply the most suitable intelligence but also to make sure the V-men were in the right places to observe and report what was allegedly going on.

Most important of them all on this occasion was 'Paul' the Dutch spy chief whom the SIPO's Major Schreieder had captured in Holland and then sent to Britain to spy against the Allies. Up to this time the 'Double-cross' Committee had not allowed 'Paul' to be used on deception. But now at the end of February 1944 they had relented and agreed that 'Paul' was to use the authority he had built up with his German controllers to hoodwink them. As an officer of the Dutch headquarters in London he was ideally suited to pay a visit to the Dutch units stationed in Scotland. And as a trained military observer he was predestined to discover 4th Army and the location of its various units. Who better than he to give the Germans an expert appraisal of its mysterious movements and unravel their significance?

In addition to 'Paul' there was yet another military observer waiting to serve the Abwehr. 'Talleyrand', the 'assistant Polish military attaché', had recently received permission from Lisbon to recruit a most promising assistant. This was an aide de camp to the young King Peter of Yugoslavia. In the eyes of the Germans his primary function was to help 'Talleyrand' with his radio transmitter.

As a consequence of his closeness to King Peter, however, he also had excellent social contacts with the snobbish British and Americans who were for ever trying to impress one so close to royalty with the extent and importance of their knowledge and influence. (Need I add that the ADC was entirely bogus, a product of the SHAEF team's fertile imagination?) The King's ADC, the SHAEF team decided, should travel to Scotland and possibly also to Northern Ireland for some shooting and fishing with friends of his royal master owning estates there.

Jorge Antonio, as ever with his ears to the ground, had heard rumours of strange goings-on in Scotland. So he had mobilised his

Venezuelan sub-agent and sent him to investigate and if possible to
watch naval exercises he had heard were being held in the Clyde.
The Venezuelan in his turn sent a sub-agent of his own (like the
Swansea ex-seaman the Venezuelan now headed a network of
sub-sub-agents!) to check up on a concentration of shipping reported to be assembling at Methil in the Firth of Forth.

And then the reports began coming in.

King Peter's ADC was the first off the mark. On March 22, two
days before MacLeod's wireless overture, he reported how while
travelling up to Scotland with one of his friends he had discovered
the headquarters of the 2nd British Corps at a place called Garter
House. Not far from Stirling, he said it was, and he gave the
ordnance map co-ordinates. The Corps headquarters had recently
moved here from Scotch Corner near Catterick in Yorkshire.

Next to report was Jorge Antonio. His message was sent about a
week after that of the aide-de-camp. It relayed a report from the
Venezuelan to the effect that he had seen troops of the 52nd Lowland
Division in Dundee as well as others from a division he had been
unable to identify. All he could say about this one was that its
divisional emblem appeared to be an oyster shell on a dark background. Jorge Antonio, forwarding this report, commented: 'This
insignia is completely unknown to me.'

Then it was the turn of King Peter's ADC once more. Back in
London from his visit to Scotland he told how he had run into an
American officer from the US Army's 15th Corps in Rosa Lewis's
sitting room at her celebrated Cavendish Hotel in Jermyn Street.*
When he mentioned that he hoped shortly to be visiting friends in
Northern Ireland the American had volunteered enthusiastically
that his Corps was in Ulster and that it would be great if they could
meet there. The Corps was made up of the 2nd, 5th, and 8th
Infantry Divisions, he said. The British 55th Division was also
undergoing training in Ulster. He was spending a week-end leave
in London because he himself was temporarily attached to the staff
in Edinburgh of General Sir Andrew Thorne who commanded
4th Army which included the American 15th Corps. General

---

* The deceivers could not have made a happier choice of a meeting place than
Rosa's sitting room in her Cavendish Hotel—as students of Daphne Fielding's
The Duchess of Jermyn Street (Eyre and Spottiswoode, 1964) will quickly see.

Thorne, he said, was a great guy. He knew him quite well, because when the general had gone to Ulster to inspect the 15th Corps he had insisted on his coming along with him. The general had been very favourably impressed with the smart turn-out of the American troops. That was quite something, for the general had commanded the Brigade of Guards. The aide was to be sure to let him know when he was visiting Ulster. He would make a point of being there and introducing him to his commanding officer.

(Sir Andrew had in fact visited the 15th Corps in Ulster, just as though it was truly part of his command. The suggestion that he should do so had come from Ralph Ingersoll, who was picking up the art of using truth to serve fiction with remarkable aptitude.)

The Germans might quite reasonably have been a little suspicious at getting so much valuable information in one single helping. But the story of the encounter in the Cavendish Hotel was so circumstantial and the American officer's invitation to the ADC to come and see him when he was in Ulster so natural, that far from doubting the ADC's word they praised him. 'Your latest message most satisfactory' signalled the Lisbon K.O. on April 12, 1944. 'Congratulations. Please continue to watch carefully. Try to ascertain exact numbers of divisions, etc., belonging to 4th Army under General Thorne. Does anything point to intended landings in German Bight, Denmark, or southern Sweden?'*

Now it was 'Paul's' turn. At the beginning of April he had informed his German controllers that he would have to visit Scotland shortly for conferences with the Dutch commanders there. By April 12th he was back in London and then he sent a series of dispatches which filled any gaps which might have remained in the deception picture. 4th Army's headquarters was at Edinburgh, 'Paul' reported, its emblem a rectangular figure 8 in yellow. 4th Army was made up of 2nd British Corps with headquarters at Sirling (emblem wavy blue lines on a white rectangle with a red fish at the top); 7th British Corps with headquarters in the Dundee area (emblem a sea shell on a blue rectangle). For the Germans receiving this report it must have been a most welcome confirmation of Jorge Antonio's Venezuelan sub-agent.

---

* See page 87.

But that was by no means all that 'Paul' had gathered on his trip around Scotland. He had also learned:

1. That 4th Army included an American corps, which, however, he had not been able to identify.

2. That the 58th Infantry Division (emblem a stag's head on a black square) was located in the district south-east of Stirling. Many men of the 58th Division were wearing the Africa Star medal.

3. At Callender he had found a Norwegian brigade.

4. In the Perth-Dundee area he had come across the Lowland Division (emblem an oblique white cross on a blue shield with a black outline).

5. He had heard that a British brigade stationed in the Orkney Islands also came under 4th Army.

Finally, as though he was doing nothing more than cross the t's and dot the i's of an obvious inference, 'Paul' concluded his report with the offhand observation that an attack on Norway should be expected in May.

That dispatch and what had been reported previously certainly gave the Abwehr men and their clients in the Department Foreign Armies West of Hitler's Army High Command plenty of material on the strength of which they could start sticking new pins into their order of battle maps of the British Isles. 'Paul's' detailed report on the troop dispositions in Scotland was referred to in Situation Report No. 1244 of the Foreign Armies West Department, dated April 23, 1944:

An Abwehr source which has so far reported accurately was able to ascertain the distribution of forces in the region of Scottish Command. His report shows that the number of British and American formations previously assumed by the department to be in this area must be augmented by one Infantry Division. As the source referred to above has carried out a comprehensive reconnaissance the presence of further formations is assumed to be improbable.

An Appendix gives further details:

1. Between Edinburgh and Stirling is situated the 50th British Infantry Division (motorised). This formation, which in the Autumn of 1943 had been transferred from Italy to Syria and was able to go

into action there several times, was presumably transferred from this area to Great Britain around the turn of the year, and is probably subordinated to the headquarters command of the 2nd British Army Corps.

2. In the same area is found the 58th British Infantry Division, which up to now had been presumed to be in the Southern Command area.(!) As for some time there had been no confirmation of the existence of this formation in that area its transfer to the area of Scottish Command must be presumed to have taken place at the beginning of this year.

3. The headquarters of the 7th British Corps whose whereabouts was hitherto unknown is situated in the area of Dundee.

4. For the presence of the British Infantry Division (number unknown) in the county of Sutherland there has been no evidence since the middle of 1943. This division is now assumed to have taken the place of the 58th British Infantry Division in the Southern Command district where troop concentrations of unknown strength have been reported in recent times.

5. The 52nd British Infantry Division, the Norwegian Infantry Brigade, as well as the 1st Polish Infantry Division, which possibly uses 2 as its number, have been confirmed in their previous quarters. In addition American troops were reported in unknown strength. Probably these belong to the American Infantry Division (number unknown) assumed to be in Aberdeenshire.

'Paul', true to his reservations about spying on his own people, had said nothing about the location of any Dutch units.

The SHAEF team, however, had not finished yet. Jorge Antonio's Venezuelan sub-agent, who had been watching naval exercises in the Clyde, now also pointed a finger at Norway as the target. He had been watching naval assault forces training off Greenock and shortly after came through with a vivid eyewitness description of a combined sea and land operation in Loch Fyne on May 10 and 11. This he judiciously concluded was in preparation for an amphibious assault and added: 'Since the troops involved have all been provided with arctic equipment it is a reasonable inference that northern Norway is the objective.' The Venezuelan's sub-agent who had been gathering information at Methil learned that the shipping being collected there was to transport supplies and troops. The troops, however, would not be embarking at Methil but at other ports.

To apply yet a further touch to this Scottish mirage, SHAEF used not a double but a triple agent. This was a Persian citizen of Armenian ancestry, who in 1943, while in Istanbul on a business trip from Hamburg, had volunteered to spy for Britain in Germany. It had not taken M.I.6 very long to discover that the Persian-Armenian was a double agent whom the RSHA wanted to plant on them. That, however, did not rule him out as an instrument of SHAEF deception, albeit an unconscious one.

Neither M.I.6 or SHAEF had used him before—except to confirm the Germans in the illusion that the British had been duped by the Persian. But they employed him on deception now. To provide yet another indication that there was to be a landing in Norway SHAEF arranged for M.I.6 to ask their Persian businessman in Hamburg for weekly reports on the density of traffic on the Hamburg–Flensburg railway line. Also would he please arrange for a watch to be kept on the Baltic ports. Was there any increase in the frequency of German troop transports to Scandinavia?

*   *   *

Nothing, however, had as yet been passed to the Germans to indicate, as the deception plan demanded, that there was to be more than one landing in Norway. Nor had anything been done to implement the plan where it called for evidence of Soviet participation in the liberation of Norway. Or of pressure on neutral Sweden from the United States and Britain to allow airfields in southern Sweden to be used by the United States Air Force and the RAF. All three tasks still remained to be completed, the first by the SHAEF team through its double agents, the second and third through diplomatic channels in Moscow and Stockholm.

For sheer ingenuity the SHAEF team's solution of their problem appeals to me quite particularly. Especially as at the back of it there lurks the kind of Central European story of intrigue, which even an Alfred Hitchcock would find difficult to improve.

It begins with a certain Dr K., an Austrian Jew, who in 1938 anticipated Hitler's annexation of Austria by fleeing to Brussels where he quickly established a thriving business. The German occupation of Belgium did not cramp his style for long. In 1941 he even received permission from the Germans to set up a business in Portugal to exploit patent rights which rather astonishingly the Germans had allowed him to keep. But perhaps not so very surprisingly after all. For soon Dr K. had arranged to supply the Lisbon K.O. of the Abwehr with political, military, and economic reports obtained by using his business agencies in Allied countries as a cover for espionage. By the end of 1942 he had managed to bluff the Abwehr into believing he had valuable sources in Britain and the United States. The M.I.6 representative in Lisbon had not been blind to Dr K.'s activities, and when, as was almost inevitable, the doctor appealed to the British for help, M.I.6 without much hesitation agreed to enroll him in the 'double-cross' network. They provided him with two businessmen, an Englishman and an Austrian, as representatives of his business in London. The Germans were delighted. The 'inside news' which the two businessmen sent written in invisible link between the lines of their business communications to Dr K. was interesting and valuable.

How did 'Potash' and 'Perlmutter', as the doctor's correspondents were facetiously code-named by their British case officer, come into the Norway scheme? On February 26 the K.O. Lisbon received a communication through Dr K., from 'Potash', the British partner. In this he announced among other things that he had taken on a war job with the Fire Office Committee. This was a committee which for a long time past had acted as a kind of meeting place for British insurance brokers at which matters of common interest could be discussed and a common policy agreed. It had many facilities useful to insurance men. For instance, it disposed of records concerning buildings and other insurable property in all parts of the world.

On April 4 Dr K. presented the K.O. with yet another letter from 'Potash'. He reported that the Ministry of Economic Warfare was requesting the loan of records dealing with northern France and the Low Countries. It had struck him that these requests might have operational significance. Should he look into this a little further? 'They are requesting urgent information on flour mills, bakeries, cold storage plants, and printing shops.' Three days later Potash came through with another message. There had been a change in priorities and similar information was now required about Norway.

'Norway', he wrote, 'has been divided into two main sectors: one in the south, the other in the Narvik area.' 'Potash' had supplied MEW with files on Aalesund, Bergen, Oslo, Larvik, Stavanger, Moss, Porsgrund, Kristiansand, and Trondheim. 'I believe from the urgency of the requests', he said, 'something must be in the offing in this direction, because strictest secrecy is being imposed. . . .' A month later he confirmed in answer to an enquiry from Dr K. that he was still working on the bakeries in Norway. He volunteered the names and addresses of some genuine ones. 'Nordby and Olsen in Oslo, Kristensen in Kristiansand, Moller in Larvik.' At the end of April, however, he reported that he had finished with Norway and was back on Belgium and northern France. I give full marks to whoever thought of the Fire Office and this beautifully indirect way of indicating there would be at least two landings in Norway.

Colonel J. H. Bevan himself, accompanied by the American Lieutenant-Colonel William H. Baumer, flew into Moscow at the beginning of February in an endeavour to interest the Russians in Anglo-American deception plans and obtain their support in such schemes as the fake Norway landing.

It had been a most unpleasant flight. Once their Liberator flew so high that lack of oxygen caused Bevan to pass out. Bill Baumer saved him, first by giving him the 'kiss of life' and then by administering liberal doses of Hine's VSOP cognac. That, however, did not banish the excruciating pain in Bevan's eardrums as the unpressurised plane descended to a lower level.

As they swept in over Moscow the sight of the Kremlin's onion-shaped domes coated with black paint cheered Bevan up a lot. 'Do you see that?' he shouted joyfully to Bill Baumer. 'They have camouflaged the cupolas! So they must believe in deception.'

On February 10, 1944, Johnny Bevan, Bill Baumer, and General John R. Deane, the Chief of the US Military Mission, presented themselves at the office of General Fedor F. Kuznetsov, of the Red Army General Staff. Bevan and Baumer had already spent several hours explaining the SHAEF deception plan to the American general. Despite the encouraging war-paint on the Kremlin towers they were apprehensive of the difficulties they would meet in explaining 'Bodyguard' to a Russian who spoke no English. Neither they nor General Deane spoke Russian. To make matters worse, General

Kuznetsov's interpreter turned out to be one of the kind who has a long and rapid conversation in Russian with his principal, and then when it comes to translating confines himself to a laconic, 'The general, he say "Yes" ' or, more usually, 'The general, he say "No!" ' If the comrade did deign to render a more detailed account of what General Kuznetsov had to say, it was in such a muddled jumble of would-be Brooklynese that neither the two Americans nor Johnny Bevan could make head or tail of it. Fortunately General Deane had brought along an interpreter of his own from the American Military Mission.

Despite dagger looks from the resentful Tovarich, Deane's man managed to whisper the gist of what Kuznetsov said to the three of them. 'I thought Kuznetsov a mental giant,' General Deane commented later, 'when in spite of the difficulties he appeared in a very short time to have mastered the intricacies of Bevan's plan.'*

Bevan explained that the contribution which the Western Allies hoped to receive from their Soviet allies was three-fold:

1. That the Russians should allow information to leak out that they could not start an offensive until July.

2. The Russians were asked to make the Germans believe that they would participate in a joint allied attack on Norway in the late spring.

3. They were also, if possible, to convey the impression to the Germans that they were planning a landing on the Rumanian and Bulgarian Black Sea coasts during May or early June.

Three further meetings followed. Kuznetsov appeared to have become most enthusiastic about Bevan's plan. 'He and his colleagues', says General Deane, 'proposed a great many changes, many of which were accepted after an exchange of cables with our Chiefs of Staff. Representatives of the Soviet Foreign Office were called in to discuss the diplomatic aspects of the matter with representatives from the British and American Embassies. Finally the Russians went into seclusion for two weeks. During this time Bevan, Baumer, and I were unable to contact them to see what was wrong. On March 5, 1944, Kuznetsov called another meeting to which he brought a 'protocol', nicely bound with silk ribbons, in which the Russians

---

* John R. Deane, *The Strange Alliance*, Viking, New York, 1947.

agreed to the original plan as presented without any of the changes
we had so thoroughly argued and agreed upon.'

In May 1944, long after the departure of Bevan and Baumer,
General Deane was informed by General Kuznetsov that the USSR
was simulating attack on Petsamo in the far north by a concentration of troops and ships in the Kola Fjord, by air and sea reconnaissance of the Norwegian coast, and by increased wireless
traffic in the whole area. Intelligence had been leaked to the Germans
that the Soviet High Command was forming a new army of
specialist troops on the central front and that it had been ordered to
complete its organisation by the end of June. Also that new Russian
reserves were being trained for use in July.

From Britain SHAEF's double agents did their stuff on Russian
participation in the coming attack on Norway. The most important
message was sent on May 4, when 'Paul' signalled his controller that
according to the Dutch Command a Soviet military and naval
mission had established itself in Edinburgh, probably in order to
co-ordinate Russian military naval operations in the far north of
Norway with General Thorne's 4th Army.

The deception team's 'Red-Army-participates-in-Allied-assault-
on-Norway' campaign culminated in a superb dispatch from 'a very
reliable V-man' which found its way into the Intelligence Digest
of the Luftwaffe of May 16, 1944 (Luft E 3017844), and was quoted
in that of 'Foreign Armies West' as well. The report itself, dated
May 14, 1944, says:

Eden has brought back from Moscow a renewed demand of the
Soviets for their participation in the assault on Northern Norway
and its occupation. Moscow has proposed a combined enterprise.
Landing of Anglo-Americans in Northern Norway, simultaneously
Russian offensive in Arctic at end of May or beginning of June.
Thereafter participation of Red Army in occupation of Norway.
Soviet Union reserves right to occupy certain districts as sole
occupying power. Eden did not commit himself on Soviet proposal
during his visit. Stettinius is reported to have assented to Soviet
proposal. According to reliable information from Foreign Office
Roosevelt favours acceptance of Soviet offer. United States Govern-
ment accordingly putting pressure on Norwegians. Among
Norwegians in Britain opinions are divided. Norwegian armed

services, the King, and part of government are against Soviet proposition while another section is for it. Attitude of British Cabinet is also split. According to Sir Alan Brooke British armed services are opposed. Whole problem was discussed at Imperial Conference. Up to May 10 no decision had been reached. Eden's attitude to the Russian proposal is very cautious and reserved. Beaverbrook above all is in favour of Great Britain agreeing to Soviet proposal. . . .

Who was the 'very reliable V-man' author of this remarkable dispatch? Was he a Soviet 'disinformation' agent backing up General Kuznetsov's directive? I doubt it. But who was he then? The one certainty is that he was not one of SHAEF's 'Knights of the Double-Cross'.

Most probably he was one of those oracles that sat around the cafés of such neutral capitals as Lisbon and Stockholm thinking up stories which could earn them kudos and money from their German clients. The Germans had a dangerous habit of allowing some of their favourite informants in neutral capitals to pick up the gist of the information being received from Britain. The idea of this was to see whether they in their turn could find out anything which would either fit in with these reports or contradict them.

There is evidence that a Stockholm V-man called Kramer earned a considerable reputation with the Abwehr and their SD successors by amplifying and embroidering the SHAEF deception stories. This Luftwaffe intelligence report, with its intriguing reference to an Eden visit to Moscow in April 1944 (which never took place) and its access to innermost cabinet secrets, smacks of Kramer at his lurid best. For the SHAEF deception team the uncontrolled agents like Kramer were a nuisance. They were always liable to send the German bloodhounds baying up a trail in the opposite direction to that which SHAEF wanted them to follow.

Immediately following the excerpt from the Luftwaffe V-man's report the Foreign Armies West Department's digest carries an item from the Swiss newspaper *Basler Nationalzeitung*: 'In Sweden and Finland the impression is gaining ground that Norway will be included in the invasion. As symptoms one sees the sweep of the Home Fleet along the Norwegian coast. One is expecting a combined British-American-Russian assault. The Russians are con-

centrating troops in the Arctic against General Dietl.' (Commander
of Hitler's army in the Far North.)

★   ★   ★

Although I have left it to the last, implementation of the plan to
suggest to the Germans that pressure was being put on Sweden to
allow the United States Air Force and the RAF to use airfields in
Sweden had begun as early as the end of March. In March 1944
Britain and the United States were already planning to persuade the
Swedes to show less favour to the Germans. For instance, the
Swedes were being asked among other things to stop their exports
of ball-bearings to Germany altogether, as these were helping the
Germans to escape the consequences of the extensive damage to
their own ball-bearings plants by Allied bombing raids.

Sir Victor Mallet, the British Minister in Stockholm, was visiting
London to discuss the demands he was about to put to the Swedish
Government in concert with his American and Russian colleagues
just around the time Colonel Bevan arrived back from Moscow.
So Bevan called on Sir Victor and asked him whether he and his
colleagues could not add to their genuine demands a couple of
requests designed not so much to be granted by the Swedes as to be
leaked by them to the Germans. Sir Victor having obtained the
assent of the Foreign Office declared his readiness to co-operate.

Accordingly on his return, the British, American, and Soviet
ministers, in addition to their other requests, asked the Swedes for
the following facilities:

1. Permission for Allied civil aircraft to land on Swedish airfields in order to avoid being molested by German fighters.

2. Arrangements between Allied transport experts and the
Swedish authorities providing for the transport of supplies to
Norway through Sweden in the event of a German withdrawal.

3. Permission for Allied aircraft to operate from Swedish
airfields for survey and photo reconnaissance purposes.

It was easy enough to arrange the leak of the information to the
German Legation in Stockholm. The gratified Ribbentrop, eager to
prove the excellence of his intelligence, passed it on to the Führer
headquarters where it was studied by Hitler and Jodl. Their pencilled

squiggles were on the margin of the message (to show they had read it) when it fell into Allied hands with other documents after the German collapse.

'The British Minister Mallet', said the signal, 'on his return from London gave a talk to the legation staff which according to a reliable source contained the following passage: "Our relations with our Swedish friends have always been good and we hope that they will remain so. We must, however, foresee the possibility that this good relationship may be put to the test. We can no longer look on passively while neutral countries deliver goods to our enemies which inflict damage on us. We will therefore make representations to the Swedish government to stop such deliveries or at least to reduce them. We must approach this task with tact. In particular deliveries of ball-bearings and iron ore help the Germans and harm us. That must not be allowed to go on. We must find ways to prevent it."' And then came an especially menacing sentence. *'Other problems too, which are of greater significance politically, may come between us and Sweden.'*

Just as though to show that the mission was carried out to the very last detail the Foreign Armies West summary (Situation Report West No. 1279 of May 29, 1944) published a dispatch to the effect that 'a high-ranking British Air Force officer had been making soundings in Sweden about the possibility of the Swedish Government permitting the use of Swedish airfields by the Allies'.*

The Germans now had it all—order of battle, operational plans, —the lot.

*   *   *

The SHAEF deception planners had hoped that the news that Britain, the United States, and the USSR were planning a combined assault on German-occupied Norway would cause a flutter in Hitler's eyrie on the Obersalzberg. But if any of them expected dramatic reactions like the dispatch of reinforcements to Norway they were disappointed. Hitler did nothing about the Norway threat. He could not. For one thing, he had no reinforcements he could send.

---

* Percy Ernst Schramm, *Kriegstagebuch des O.K.W.*, IV 1, page 316.

The deception served its purpose, however. It frightened Hitler out of withdrawing troops from Norway and Denmark. No troops were moved to France from Denmark and Norway until June 16, when it was much too late for them to do any good.

On June 16 Hitler ordered the 89th Infantry Division to be sent from Norway to reinforce the 15th Army guarding the Pas de Calais area in France and so too the 363rd Infantry Division from Denmark.* An indirect effect of the Norway deception was its contribution to making the Germans accept a July date for the invasion. Most important of all was that it achieved its purpose in teaching German intelligence to rely for their information about the Allied order of battle on the SHAEF-controlled V-men. A post-war comparison of the messages put out by the V-men with the intelligence summaries circulated by the Foreign Armies West Department shows that as far as the order of battle was concerned the German intelligence officers swallowed them in their entirety, fictitious corps, fictitious divisions and all, even the fictitious army.

The only important Order of Battle report which finds no echo in the summaries of Foreign Armies West is that by King Peter's young ADC which—quite accurately—placed the American XV Corps in Ulster. He had been congratulated on this report by the Abwehr, so there is no reason to assume the omission was due to doubt or distrust. More probably it never reached Foreign Armies West owing to some breakdown in communications. Poor Colonel MacLeod's labours with his signals units also show no first-hand evidence of having been rewarded. No intelligence is recorded as having been received from 'a sure source', the phrase habitually used to indicate radio interception. But then it is likely that un-deciphered signals traffic indicating by its volume a concentration of forces in certain areas would not find its way into the situation reports of Foreign Armies West.

While the German intelligence swallowed the reports of their SHAEF-controlled V-men without reserve, what they did not always accept was the interpretation the V-men at the behest of their SHAEF masters attached to the information they were supplying.

The reason for this, as I see it, is that in the case of the fake Norway

---

* Percy Ernst Schramm, *Kriegstagebuch des O.K.W.*, IV 1, page 316.

assault the SHAEF deception planners had unwittingly broken one
of their own cardinal rules, established in the early days of 'A' Force
in Cairo. This laid down that the finest deception plan is unlikely
to succeed unless it has been framed to fit the enemy's own appreciation of the situation. The excellence of the later Pas de Calais
deception was that it did exactly that. It fitted the preconceptions of
Hitler and those of the OKW intelligence.

Not that I attach any blame to Colonel Bevan and Colonel Wild
for their failure to put over the Norway deception in its entirety.
For the German staff officer evaluating the intelligence supplied by
the SHAEF-controlled V-men was so far as the Norway operation
was concerned in a class all of his own. Not unless they had known
who was in charge of the Foreign Armies West Department of the
Army High Command's Intelligence Branch could they have
anticipated his reaction to the scheme and allowed for it. For Colonel
Alexis von Roenne was a Baltic nobleman whose family had lived
for generations within the Russian orbit. He had been brought up
with strong convictions about the political mentality of Russians—
Tsarist and Bolshevik alike. And these convictions caused him to
dismiss out of hand any suggestion, however authoritatively put
forward, that the Russians would tolerate, let alone support, an
Anglo-American intrusion into northern Norway, an area which they
considered of vital military interest to themselves. They would oppose
it, he argued, as resolutely as they had been opposing British attempts
to set foot in the Balkans. The Anglo-Americans would never dare
to undertake such an operation in the face of Russian hostility.

Roenne's disbelief in the reports identifying northern Norway
as the target of Allied invasion plans was so strong that for an
agonising moment he even permitted himself to question the
reliability of the source of the reports.

'The Allied movements of troops and shipping in Scotland,
reported by an Abwehr source *which has otherwise proved reliable ...*'
he says in a first evaluation. And he comes to the conclusion: 'As
the target of this operation the coast of Norway is suggested. The
department considers it absolutely improbable that the Russians
would agree to a Petsamo-Murmansk enterprise. The total nature
of the Russian claims to Finland has been evident for years. Without
doubt they even go beyond the Russian claims to the Balkans. If

the Russians jealously blocked any large-scale operation by the Anglo-Saxons in the Balkans, a similar reaction by them can be assumed with certainty concerning Finnish territory.'

But he is careful to qualify his 'absolutely improbable' verdict. 'None the less,' he says, 'an increase in the defence preparations along the Norwegian coast is indispensable and so is an intensification of aerial reconnaissance over the entire North Sea area. This is the only way to prevent surprises like those in the case of the landings in Sicily and at Nettuno. Air reconnaissance of ports in Northern Scotland and the dispatch of naval forces (U-boats) in the direction of Scotland with an exclusively reconnaissance task are to be regarded as important additional measures.'

A further memorandum by Roenne (prepared on April 12, 1944) dismissed as 'diversionary nerve war propaganda' reports of Allied intentions to stage assault landings in western Sweden or Denmark. Sweden he ruled out because State Secretary Cordell Hull had expressly pledged that the United States Government would only exert moral pressure on neutrals, not use violence on them to gain their end. Denmark he excluded as well, because the narrow neck of the Jutland peninsula would be easy for the Germans to defend, and because of the difficulty for the Allies to provide air cover. Nor did the dispositions of the Allied Order of Battle in Britain suggest to him any intention on the part of Eisenhower to seek a decision in the North Sea area. But then having said that he hedges once more and declares that the Allies might perhaps stage a diversionary attack on southern Norway and Denmark with a view to inducing a withdrawal of troops from France before the big invasion. He concludes emphatically: 'This department therefore now as before is convinced that while diversionary enterprises are conceivable in the North Sea area, the main attack must be expected on either side of the Pas de Calais with the heaviest concentration on the Northwestern French coastal sector. . . . The department sees no occasion to change the view it has held for months about the target area [of the invasion] and the deployment of the enemy attack from Britain. It considers the enemy's dissemination of other targets to be attempts to cause uncertainty on the German side.'

By April 27, when he releases another assessment of enemy intentions, Baron von Roenne has become aware of 4th Army in

Edinburgh and he is modifying his views about the possibility of a
Norway venture. 'In Scotland and Iceland', he says, 'the probability
of Norway plans has been increased by the presumable transfer of
the 55th American Infantry Division from Iceland to Scotland. The
command of the British 4th Army, which is being held available to
take charge of a Norway operation, is apparently expecting the
assault to begin at the beginning of May.

'For the presumable target there continue to be few indications.
The idea of a Narvik operation with a view to an occupation of the
Swedish iron-ore area and an advance to the Aaland Islands is
considered out of the question [abwegig] as the Anglo-Saxon Command will in these regions respect the Russian Veto just as in the
Balkans. The interruption, however, of German sea communications,
along the Norwegian coast, the containment of German armed
forces, and an insurrection of the Norwegian population are to be
seen as objectives which could be attained by landings in southern
as well as in northern Norway.'

By May 23, however, he no longer believes in the possibility of a
Norway assault. While calling attention to large-scale troop movements to the South of England from the Midlands and the North he
points out: 'It is worthy of remark that Scottish Command in
particular has been effectively weakened by the withdrawal of as
many as four formations (the 3rd and 50th British and the 1st
Polish Armoured Divisions and possibly also the 52nd British
Infantry Division). . . . The Scottish group of forces has sunk to a
strength which rules out operations of any importance.'

Colonel von Roenne was pretty near the truth in his analysis of the
Norway threat. But he was to be proved hopelessly wrong when
he put all his money on the Pas de Calais as the target of the main
Allied assault. Both he and his master had been conditioned over the
years by Allied Deception to accept Calais as the Allies number one
objective. As a consequence the Pas de Calais deception fitted in
perfectly with their own appreciation. Just as Colonel Dudley
Clarke, the great master of deception, had laid down that the model
deception should!

9

George Patton's Phantom Army

Long before the autumn of 1943 everyone knew that it was healthier not to report unpleasant truths to Hitler. What the Führer required from those serving him was faith, not unpalatable facts. Faith in the infalliability of his decisions and confirmation of their wisdom. Faith in Germany's final victory. Above all, he wanted optimism from them, unswerving optimism. By and large he got it.

There was, however, one officer who seemed to go out of his way to demonstrate his scepticism. In the outward appearance of Colonel Alexis von Roenne, chief of the Foreign Armies West Intelligence Staff, there was little to suggest the soldier hero leading a rebellion. Indeed, there was little to suggest the soldier. Of slender, frail-looking build, grey eyes peering appraisingly from beneath a pair of gold-rimmed spectacles, he looked more like a university don or a Jesuit Father than a professional soldier. But the broad scarlet stripe of the General Staff on the grey-green breeches of his uniform showed that he was a professional, all right. Nor was von Roenne's refusal to toe the line due to neurotic exhibitionism or a hankering after a martyr's crown.

Two excellent reasons made him decline to conform. The first was that as a member of the Prussian officer caste he was nauseated by the sycophantic rosiness of the military intelligence being peddled to Hitler by Himmler's Security Service, the SD. By rights, the SD had no business to be supplying such intelligence. Military intelligence, under a ruling of December 21, 1938, was the exclusive preserve of Admiral Canaris's Abwehr. In theory the SD and the Gestapo dealt only with Home Security and certain aspects of counter-espionage. But the power-hungry Himmler was trying to expand his empire to include all intelligence, home and foreign alike. To ingratiate himself with Hitler and prove how superior to the Abwehr the SD service would be Himmler was sending Hitler samples of SD intelligence specially flavoured to appeal to the Führer's sweet-tooth craving for reassuring news.

It so happened that the Foreign Armies West Offices were housed in the same bomb-proof underground citadel at Zossen outside Berlin as the Abwehr headquarters. As a consequence Roenne saw a lot of his Abwehr colleagues and came to learn a great deal about the intrigues of the SD. So he decided to join in the battle against the SD and discredit their intelligence wherever he could.

His second reason for flouting the Führer's appetite for optimism was strictly military. As head of the department evaluating intelligence from all countries except Russia, von Roenne was deeply concerned lest the euphoria induced in the Führerhauptquartier by the extravagantly complacent reports of the SD should lead to an underestimation of the danger from the coming Anglo-American assault in the West and an overestimation of such vital elements in the German defence against it as the Atlantic Wall.

That bastion had been praised by the Goebbels propagandists as impregnable. Colonel-General Kurt Zeitzler, the chief of the General Staff, had told Hitler that the repulse of the Dieppe Raid in 1942 had proved this, and Hitler had gratefully accepted Zeitzler's assessment.

'The fortifications at Dieppe', he told his reverent listeners in the Führerhauptquartier towards the end of 1943, 'are a thousand times stronger today than they were a year ago. I am constantly devising ways to improve them. . . . The assault will be broken on the Atlantic Wall.'*

Colonel von Roenne, in his self-assigned role as debunker of the Führer's wishful thinking, decided to carry out a quick reconnaissance of the fortifications. He therefore paid the wall a five-day visit from October 29 to November 2, 1943. On November 12, 1943, he made his report. It was shattering. Roenne came to the conclusion that with the exception of the fortified ports, the Allies could force a landing wherever they pleased on the Channel coast and then go on to capture from the land side any port they had set their hearts on. (This constituted a noteworthy revision of Roenne's

* Führer Conference, December 20, 1943. From *Lagebesprechungen im Führerhauptquartier*, edited by Helmut Heiber.

own assessment only a month earlier that the Allies were 'under no illusion about the difficulties of a large scale assault against the *by no means numerous coastal sectors suited for a landing*'.*

Here is the text of the German colonel's report.

1. Defensive power of seafronts of the big and medium harbours (Dunkirk, Boulogne, Le Havre, Dieppe) is considerable. Guns of all calibres, mostly under concrete or rock. Minefields and other barriers inhibit access.

Harbour demolition charges have been widely prepared.

The habour garrisons (military and naval) are not entirely adequate, neither in quality nor in quantity. (About 60 to 70 per cent of what is required.)

2. The terrain between the ports is only sparsely defended by guns and men. The defences lack depth and density. Landings, particularly if covered by smoke screens, will be possible almost everywhere, if the enemy employs strong naval and air forces. The steep cliffs will not prove a decisive obstacle to the landing of light units which could open up the valleys and smaller harbours from the flank and the rear.

3. The defence of the land fronts of the larger and medium-sized ports is weak. Its cover by troops, artillery, and anti-tank weapons is altogether insufficient. Munition supplies are not equal to the demands of a battle lasting several days.

4. The operational reserves of the armies (single motorised divisions) which have been placed further in the rear must expect to be hindered in their movements by strong bombing attacks from the air as well as by airborne troops. It can hardly be expected that they will be available in time to take part in a concerted counter-attack.

5. The picture of a large-scale enemy assault (outside the harbours) is seen as follows: forced landings in the terrain between the harbours under cover of artificial smoke and strong air attacks. After the enemy has formed correspondingly strong armoured assault groups pincer attacks against the harbour. Assault will be supported by waves of bomber aircraft which destroy every attempt to bring up German reserves. The bombers smash the land defences of the port fortresses.

6. In view of the impossibility of obtaining troop reinforcements

---

* Author's italics.

a considerable increase in minefields and anti-tank defences seems the very minimum of what is urgently required. In view too of the extraordinary scale of the enemy air attack to be anticipated all heavy weapons from anti-tank guns upwards must either be placed under concrete or given some provisional shelter to protect them from being discovered from the air and destroyed.

7. The above views were put orally to the Chief of Army Group D (C-in-C West), as well as to the Wehrmachtführungsstab and the Chief of the General Staff. They found the approval of all of them, particularly that of the last mentioned.

The rest of the page is taken up by an additional note. In order not to involve his typist in such dangerous heresy Roenne wrote it in his own hand.

8. To sum up: the chief of Foreign Armies West gained the impression that the enemy command can force a landing at any point it chooses on the Channel coast outside the harbours and then capture whichever harbour is its target. The course of events therefore depends solely on the time picked for the landing, not on the development of the battle which is beyond doubt. (This view, too, was advanced in the above form. For security reasons it has been set down here in handwriting.)

Freiherr v. Roenne*

Amazingly, von Roenne suffered no untoward consequences from his 'defeatist' memorandum. Indeed, his criticisms may have had a share in persuading the Wehrmachtführungsstab to call Rommel from north Italy to make a similar inspection of the Atlantic Wall. (After which, it will be recalled, Rommel was in January 1944 appointed to the command of Army Group B defending the critical invasion coast from the Zuyder Zee in Holland to the Loire river in France.)

While Hitler and his generals continued to indulge themselves in midnight orgies of optimistic speculation Roenne went on warning of the seriousness of the Allied threat and its imminence.

On February 8, 1944, he wrote to Colonel Meyer-Detring, the G.2 at Field Marshal Rundstedt's headquarters in St Germain, to tell him that the 'Overlord' assault was certainly coming in the first

---

* Freiherr = Baron.

half of the year. His trip around the 'Atlantic Wall' had shown him, he said, that among both officers and men of the forces in the West there was widespread scepticism about this assault. He begged the colonel (who must have been irritated at being addressed as 'Dear Meyer' by the Baron) to do all in his power to rouse the troops out of their scepticism. 'A soldier who doubts the imminence of an attack . . . will not show that ardour and watchfulness which should be the characteristic of the Western Army.'

Even greater concern about coming events was shown by him in a long letter addressed on March 3, 1944, to Colonel Beelitz, Field Marshal Kesselring's Chief of Staff on the Italian front. Roenne begged Beelitz to use his influence with the field marshal to persuade him that the Germans should abandon their Italian positions in order to reinforce their armies in France.

The decision in all the West European fighting, and therewith of the war as such, will fall where the enemy command brings the mass of its forces to bear. This point is not Italy. For the German Command it is vital to oppose the enemy assault at the decisive point with the greatest possible strength. If we succeed in repelling the Western invasion, even the loss of Italy would pale to insignificance. If we manage to hold Italy, this will be without importance, should the Western invasion succeed. The decision, whether we can dare to leave our forces tied up in a long term defence of Italy, depends on how we gauge our own fighting strength in France. . . . If our chances of repelling the invasion in France seem low in view of the present strength of our forces, then the consequences from this must be drawn in Italy. Should the Western invasion succeed then without doubt history will one day pose the question what forces did Germany have available in Germany itself and in secondary theatres of war at the time of the assault, which were not used against it. . . . The measures I advocate are of course based on my own opinion of the German defences in the Atlantic area, of which I gained an impression in the course of an inspection lasting several days. . . . These, dear Beelitz, are in rough outline my private views which bear no official character. The only reason for doubting that you share my main conclusions is that you perhaps have insufficient acquaintance with the 'Atlantic Wall'. . . .

In his anxiety about the coming invasion and what seemed to

him the dangerous complacency of the High Command Roenne even went so far as to telephone to officers in Hitler's entourage giving them the benefit of his gloomy forebodings. For instance, we still have his minute of a call he put through to Colonel (as he was at that time) von Buttlar-Brandenfels in the Wehrmacht-führungsstab. Roenne predicted to him that RAF Bomber Command, the Tactical Air Force of the RAF and the US Tactical Air Force were about to form a joint command for operations over France.

'As a consequence of the enemy's overwhelming superiority in the air', Roenne told Buttlar-Brandenfels, 'the operational mobility of our own forces will be reduced to nil, while their tactical mobility will be seriously cut down.'

Buttlar-Brandenfels, presumably conscious that the Führerhaupt-quartier telephones were liable to be tapped by Himmler's SD, was cautiously orthodox in his reply. 'The Allied Air Force did not succeed in paralysing German mobility during the Allied landing at Salerno [in Italy],' he said.

'And mark my words. If the Anglo-American Air Force attacks us in France we shall reinforce with fighters from the Reich. The Allied bombers will be decimated!'

But Roenne refused to be cheered up. 'The Salerno landing', he insisted, 'can't be compared with what must be expected in France. Salerno involved an infinitely smaller number of aircraft. What is more, over France the Allied bombers will be escorted by fighters, masses of them, their latest and most up-to-date machines against which ours will not stand a chance. There will not just be a few Lightnings and Mosquitos to escort the bombers as during the bombing raids over the Reich.'

There is no record of what Buttlar-Brandenfel's comment was on that. My hunch is that he just rang off without trying to argue any further with his impulsive young comrade.

Conversations like this one with von Buttlar-Brandenfels were extremely dangerous in view of the Führer's allergy to 'defeatist' talk.

But in courageously advancing his opinions Roenne believed, and rightly, that he was doing his patriotic duty as a German officer. Roenne, however, did more than just talk. In his eagerness to dissipate the Führerhauptquartier's euphoria and defeat the SD's intrigue against the Abwehr, Colonel von Roenne went a step further. He began to fake and exaggerate his reports. Not unconsciously but quite deliberately.

With the connivance of Lieutenant-Colonel Roger Michael, the officer commanding Group III in the Foreign Armies West Department (Group III was in charge of intelligence concerning the British and Allied forces being concentrated in Britain for the invasion), Roenne began to accept uncritically reports of the build-up of the invasion army in Britain. These were the reports put about by Storey's Gate during 1943 as part of 'Operation Cockade'* and others spontaneously generated out of the climate of opinion created by 'Cockade' among the host of free-lance agents in the neutral capitals who earned their living by inventing reports from 'sources in Britain' for the benefit of Abwehr and SD. Roenne himself had disparaged them as 'utterly fantastic' as recently as October 2, 1943. Now he began to use them as a basis for his 'Allied order of battle in the United Kingdom'.

Major Staubwasser, an officer on the staff of Foreign Armies West, had misgivings about the new method. He remonstrated with the colonel. But Roenne dismissed his protests with a laugh. 'The SD in their superior wisdom will as usual persuade the Führer to cut down our figures. By the time they have finished their whittling, the total arrived at should be just about right!'

Staubwasser was not satisfied. He continued to protest against what he called unprofessional methods. He went so far as to say he wanted no part in them. But Roenne was adamant.

'I should hate to lose you, my dear Staubwasser,' he said. 'I value you as a friend and a comrade. You are a very able intelligence officer. But I have thought this thing over very carefully. If you will not accept these findings I shall, most reluctantly, be forced to have you posted elsewhere.'

In the end Staubwasser decided to give in and remain with Roenne, whom, as he told me many years after the war, he liked and admired. The decision to yield was made all the easier as at this time (before the SHAEF-controlled V-men had got into their

* See page 87, footnote.

stride) the Germans had no coherent intelligence from Britain. 'It was all guess-work. And,' says Staubwasser, 'one guess was as bad as another!'

The effect, however, of the Roenne-Michael order of battle on the strategy of Hitler and his generals was catastrophic. For it led them straight into the trap being set for them so thoughtfully by the Anglo-American deception unit at SHAEF. Von Roenne's faked battle order provided the foundations on which the SHAEF team was able to build up a fictitious army group in south-east England and make Hitler believe in the possibility of several widely separated diversions in addition to a main assault in the Pas de Calais.

For the purposes of the SHAEF Deception Unit Roenne's faking of the invasion force's order of battle could not have been begun at a more opportune moment. On December 31, 1943, Foreign Armies West issued its monthly survey of the Allied forces in Britain. This showed fifty-five Allied divisions waiting in Britain to embark on the invasion. It was an impressive figure, impressively accompanied by a map revealing the identity of the various divisions, their locations and the commands to which they belonged. It was so convincing that not even the SD dared challenge it. The figure was accepted. In fact it was wildly overdone. Not fifty-five divisions were in Britain at the beginning of January 1944 but only thirty-seven. And even this figure included garrison troops and training divisions which could not be used in crossing the Channel.

Once the intelligence supplied to Roenne and Michael through the SHAEF-controlled V-men began to trickle in, the size of the Allied build-up in Britain became even more sensational. In his 'note on the enemy situation' No. 2798/44 of May 8, 1944, Roenne reported that the Anglo-American forces in Britain had a strength of 'between seventy-five and eighty large formations'. On May 31, a week before D-day, he said* that the Allies had the equivalent of eighty-seven combat divisions in Britain. Eight of these, he claimed, were airborne divisions. The truth, however, was that fewer than fifty-two British and US divisions were in Britain on D-day. And only thirty-seven of them were available for cross-Channel operations. The remainder were mostly non-operational divisions.

---

* *Überblick des Britischen Reiches*, No. 30.

Even of the thirty-seven divisions a good many could not be sent into action until seven weeks after D-day, a point to his advantage of which the unfortunate Field Marshal Rundstedt, commander-in-chief of the German forces in the West, was completely unaware.

But it was not through his exaggeration of Allied resources compared with Rundstedt's that, what Roenne had begun as a trick to discredit the SD and free German strategy from Hitler's wishful thinking, did the greatest damage. Hitler became convinced—as the SHAEF team intended—that the difference between the strength of the forces committed by Eisenhower in Normandy and the number of divisions German intelligence credited the Allies with having available in Britain confirmed the reports that the Allies were holding the 1st US Army Group (FUSAG) in reserve for the main assault across the Straits of Dover. Despite the entreaties of Rundstedt and Rommel, Hitler therefore insisted on holding an army ready to meet and beat them. He held the 15th Army in its positions around Calais. For seven decisive weeks he kept nineteen of the best German divisions kicking their heels in north-eastern France, waiting for an army that did not exist to make an assault that had never been intended.

It was the biggest and most decisive hoax of the war. And Colonel the Baron von Roenne, chief of the Foreign Armies West Department of the German intelligence staff, had unintentionally played a part in it which was almost as important as that of Jorge Antonio, 'Paul', and the British and American officers who had planned it.

But Roenne was no traitor. Like Hitler, he wanted to defeat the invasion. Roenne wanted to defeat it, so that he and his fellow conspirators in the plot to get rid of Hitler could negotiate with the Allies from a position of comparative strength.

*　　　*　　　*

The London Controlling Section and after them the SHAEF Deception Unit at Norfolk House were on to a good thing when they plumped for the Pas de Calais as the area where Hitler was most likely to expect the Allied invasion.

From March 1942 onwards, when he first began to build the Atlantic Wall in anticipation of an Allied assault in the West, Hitler had put his main emphasis on the Pas de Calais sector. During 1942 four times as much concrete had been allotted to the defences of the Pas de Calais sector as to the whole of the Normandy–Brittany coast. By May 1943 the concentration of troops along the littoral from the Seine to the Scheldt was almost three times as heavy as that in the Normandy–Brittany sector.

Fresh importance was given to the Pas de Calais area when in the summer of 1943 Hitler began to install the launching sites here for the long-range rockets and pilotless aircraft with which he expected to reverse the course of the war. He was convinced that the V-weapons (V for *Vergeltung* = Retribution) would wreak such destruction in Britain that regardless of what other plans the Allies might have made previous to the missile bombardment they would be forced to make a direct cross-Channel assault in order to capture the missile sites and put a stop to the bombardment.

In logical pursuance of this thinking, Hitler in June 1943 assigned priority to the construction of those portions of the Atlantic Wall protecting missile sites. And when in November 1943 he took his eyes off the Russian battlefield to issue his famous 'Directive No. 51'* for the decisive battle in the West his attention was still firmly riveted on the Pas de Calais.

. . . The threat from the East remains. But an even greater danger looms in the West: the Anglo-American landing! In the East the vastness of the space will, as a last resort, permit a loss of territory, even on a major scale, without a mortal blow being inflicted on Germany's chance for survival.

Not so in the West! If the enemy succeeds here in penetrating our defences on a wide front, consequences of staggering proportions will follow within a short time. All signs point to an offensive against the Western Front of Europe no later than the spring, perhaps earlier.

. . . I have therefore decided to strengthen the defences in the West *particularly at places from which we shall launch our long-range war against England. For that is where enemy must and will attack. That is where—unless all indications are misleading—the enemy will attempt his landing and the decisive battle will be fought.* [Author's italics. The reference to the Pas de Calais could not have been

---

* Percy Schramm, *Kriegstagebuch des OKW*, IV 2, page 1530.

clearer.] Holding attacks and diversions on other fronts are to be expected. Not even the possibility of a large-scale offensive against Denmark may be excluded. . . .

Hitler, as a result of Colonel Bevan's 'Cockade', was intensely worried about the possibility of such diversions and the difficulty he would have in deciding which assault was a diversion and which the main assault. First-hand evidence of his perplexity is contained in the record of the Führer Conferences captured after the war. (Most of the records had been burned, but some escaped undamaged, others part charred.)*

After supper in the Führerhauptquartier it was Hitler's custom to sit talking with his staff into the early hours of the morning, reminiscing about his experiences in the First World War, discussing the difficulties of the enemy (e.g. the diminution of Britain's steel output), asking questions to which he required immediate answers from the appropriate Reich authorities no matter what the hour of the night, issuing orders and giving his view of the military situation. A group of parliamentary stenographers from the Reichstag parliament sat in on the chit-chat, taking down every word that was uttered. It is their records that have partially survived.

On December 20, 1943, Hitler had spent some hours studying a batch of British Foreign Office telegrams dealing with the Teheran Conference between Stalin, Roosevelt, and Churchill, at which the launching of 'Overlord' had been agreed. The telegrams had been sent to Hitler by Admiral Canaris, who in turn had received them from his man in Ankara. They were some of the telegrams which the Albanian valet of Sir Hughe Knatchebull-Hugessen, the lamentably insouciant envoy of His Britannic Majesty in Ankara, had removed from the ambassador's bedroom safe while His Excellency was asleep. Before putting them back in the safe the valet had photographed them. He then sold the negatives to the Abwehr.† Now Hitler had just finished browsing through them and was mentally brimming over with the prospect of the coming showdown in the West. There was no doubt in his mind now, he announced portentously to his staff, that the assault would

---

* *Lagebesprechungen im Führerhauptquartier*, edited by Helmut Heiber.
† They paid him in forged fivers.

come in the spring. He looked forward to it with pleasurable anticipation.

The Führer: 'If they attack in the West, then this attack will decide the war. . . . If this attack is repelled the whole thing is over. Then we can withdraw our forces from there.' And, he implied, with that increase in our strength settle the hash of the Russians. But he did not actually say so, for before he could do so his volatile mind switched to the Pas de Calais and its missile ramps. The Allies had begun bombing them on December 5, 1943. Jodl reported that the raid of the previous night had been the heaviest yet.

Jodl: 'But they did comparatively little damage from what I hear.'

The Führer: 'It's not all that simple to hit small targets.'

Jodl: 'They say the bombs did not hit the installations themselves but only the railway sidings.'

The Führer: 'It is quite clear those missile sites have given them [the Allies] the jitters. If anyone was building installations of which we knew they could smash up Berlin, we would also become pretty nervous. They are fully informed about everything that is going on. . . . When the installations are completed, it will be quite impossible for them to bomb each one of them.'

The unspoken implication was that the Allies would be forced to attack across the Channel because that was the only way to eliminate both the missile sites and the missiles.

His mind jumped from the Pas de Calais and its missile sites to the threat of diversionary assaults. Assaults on Norway, the Biscay Coast, the Balkans. He discussed every target mentioned in the 'Cockade' directive. Particularly Norway.

The Führer: 'There's every chance they will make a landing up there in northern Norway. Up there in northern Norway one must operate with a mass of U-boats. And one mustn't leave it too late. There's no knowing what the ice conditions are. . . . It would, of course, be nothing more than a diversion. Then there is Biscay. The mass of U-boats must be deployed in the Bay of Biscay.'

Admiral Voss*: 'That is all provided for, my Führer. If anything happens in the West everything will be mobilised against it. That is all prepared.'

---

* Former Commandant of the cruiser *Prinz Eugen*, now naval representative at FHQ.

The Führer: 'We must start right away to send U-boats up to Norway, otherwise it will be too late.'

Admiral Voss: 'There are many U-boats in Brest, Lorient, and St Nazaire.'

The Führer: 'But they won't get to Norway in time. We cannot send any military formations up there. And the Luftwaffe does not look too good either. Perhaps you could think this over. There must be a massive concentration of U-boats off Norway. In the West, too, one must think things over.' His thoughts switched to the Atlantic Wall and the Pas de Calais.

'I am constantly thinking about things that would improve our defences. Flame-throwers, for instance, which go into action automatically, tubs of oil which are thrown into the Channel and start to burn. . . .'

Then his mind was back on the problem of how to decide which was the main assault.

The Führer: 'Every month that the assault is postponed things get better for us. With every month that passes our chances improve of getting a group of jet-fighters into the air. The decisive thing is that the moment the enemy lands he should get a load of bombs on his head. That'll force him to take cover. And even if only one of our aircraft is in action the enemy will have to take cover. And that will make him lose hour after hour. But in half a day we can call up our reserves. If he is nailed to the beach for only six or eight hours one can imagine what that will mean for us. He will be nailed down until our reserves are brought up.' And here it came once more, the nagging doubt: 'Moreover, one would get an idea. It would be splendid if one could get a good idea in the first moments of the landing: which is the diversion, and where is the real full-scale assault.'

From time to time Hitler got up to walk over and inspect the six-foot-long coastal map of Europe which ever since November 1943, when Hitler issued his directive for the defence of the West, Colonel-General Jodl had prepared daily for his Führer. Semicircles in yellow crayon pointing inland showed where Allied assaults were expected in the event of invasion. From the size of the semicircle and the intensity of the shading Hitler could see at a glance which areas were being mentioned most frequently in the latest V-man reports.

But however much he studied Jodl's intelligence map, the general picture of how he expected the invasion to develop underwent little change during the next six months. In an interview with Baron Hiroshi Oshima, the Japanese ambassador to Berlin, on May 28, 1944, Hitler said that he expected the Allies to begin the invasion with diversionary operations in Norway, Denmark, and the southern part of the west coast of France, and in the Mediterranean. After that they would establish a bridge-head in Normandy or Brittany. Only when they had seen how things went would they set about the establishment of a real second front in the Pas de Calais. Germany, Hitler told the ambassador, would like nothing better than to have a show-down with large forces of the enemy as soon as possible. If the enemy operated in the way he expected he would be dispersing his forces in small parcels, doing exactly what he, Hitler, wanted him to do.

Fascinating, this. For that was exactly what 'the greatest strategic brain of all times' did himself with his by no means excessive forces, as a result of the false information passed to him by the Anglo-American deception team.

Oshima, ignorant that the Americans had cracked the Japanese diplomatic cipher months before Pearl Harbour, reported his talk with Hitler to Tokyo in a long dispatch transmitted by radio. Great was the satisfaction of the Anglo-American deception team when they read this unsolicited tribute from the Führer to the persuasiveness of their work.

*   *   *

The deception operation designed to mislead Hitler about the timing, direction, and weight of the Anglo-American assault was code-named 'Fortitude'. And that operation in turn was sub-divided into 'Fortitude North', which represented the threat to Norway, and 'Fortitude South', representing the plan to deceive the enemy with fictitious preparations for a massed assault against the German positions in the Pas de Calais.

Just as 'Fortitude North' had been given the task of convincing the Germans that an Anglo-American expeditionary force was being assembled and trained in Scotland for a descent on Norway, so now 'Fortitude South' was to lead von Roenne and Michael step by step into the belief that a vast expeditionary force of American, British, and Canadian troops was being moved into south-east England, together with supporting bombers, fighters, airborne troops, cooks, canteens, and landing craft. Once more, as in the case of the Norway hoax, the plan of the deception team was not simply to tell the Germans: 'Look out, chaps, that fellow Eisenhower is building up an army in East Anglia for a super-colossal assault on the Pas de Calais area.' Instead the evidence was to be insinuated piece by piece, formation by formation, move by move, until, when it was all assembled on the maps in von Roenne's underground war room at Zossen, the Germans would be confronted with a great Anglo-American Armada, entirely separate from the other invasion force, based on southern and south-eastern England. It would be revealed to have a separate command, and, by implication, a separate mission.

To determine what that mission was would be left to the German intelligence staff and the German High Command. They would be given all the evidence, faked and genuine, calculated to make them believe in the vast Armada in East Anglia. But none of the SHAEF-controlled V-men would expose themselves before D-day by naming a date or a place for the assault. It was vital to the success of the SHAEF deception—and with it to the success of the assault—that the credibility of the V-men under Allied control should not be questioned at the very time it was essential their information should be accepted and believed.

Unfortunately Field Marshal Montgomery and his 21st Army Group did not quite see things this way. They had insisted—and SHAEF had reluctantly yielded to them—that such time as the real preparations had reached a stage when the Germans could no longer be in doubt the assault was imminent, the threat to the Pas de Calais was to be stepped up. What could no longer be concealed, they argued, should at least be wrongly interpreted. This meant the V-men would almost certainly be committed to saying things which would be quickly contradicted by events. But even here that 'Providence', on which the agnostic Hitler pretended to place such great reliance, proved a fickle ally, as far as he was concerned. The German Secret Service in Lisbon, embroiled in the feuds accompanying the takeover of the Abwehr by Himmler's SD, shanghaied a double-cross agent of the Allies and abducted him to Berlin. The man almost certainly was in the know about the activities of his associate, the Pole known as 'Talleyrand' who was deeply involved in 'Fortitude South'. If the Germans were to learn that the threatened Calais assault was a hoax, they would have little difficulty in deducing that the genuine attack was to be made in Normandy. For the Pas de Calais and Normandy were the only areas suitable for a landing. Under the circumstances the request for a 'stepping up' of the threat to the Pas de Calais was withdrawn—to the immense benefit of 'Fortitude South's' ultimate success.

*   *   *

As in Scotland, and before that in North Africa, it was decided to use fake wireless traffic to support the intelligence transmitted to the Germans by the SHAEF-controlled V-men, wireless traffic providing audible evidence for the German radio interception units of the movements of the various formations. Visual evidence was to do the rest. This took the shape of dummies representing landing craft, hangars, loading ramps, assemblies of armour and much else, all of them placed where German reconnaissance planes were expected to observe and photograph them.

It turned out, however, that the efficiency of the German radio interception services had declined since the days of Captain See-bohm's triumphs in the Western Desert. Comparatively few fixes seem to have been picked up by the Germans from the deception signallers. The reconnaissance flights of the Luftwaffe were so few and far between that—as Foreign Armies West never ceased complaining—the intelligence produced by them was lamentably incomplete and unreliable when they did report, as at the end of May, that the Allied invasion fleet observed along the coast was sufficient to carry $15\frac{3}{4}$ divisions across the Channel in one lift, even Roenne was cautious. For his main information from England he preferred to rely on the V-men. That suited SHAEF quite well.

The V-man entrusted with the overture for 'Fortitude South' was 'Talleyrand', the young Polish officer whom the Abwehr (with the secret knowledge and approval of the British) had recruited in

Bucharest as long ago as 1940 and who was now serving as an assistant military attaché in his country's legation in London.

Towards the end of February 1944 'Talleyrand' flew out to Lisbon to meet his German controller. Colonel Wild and the other SHAEF officers who had worked out what 'Talleyrand' was to tell the Germans were full of doubts as to how his story would go down with the Germans. So, too, was 'Talleyrand' himself.

And indeed, as I have already mentioned, the atmosphere was distinctly frigid the first time 'Talleyrand' met his German boss, Colonel Schreiber, chief of the Lisbon K.O. Schreiber told 'Talleyrand' to his face that the Abwehr was not satisfied with his work, that the reports he had been sending them were not worth the money he was getting for them. 'They are the sort of trash which the British leak to foreign diplomats for propaganda or deception. If you want to go on working for us, you must get out and about yourself. Do your own scouting and observing. Don't just sit on your bottom accepting hand-outs from the attaché service or whatever it is the British call the office distributing their phony material.'

'Talleyrand' kept his head. Despite his own misgivings about his brief, he pretended to be full of hurt pride as he protested that 'getting out and about' was exactly what he had been doing, that Schreiber would realise that, when he had heard what he had to report. 'Things are hotting up in England and I have been all over the place checking on what I have learned. Listen carefully to what I tell you and report it accurately to Berlin. They are well informed there, I am sure. And they will appreciate the importance of the intelligence I have for them!'

His bluff succeeded completely. And when Schreiber and 'Talleyrand' met again two days later the clouds had disappeared, the sun was shining once more, and Schreiber was at his friendliest and most affable. Full of bonhomie and humour, he apologised most humbly for having doubted 'Talleyrand's' industry and enterprise. 'Berlin is delighted with the information you have brought us. Pity you are not a German. If you were, the Führer would award you a medal! Ha! Ha!'

Schreiber spoke the truth. Roenne and Michael were so happy over V-man 'Talleyrand's' report that excerpts from it were published in a special appendix attached to the very next situation report to be circulated:

Appendix to situation report West, No. 1199 of 9.3.1944.

A V-man dispatch which reached the department on 7.3.1944 has brought particularly valuable information about British Forces in Great Britain.

The authenticity of the report was checked and proved. It contains information about three armies, three army corps* and twenty-three large formations among which the location of only one need be regarded as questionable. The report confirms our own operational picture.

The sentence about the report 'confirming' their own operational picture was a bit of departmental window-dressing for Foreign Armies West and for the Abwehr in its fight with the SD. In reality the captured files of the department show that 'Talleyrand's' information filled in many gaps for Foreign Armies West†—and, I fear, not always accurately.

Most of what 'Talleyrand' told his German controller in Lisbon was slanted to fit 'Fortitude North' rather than 'Fortitude South'. It referred to formations like the 3rd Infantry Division being moved from Southern Command to Inverness and the 47th Infantry Division to Scarborough from Dorset. 'The English Guards Armoured Division', says the note, 'which had been in Eastern Command has been moved to north of Hull.' But the indisputable fact that 'Talleyrand's' information had been found so acceptable augured well for 'Fortitude South' in the future. And the Foreign Armies West picture based on what 'Talleyrand' had said in Lisbon did show formations in positions from which they could easily be moved to locations appropriate to the fictitious build-up in an area

---

* In the German text it says: '... *Angaben, über 3.AOK, III.A.K. und 23 grosse Verbände* ...' which would mean '... information about the 3rd Army, the 3rd Army Corps and twenty-three large formations ...' Internal evidence, however, suggests the ordinals are misprints for cardinal figures.

† That Foreign Armies West report of December 31, 1943, for instance, which gave the Allies fifty-five divisions in Britain when in fact they only had thirty-seven. Examination in detail reveals that of the fifty-five only twenty-two were correctly named and of those only ten were located correctly.

east of an imaginary line drawn from Oxford to Brighton. For instance, the report says:

South Eastern District
The 34th British Armoured Brigade hitherto in an unknown location has been ascertained in Kent.

Southern District
The 42nd British Armoured Division presumed hitherto to be in Devonshire, has been sent to the Mediterranean. The 42nd Division, hitherto reported as being in North Africa, is presumably the 42nd British Armoured Division and not, as had been assumed, the 42nd Infantry Division. The 42nd Infantry Division must therefore for the present be consigned to the category 'location unknown'.
Confirmation awaited.
In place of the 42nd Armoured Division which has been sent overseas the 7th Armoured Division has arrived in Britain from the Mediterranean.
Location unknown. Confirmation awaited.
Apart from this a large number of British formations are confirmed in locations previously accepted for them by the department.

Before SHAEF began to educate it, Roenne's department divided the Allied forces in Britain into three main groups, a northern, a central, and a southern group. The northern group was a good start for the mythical 4th Army in charge of 'Fortitude North's' Norway expedition. The southern group was well placed to give birth in its eastern sector to what the SHAEF V-men would in due course reveal to the Germans as FUSAG, the independent army group of assault forces in East Anglia, or, more accurately, in an area of southern England east of that line running from Oxford to Brighton.

The central group, however, did not fit in at all with the picture which the SHAEF Deception Unit were anxious to sell to the Germans. To the unit's irritation it was discovered that the Germans insisted on clinging to their conception.

A free-lance agent code-named 'Josephine', who worked out of Stockholm and ran a mythical network of agents in Britain, all of whom had female code-names, had sold them the 'central group', and Foreign Armies West gallantly refused to abandon it. 'Josephine' had persuaded the Abwehr that the 'central group' was spread over a wide area of central England. It had a strength of some twenty divisions, she said, and included United States formations as well as strong parachutist units.

So devoutly did Foreign Armies West believe in 'Josephine' and her 'central group' that they twisted the intelligence from the SHAEF V-men to fit in with the picture 'Josephine' had given them. When, for instance, as part of 'Fortitude North', they were informed of concentrations of shipping in the far north-east of Scotland, they did not interpret this as being a preparation for the expedition to northern Norway. Instead the department solemnly 'emphasised the probability' that the shipping was being held in readiness for the 'strong group of forces known for some time to be in central England'.

Fortunately the Germans had an equally strong belief in the 'southern group of armies'. The only trouble here was that they were in two minds about its point of concentration. At one moment they placed this in the south-west, at other times in the south-east. When the full campaign for 'Fortitude South' opened on April 24 with a barrage of bogus wireless signals, the weather vane of Foreign Armies West opinion had once against swung round to the south-west. So it was the business of the SHAEF-controlled V-men building FUSAG to rivet German attention on the south-east.

Jorge Antonio was the first to score. He relayed to Kühlenthal two successive messages from the Swansea seaman's 'Welsh Nazi' sub-agents. The first message reported how the agent whom Kühlenthal had code-named 'Desmond' had visited Ipswich at the beginning of May and found the 6th American Armoured Division ensconced there. Kühlenthal's office in Madrid had hardly had time to signal this to Berlin when another 'Welsh Nazi' (this time the one code-named 'Dick' by Kühlenthal) reported that the 28th American infantry Division had moved to Folkestone. Foreign Armies West promptly recorded both items in situation report No. 1256 of May 5, 1944:

The 6th American Armoured Division hitherto believed to be in Worcestershire is according to an as yet unconfirmed Abwehr report said to be in the East of England in the Ipswich area.

The 28th American Infantry Division according to a further Abwehr report has been moved from its location around Swansea

(South Wales) to south-east England into the neighbourhood of Folkestone. Confirmation awaited.

This was followed by a comment in the appendix to 1256:

. . . The move of the 6th American Armoured Division to Ipswich, reported by a good source, and of the 28th American Infantry Division to Folkestone as well as of the 7th American Army Corps to the Torquay area points to the already known areas of concentration and rounds off the picture of the completed deployment.

The pinpointing of the American 7th Army Corps in the Torquay area was owed to 'Paul', the Dutch staff officer, who had reported to his controller in Hamburg that 'while on my way to Torquay I quite by chance encountered troops of the American 7th Corps in Salisbury'. It is quite a way from Salisbury to Torquay and Salisbury could hardly be described as being in the Torquay area. So someone at Foreign Armies West or the RSHA signals in Hamburg must have been a little slipshod. Next 'Dick' (relayed by Jorge Antonio) reported that he had found the 8th American Corps in the same Folkestone area where he had already located the 28th US Infantry Division. That too was ecstatically recorded by Foreign Armies West—on May 11, 1944, in situation report West No. 1262.

According to the observation of a useful source the 8th American Army Corps is said to be in South East England. Its location is given as the Folkestone area.

This was followed on May 12, 1944, by a comment:

The probable arrival of the 8th American Army Corps in the Folkestone area, established by a useful source, makes it seem likely that apart from the 28th American Infantry Division already reported there, one or two further American formations should be presumed here which have not yet been located. The general picture emerging thus shows that apart from the strong American forces in south-west England one must expect individual American divisions to be launching attacks from all the other jumping-off bases.

In other words while Foreign Armies West still believed the south-west to be the main base for the assault, they had now come to the conclusion that a number of diversionary attacks by individual American divisions would take off from south-east England.

During the next days a series of further messages from the SHAEF-controlled V-men reached Foreign Armies West. Most of these reported quite accurately the movement of British divisions belonging to 21st Army Group to positions in southern England. A message, sent on May 9 by 'Paul', gave strong support to the American build-up in East Anglia. 'In the Bury St Edmunds area of East Anglia are located both the 20th American Army Corps and the 4th American Armoured Division.'

'Paul's' intelligence had the effect of pushing Foreign Armies West still further along the road the SHAEF deception strategists wanted them to travel in their appreciation. Says the appendix to situation report No. 1264 of May 13, 1944:

The main concentration of the enemy deployment is showing itself more and more clearly to be in the south and south-east of the island. Apart from the recently recognised move of the 3rd British Division to southern England the advance of the 47th British Division from the region north-east of York into the Portsmouth area is credibly reported.

And on May 15 Roenne claims that this south-eastern direction of the concentration is further supported 'by the introduction of American formations into the British build-up of forces in south-east England'. This was progress indeed. The south and the south-east were now the main invasion bases with the south-east as important in the opinion of Foreign Armies West as the south. Point three of an extract from the Luftwaffe intelligence staff's situation report built up the south-east even further:

Partial transfer of the 9th US Airfleet from south-west England to south-east England.

. . . The increased Interception Patrols by the US Air Force and the RAF off the south-east coast between Beachy Head and the Thames Estuary also deserve attention. Presumably their purpose is the defence of the concentration areas in this region.

Foreign Armies West were now accepting the reports of the SHAEF-controlled V-man network as uncritically as they had previously accepted the intelligence of such old favourites of the Abwehr as 'Josephine' and her ladies 'orchestra'. The 'Survey of the British Empire, No. 30' issued punctually by Roenne on May 31, 1944, showed that he and Roger Michael had accepted all the formations and their locations which SHAEF had passed to them in preparation of FUSAG. But owing to their habit of arbitrarily assigning formations to commands which did not exist but had been created in their own and 'Josephine's' imagination they were assigning formations, which the SHAEF deception team's fictitious order of battle had wanted them to assign to FUSAG, to other commands from which it was going to be difficult to disentangle them. For instance they readily accepted the 4th and 6th US Armoured Divisions as being in East Anglia. But Foreign Armies West assigned them to Eastern Command which on their own idiosyncratic map of the Allied order of battle was the 6th Army. The 28th and 83rd US Infantry Divisions, likewise intended by the deceivers for FUSAG, were assigned by Roenne and his officers to what they called the Fifth Army, although they had willingly accepted the locations given for them by the SHAEF-controlled V-men. The 11th Armoured Division, whose move from Yorkshire to Sussex had been reported by 'Paul' on May 25—he had observed it 'passing through Dorking'—they had arbitrarily put with the Guards' Armoured Division under the command of the 1st Canadian Army, presumably because their locations were close to each other.

Added to all these divisions moving into what the Deception Unit had designated as the FUSAG area was a liberal helping of nonexistent ones. Some had a number, some had none. All, however, had locations in East Anglia: in Norwich, Harwich, Lowestoft, Chelmsford, Colchester, etc. Most of these divisions had been invented by the SHAEF unit. But some, I fear, owed their existence to von Roenne and his helpmate Roger Michael.

These two officers had seen their worst fears confirmed with the take-over of the Abwehr by its old rivals of Himmler's RSHA, the Chief Reich Security Office. In its fight against 'defeatism' the RSHA had ruled that in order to protect the morale of the 'politically unschooled' Officers' Corps foreign and military intelligence reports should from now on be circulated only after they had been censored by SD experts and purged of anything undermining confidence in the Führer and his conduct of the war.* Roenne, like Michael and a number of other officers of the German General Staff, regarded this ruling as a challenge to their ingenuity.† Were the divisions 'number unknown' Roenne's answer? It is conceivable.

*   *   *

The take-over of the Abwehr by Himmler's men caused consternation among the SHAEF deception men, now sharing offices with the rest of Eisenhower's headquarters staff in the south-western outskirts of London at Bushy Park near Kingston-on-Thames. Like Colonel Wild himself, they feared there would be a shake-up among the Abwehr staff in the course of which the V-men would be handed over to a new set of controllers who might smell rats where an old hand like Erich Kühlenthal had remained unsuspecting.

And indeed their apprehensions appeared to have been realised when on April 29, 1944, a signal was received from the M.I.6 representative in Lisbon reporting that 'Talleyrand's' friend and associate 'Scherer'‡ had been shanghaied from his villa in Estoril by a posse of Schellenberg's strong-arm toughs. The unfortunate 'Scherer', a 'Folk-German' from Transylvania, had been doped by Schellenberg's 'commando' squad, bundled unconscious into a car with Corps Diplomatique numberplates, and driven across the frontier into Spain. 'By now', the M.I.6 report surmised, 'he must be in Berlin and undergoing rigorous interrogation.'

That report caused near-panic in SHAEF's Deception Unit and the LCS. Looking back both Noël Wild and Johnny Bevan today regard 'Scherer's' abduction as their worst moment of the war. Had 'Scherer', as was to be feared, broken down and revealed to his

---

* Gert Buchheit, *Der Deutsche Geheimdienst*, p. 432.

† The pretext for the crack-down on the Abwehr had been provided by the defection of Dr Vermehren, a junior Abwehr man in Ankara. With his wife he took refuge in the British Embassy and was flown first to Cairo, then to London. About the same time Fräulein Neele Kapp, secretary to the SD chief at the German Embassy, went over to the Americans. Hitler ignored the defection of the SD girl and concentrated his fury on Admiral Canaris. The Abwehr chief was fired and then consigned to Castle Lauenstein, the headquarters of Germany's Economic Warfare unit of which the Admiral was put in nominal charge. In fact he was in custody.

‡ 'Scherer' was the Abwehr's code-name for this agent.

German interrogators all he knew about the Allied deception in which his friend 'Talleyrand' was playing a major part, not only would 'Fortitude' itself be blown, but all the double agents employed by SHAEF and—as I have already shown—the invasion plan itself. 'Scherer', however, did not break down. He never betrayed either 'Talleyrand' or 'Fortitude'. It is conceivable that he was never examined about 'Talleyrand's' Abwehr mission in Britain. Whether he was or not, the fact is, that the reliability and integrity of 'Talleyrand' as a V-man was never questioned by the Germans.

Skilful enquiries by M.I.6 in Lisbon revealed that not doubts concerning 'Talleyrand's' loyalty as an agent had led to 'Scherer's' arrest, as was at first feared, but a typically squalid intrigue of the SD against the Abwehr. The SD men in order to 'get something' on the Abwehr had accused 'Scherer' of financial dishonesty and anti-Nazi conspiracy with the family of Dr Vermehren, the Abwehr officer who had defected from Hitler in Ankara. So far were they from suspecting the truth that they feared 'Scherer' might denounce 'Talleyrand' to the British as a spy!

'Scherer' had been an agent of the Abwehr even before the occupation of Rumania. It was he who (in Bucarest in 1940) had recruited 'Talleyrand' for the Abwehr after 'Talleyrand's' escape from Poland during its 1939 collapse. 'Talleyrand' in due course had repaid the compliment by recruiting 'Scherer' as a double agent for the British. The Germans had sent him to Lisbon. There, with the blessing of M.I.6, 'Scherer' claimed he was fooling the British. He had conned them, he boasted to Schreiber, the chief of the Lisbon K.O., into accepting him as an Anti-Nazi. (A profitable hobby indulged in by many members of the Lisbon 'Corps d'Espionage'.) To the Abwehr 'Scherer' pretended that he was helping 'Talleyrand' with his 'escape-organisation' subterfuge. And this was the explanation he gave his Abwehr chiefs for his frequent meetings with the local representative of M.I.6.

When 'Talleyrand' called on Schreiber at the Abwehr's Lisbon headquarters, during his visits to Lisbon—he made several after that first successful one at the end of February—he was usually accompanied by 'Scherer'. Schreiber welcomed 'Scherer's' presence and was only too glad to have him sitting in on the meetings. 'Talleyrand' was equally pleased, for 'Scherer' had a wonderful technique in steering Schreiber away from dangerous topics by interposing inquisitorial questions, phrased in a misleadingly challenging and hostile manner.

When 'Talleyrand's' reports were praised by Rohleder and Roenne, 'Scherer' came in for his share of the glory. And then, just when 'Scherer' was at the acme of jubilant self-confidence, Nemesis stepped in and crushed him with one shattering blow.

A free-lance agent using the name of 'Brandes' was jealous of 'Scherer's' renown and apprehensive of 'Scherer's' probing into his own activities. This man denounced 'Scherer' to the SD. He declared that 'Scherer', apart from being engaged in illicit currency dealings, was having secret meetings with the mother of Dr Vermehren, the traitor and defector. True enough, Frau Vermehren had indeed resided in Portugal until recently—although after her son's defection she had been forced to return to Germany where she had been imprisoned by the Gestapo. It was true too that she had been on friendly terms with 'Scherer' who had visited her frequently. Once these facts were established they were enough for the SD to go into action against 'Scherer'.

There had been some trouble over money owing to 'Talleyrand' from the Abwehr. To straighten things out—that was the pretext thought up by the SD—Schreiber and 'Scherer' were invited to come to Biarritz and discuss the matter with von Bohlen, an Abwehr officer in charge of the organisation's finances. Major von Bohlen, 'Scherer' was told, wanted his advice because he ('Scherer') knew best how to handle 'Talleyrand' in so delicate a matter. Bohlen did not want to take a false step with so valuable a V-man as 'Talleyrand'.

Flattery, however, was not enough to snare 'Scherer'. He was far from eager to cross into France where he would have been in the complete power of Himmler's men. He excused himself from making the trip on the very reasonable ground that it would smash to smithereens his cover with the British. How could he go on pretending to them that he was an anti-Nazi if he travelled to occupied France, a thing that no genuine anti-Nazi would dare to do? So Schreiber had to travel to Biarritz alone. The SD, convinced now that in 'Scherer' they were on to a good thing, organised his shanghaiing. Without great originality they code-named it 'Opera-

tion Dora'.* On May 2 Schreiber received a signal from Berlin,
' "Operation Dora" successfully completed.'

After their interrogation both 'Scherer' and Frau Vermehren
were consigned to Oranienburg concentration camp. But while
Frau Vermehren survived and was able to tell Allied intelligence
officers after the war how she had met 'Scherer' in the camp and
talked with him, 'Scherer' himself disappeared without trace.
Whether he was liberated by the Russians only to be rearrested and
consigned to some death camp in Russia—as happened to so many
non-Communist prisoners found in National Socialist concentration
camps—or whether, like other members of the Abwehr accused
of treason, he was shot by Himmler's black guards during the
final agony of the Third Reich, no one knows. 'Scherer' was
gone.

But in May and June 1944 his situation was far too unclear for
the Allies to take any risks. The 'Double-cross' Committee therefore
decided against letting 'Talleyrand' pass any further deception messages in case the Germans should get on to their real meaning
through 'Scherer'. But they did not take him off the air right away.
'Talleyrand' went on sending messages as though nothing had happened, harmless messages free of poison, devoid of interest. Until
the right moment arrived for him to make his farewell.

'Talleyrand's' farewell was contrived with an elegance characteristic of his whole performance. At the request of 'A' Force, acting
on behalf of LCS, SIME (Security Intelligence Middle East) sent a
wireless message to the War Office in London in a cipher which
they were certain the German interception services would read. The
message (sent around May 15) said that the guerilla headquarters of
General Mihailovic in Yugoslavia had learned from a well-placed
source that the ADC to King Peter was a spy working for the
Germans. On May 20 'Talleyrand' reported to Lisbon in a letter
(written in invisible ink) how he had been called to the War Office
and asked a lot of searching questions about his young friend, the

---

* The Germans had a passion for giving female code-names to plans for
violent assault, e.g. 'Gertrud' (assault against Turkey), 'Gisela' (occupation of
Spain and Portugal), 'Ida' (assault on Istrian coast), 'Isabella' (seizure of Canary
Islands), 'Margarethe I' & 'II' (occupation of Hungary and Rumania), 'Marita'
(assault on Greece), etc., etc.

ADC. 'The interrogating officer wanted to know what were my friend's political views, how and why he had come to England. I gathered that the cause of these questions was a message from British intelligence in the Middle East passing on information which had come from Mihailovic circles in Yugoslavia. It was not stated clearly during the interview but the implication of the questions put to me was that he was accused of working for the Germans. I got the impression that the British do not take information from such a source too seriously, so I do not see any reason for panic. But it is possible they will be making further investigations. My friend and I decided therefore to take the radio set to pieces and hide them in case the place is searched. My friend expects the King to use his influence on his behalf. So keep a watch for signals. We shall resume our reports as soon as feasible.'

Schreiber's operators watched for 'Talleyrand's' signals for more than two months. In vain. Not one word was received from him. But on June 30 the ADC sent Lisbon a message. 'Had to keep silent for reasons stated in letter of May 20. Expect to be sent away shortly on unavoidable mission for my master. Thanks to him British doubts about me mainly dispersed. But some still exist.' An indignant reply came from Schreiber on July 4. 'Do not understand sudden interruption. Letter of May 20 not received.'

Poor 'Scherer'! He had kept faith. But 'Talleyrand' and 'King Peter's ADC' did not resume their work.

*　　*　　*

The kidnapping of 'Scherer' and the subsequent closing down of 'Talleyrand' was the only set-back the SHAEF Deception Unit had to suffer as a result of the change of masters at the Abwehr headquarters. To the immense relief of Wild's team, Himmler and his satraps, having satisfied their empire-building ambitions, soon gave up reorganising and reforming and left things much as they had been. The only real changes were that in place of the somewhat easy-going Admiral Canaris the brash and ignorant careerist Walter Schellenberg, now a major-general of the Waffen–SS, was put in charge of the integrated German intelligence services, and that the Abwehr officers were now called SD men. Jorge Antonio was gratified to note that his old boss 'Alfonso'* still signed the messages from the Madrid K.O., Schellenberg, Jorge Antonio happily concluded, certainly was not making things more difficult as far as he was concerned.

Nor was the SD harder to dupe than the Abwehr. If anything, the reverse was true. Which was just as well. For with D-day approaching 'Fortitude South' was about to face its 'moment of truth'. Or, more accurately, the moment when its great lie would be put to the supreme test.

*   *   *

When 'Fortitude South' was planned in January 1944 the Deception Unit's most sanguine hope had been that their hoax would manage to keep Hitler fooled for just forty-eight hours after the landing. Eisenhower had told Wild that he would be well satisfied if for the first two days after D-day the OKW could be induced to go on believing that the main blow was coming later with the Pas de Calais as its target. 'Just keep the 15th Army out of my hair for the first two days. That's all I ask. That will give us time to establish ourselves firmly in the bridge-head.'

By the middle of May, however, enough intelligence about the German reaction to the deception had been received by SHAEF to make the Deception Unit more confident about the durability of their hoax. Things looked as though with some luck its life might be prolonged. It became imperative therefore not to prejudice its chances of survival by any ill-considered word or careless action. Nothing must be allowed to arouse German suspicion that the threat from the Armada in south-eastern England might not be as real as Luftwaffe reconnaissance (such as it was), radio interception, and the V-man reports had led the Führerhauptquartier to accept. No personalities and no formations connected with the forces the Germans had been led to assume would be entrusted with the main assault must therefore be allowed to play a part in Normandy. Not until Eisenhower was ready to abandon the deception. That decision pointed a warning finger straight at one man: the commander of the

---

* Kühlenthal's cover-name was 'Alfonso', see page 57.

American contingent landing in Normandy, General Omar Nelson Bradley himself.

Shortly after he had arrived in Britain in January 1944 it had been announced publicly that General Bradley would command the 1st United States Army. What had not been announced, although it was already decided, was that Bradley would also command the 1st United States Army Group. This FUSAG—unlike the dummy formation in south-east England which had borrowed its name for deception purposes—was a genuine formation and included Bradley's own 1st United States Army as well as the 3rd United States Army commanded by General George S. Patton.

Wild and his fellow deceivers had to face the disagreeable possibility that as the 1st United States Army was in the first wave of American troops landing in Normandy Bradley's presence in France might become known to the Germans. Therefore, if his name remained linked with FUSAG, the whole deception scheme might be given away. This was all the more likely as Jorge Antonio in a signal sent to Madrid—before it had been decided that 'Fortitude South' might be prolonged—had quoted a fictitious American informant to the effect that Bradley was 'provisionally' the commander of 1st United States Army Group. It was a nasty problem.

Its solution, however, was as simple as it was brilliant. This was to change the name of Bradley's Army Group. It was re-named '12th Army Group'. And the bogus FUSAG was given a new commander, none other than the flamboyant General George S. Patton.*
In the eyes of the Germans no one could have been a more natural choice to command the main assault. Patton was senior to Bradley and therefore ideally fitted to take charge of what was clearly intended by Eisenhower to be the decision-forcing Army Group. Moreover his dashing generalship was just the kind needed in the German view for the break-through he was to lead. From the viewpoint of the SHAEF deception team there was yet another consider-

---

* This was not the first time that General Patton had been used in a deception operation. In July 1943, just before the landing in Sicily George Patton was brought to Cairo from Algiers. Dudley Clarke and Noël Wild took him in tow. Together they toured the town, dined at Shepheard's in full uniform, and took the trouble to attract as much attention as possible. The idea was that Axis agents should report Patton's presence in Cairo, thus helping to support the story of an intended Allied landing in Greece.

ation that spoke in George Patton's favour: he was not due in France until the beginning of July.

Nevertheless, when 'Paul'* in a message transmitted to his controller in Hamburg on May 31 spelled out to the Germans the complete FUSAG story in the terms SHAEF wanted the Germans to accept-there was just one point on which Roenne had reservations: General Patton's command of FUSAG. Roenne had accepted Jorge Antonio's earlier report that Bradley was in command of the 1st United States Army Group. And Roenne was like intelligence officers all the world over. Once he had accepted a piece of intelligence as a fact, he was mesmerised by it and stubbornly refused to change his mind. But Carlos Reid remembered the message about Bradley's command of FUSAG and realised the need to put it right. He helped Jorge Antonio to concoct a truly classic 'correction'. The fictitious American source who had given Jorge Antonio the original tip about Bradley's 'provisional' appointment to command FUSAG (he was a sergeant who worked in an unidentified headquarters staff and appeared to have access to a startlingly wide variety of information), was called in to help once more. Signalled Jorge Antonio: 'I asked 14/3' (the sergeant's code-number in communications from Jorge Antonio to Madrid) 'where I could find the headquarters of General Bradley. But as Bradley is at present under Montgomery in 21st Army Group, 14/3 could not tell me where his headquarters was. I enquired who might be in charge of FUSAG. He said General Patton had taken over the command that had been temporarily held by Bradley during the army group's formation. In the course of the conversation I learned that the headquarters of General Patton, that is of FUSAG, is at Wentworth.'

Wild assumed that would do the trick. And—as the SHAEF officers were able to assure themselves from the records of Foreign

---

* 'Paul' was now in a position of exceptional authority with regard to Allied plans. On May 18 he had announced to his Abwehr controller in Hamburg that he had been appointed to FUSAG headquarters. He was to be a member of a liaison section of French, Dutch, and Polish army and airforce officers. Under the command of an American they would have the job of recruiting their nationals who had been working for the Germans into an Allied Labour Corps, if they found them suitable. He was thus in a position to pick up much that was of interest without being bound to know everything that was going on. An ideal position for a deception agent.

Armies West when they went through them after the war—it did. From now on, until it underwent further changes of command, the phantom army was as often as not referred to in the reports of Foreign Armies West as the 'Patton Army'.

The message transmitted by 'Paul's' radio operator to Hamburg on May 31 created a tremendous impression at Foreign Armies West Headquarters in the underground 'Zeppelin' citadel in Zossen. Roenne used the information it gave in his situation report on D-day. It is an historic document. I therefore reproduce the text of the section dealing with the invasion in full.

Appendix to situation report West No. 1288 of 6.6.1944.
England
While the Anglo-Saxon enemy landing on the coast of Normandy represents a large-scale operation, the forces employed comprise only a relatively small portion of the formation available.

Of the sixty large formations held in Southern Britain only ten to twelve divisions including airborne troops appear to be participating so far.

The execution of the operation followed the established technique for large-scale landing operations. It included Bomber raids at night on coastal fortifications, parachute and glider landings making use of the moonlight, and most remarkable of all, landings on the beaches without consideration of the state of the tide. The weather must have caused the operation some difficulties. In particular it is bound to have interfered with the operations of the enemy airforce.

The progress of the landing so far can hardly have lived up to the expectations of the enemy command as it included numerous setbacks and many abortive attempts to reach land. All the same the success should not be underestimated. The enemy has gained a bridge-head which is thirty kilometers wide and in places up to eight kilometers deep. The weakness of this bridge-head must be seen in its shallow depth in some places and the lack of an efficient port. Nor does the successful landing of armour make up for this as yet.

The main object of the landing is to take possession of the harbour of Cherbourg and to seal off the Cotentin peninsula.

Points worthy of special note are:

(a) the confinement of the air attack to limited areas which contrary to expectation did not include the main German command posts in the West.

(b) the only partial commitment of the sabotage organisations. Vast areas have been left untouched.

(c) the uniform origin of all the formations engaged to date (2nd Canadian, 50th British, 79th British Armoured Divisions, the 6th British Airborne, 82nd US Airborne, and 101st US Airborne Divisions).

The factors enumerated under (a) to (c) all indicate that further operations are planned and confirm statements to that effect by Churchill and Eisenhower.

In this respect the areas (in England) in which the formations were stationed before being committed to battle seem particularly relevant.

According to a believable Abwehr report of June 2nd the forces in southern England are divided into two army groups, the 21st British Army Group and the 1st US Army Group. Of these the 1st US Army Group appears to comprise the 1st Canadian Army, which has been ascertained in south-east England (with thirteen large formations), as well as the 3rd US Army (about twelve large formations) between the Thames and the Wash. Whether this US Army Group is under General Bradley or under General Patton is not yet clear. 21st Army Group, commanded by General Montgomery, seems to comprise the formations in south and south-west England which are divided into three army corps. All formations which have so far appeared in the beachheads come from this group of forces stationed in an area west of the line Brighton–Oxford. At the same time numerous British official announcements confirm that Montgomery commands the forces engaged in the landing.

This would suggest that Montgomery has at his disposal a further twenty large formations, which allows us to expect further attempts at landings from air and sea in the area of the Cotentin peninsula. Assaults against the Channel Islands and the west coast of Normandy seem possible, also raids in the direction of Brest.

Not a single unit of the 1st United States Army Group, which comprises around twenty-five large formations north and south of the Thames, has so far been committed. The same is true of the ten to twelve combat formations stationed in central England and Scotland.

This suggests that the enemy is planning a further large-scale operation in the Channel area, which one would expect to be aimed at a coastal sector in the Pas de Calais area.★

In connection with this operation one must expect to see the

★ '. . . in Gegend der Kanalmitte'.

strong forces of the Anglo-Saxon Air Arm deployed. They have
been held back until now. Presumably these air fleets will then
attempt to smash the German command posts.

Whether and to what extent, in addition to these plans, small-
scale diversions are still envisaged in the North Sea area, cannot be
established.

It must be reckoned with, however, that strong forces are being
held ready with, the necessary shipping in eastern seaports of the
USA to be transported directly to any Atlantic port of sufficient
capacity which might fall into enemy hands.

Well, there it was, the FUSAG story: the super-armada in south-
east England, lying in wait with its 'twenty-five large formations',
and who knows how many airborne divisions, waiting for the order
to pounce on Calais. It had been served up on a platter to the
RSHA. Foreign Armies West had swallowed it whole. To Hitler,
too, it must have been irresistible.

No wonder. The FUSAG deception had been specially tailored
to fit Adolf Hitler's psychology. It had everything to appeal to his
long-displayed lust for self-dramatisation.

Here he was, the hero Führer, faced with the supreme challenge
of the Anglo-Americans. And behold! Just as Prussia's hero King
Frederick the Great was saved in his most critical hour (Hitler was
never tired of this parallel with Frederick the Great) by the provi-
dential death of the Tsarina Elizabeth and the accession of the Pro-
Prussian Tsar Peter, so now a spy had providentially come forward
at the last moment to reveal to him, the Führer, the secret plans of
his enemies. Ha! He would show the wily Eisenhower that he could
not be tricked into sending his armour to Normandy. With his
'iron will' and 'unshakeable resolution'—two of Hitler's favourite
phrases—he would keep his troops in position around Calais no
matter what the temptation to move them. When the enemy struck
there, as strike he must—the V-missile bombardment was planned
to open on June 12, and Patton would be forced to strike—he,
Hitler, the hero Führer, would have his armour waiting for him in
the strongest and most lethal sector of the Atlantic Wall. Patton
would be smitten 'hip and thigh'! The invaders would be destroyed.
The war would be won.

The SHAEF Deception Unit's was a brilliant piece of psychology. Better than anything thought up during the war by us Psychological Warriors, 'white' or 'black'.* And it worked. But very nearly it did not. For Hitler, vacillating as ever, despite his iron will and unshakeable resolution, could not quite make up his mind. When Rundstedt and Rommel bombarded him with appeals for reinforcements he very nearly gave way.

In fact he had given way. And then another message arrived. A message from the Spaniard he knew as 'Cato'—his most trusted spy. Hitler changed his mind again. He recalled the Panzers to Calais— and lost the war.

---

* The Psychological Warriors divided their production into 'white' and 'black'. 'White' propaganda openly avowed its Allied origin. 'Black' propaganda sought to disguise its source.

10

Madrid's D-day Bungle

It was Carlos Reid who had the idea to give Jorge Antonio a scoop on the invasion. We even know the day on which he conceived it and the approximate hour: somewhere between half-past nine and noon on the morning of Thursday, May 4, 1944.

For the first time that year Charlie had breakfasted under the chestnut tree in the garden behind his London home. There had been a shower of rain just before dawn and now the sun was shining. Everything was bright and green and clean, as bright and clean as things could be despite the grimy debris left by the bombs. Charlie felt good. He was enjoying the scent of the freshly mowed lawn and the warm fragrance of the blossoming shrubs. Mimosa and lilac. He had brought them from his casa at Pollensa and planted them here in his garden the year the war broke out.

Thinking of Pollensa reminded him that Jorge Antonio would be coming around to see him that morning. They had agreed to draw up a plan of campaign together for the 'network's' activities in the decisive weeks ahead. He must get something down on paper before the Spaniard arrived.

Charlie went indoors and sat down at his typewriter.

'During the remaining weeks before D-day,' he tapped out, 'and indeed during the period immediately following D-day, there is likely to be considerable divergence of opinion among the members of the German High Command regarding the Allied intentions. The design and scope of "Neptune"* will not have been revealed to them in its early stages and they will still be guessing. We may perhaps be permitted to hope that there will be some among them who will draw the conclusions we have been trying to suggest by

---

* Code-name for the landing in Normandy.

means of "Fortitude South". If through "Vandal"* we can continue to supply those circles which are already disposed to accept "Fortitude South" with further arguments in its favour we shall perhaps be able to give decisive support to "Neptune". It is important therefore that we should consider carefully the arrangements for "Vandal's" operations in the period immediately preceding D-day, during D-day, and during the days immediately following D-day.'

Charlie looked up and chuckled. What a pity that he could not show this paper to Kim Philby.† Kim had liked his *Don Juan weeps and other poems* and he would enjoy the irony of its author writing this kind of Whitehall gobbledegook. But Philby was not 'Bigotted'‡ and, although as head of M.I.5's Spanish desk he knew about Jorge Antonio, he was not in the picture on 'Fortitude South', nor aware of Jorge Antonio's share in it.

And then suddenly, completely out of the blue, Carlos had his idea. How would it be if on the eve of D-day Jorge Antonio was allowed to warn the Germans that the invasion was on the way? A couple of hours or so before the first landing from the sea would do. Not long enough ahead to allow them time to prepare for the assault, but long enough to give him the scoop. That would bolster his prestige with the Germans enormously and make them ready to accept anything else he had to tell them. But would Ike ever agree to a scheme like this? Well, the colonel would have to persuade Bedell Smith. And Bedell would then persuade Ike.

Charlie, feeling even better than he had felt in the garden, got down to his paper once more. When he had finished it, his memorandum contained two main proposals. The first, that two hours before the expected time of landing 'Vandal' should signal Madrid that the invasion was on its way; the second, that forty-eight hours after the troops had stormed ashore 'Vandal' should send a further message. This would say that he had been thinking over the developments of the last two months. He had also discussed them with

---

* SHAEF code-name for Jorge Antonio.
† Kim Philby, who in the sixties defected to Moscow and later boasted that he had been a Kremlin agent all his adult life, was at this time head of the Iberian sub-section of M.I.5. Carlos Reid and he had become close friends.
‡ Persons entrusted with the top-secret details of the D-day plans carried passes inscribed with the code-word 'Bigot'. They were 'Bigotted'.

the sub-agents who had been reporting to him from the embarkation points and the assembly areas. They had agreed with him that
despite its imposing scale the present operation represented only one
prong of an assault that was at the very least two-pronged. Having
said that, he would then go over the evidence once again that led
him to this conclusion.

Colonel Wild was delighted and excited when Reid presented
him with the paper in his pre-fab office hut in Bushy Park's 'SHAEF-
ville' the following day. 'First class!' he said. 'I am sure we can get
approval for this. Bedell and Ike will love it!'

He grinned happily before going on. 'Meanwhile I have a little
idea of my own. You know those long-haired Political Warfare
chaps in Bush House? Every week they issue a thing they call the
"Central Directive". It's a dreary document on which they spend
hours of arid nit-picking. They debate and rewrite every sentence
phrase by phrase several times over before they're satisfied. Well
this "Central Directive" contains the guide-lines for the Propagandists telling them how to handle the political and strategic situations
that may come up in the near future. They lay down what shall be
said and what shall not be said in the various media—BBC broadcasts, propaganda leaflets, newspaper articles and so forth. Well, I
have been having this directive sent to me for the past few weeks.
And it gave me an idea. Why don't we fake a few copies of the
PWE* "Central Directive" and pass them to the Germans? The
German intelligence chaps could then submit the directives to close
analysis and draw all manner of fascinating conclusions. For instance, imagine that around D-day the directive decreed that there
must be no public speculation about the possibility of a further
landing. The inference should be fairly obvious that there *is* going
to be a further landing and that Eisenhower is trying to keep it from
being talked about in order that it should take the Germans by
surprise.'

It was Reid's turn to be enthusiastic.

'Is this a little job you have in mind for "Vandal", Noël?' he
asked. 'If it is, I think he should manage to put it over quite nicely.
That friend of his at the Ministry of Information might recruit him

* PWE= Political Warfare Executive.

to the M of I and have him made a temporary Civil Servant. That would give him access to many interesting secrets. And he ought to be able to pinch a copy of the PWE Central Directive there. Of course, "Vandal" will have to obtain Madrid's approval before joining the M of I. But Kühlenthal is bound to jump at the chance of getting "Vandal" into a position with direct access to the innermost secrets.' Wild and Reid both laughed at this description of the Ministry of Information for which they had no very great respect. 'But "Vandal" in his approach to Kühlenthal should, of course, show becoming qualms at signing the British Official Secrets Act and reluctance at even going through a pretence of betraying his beloved Führer.'

'Splendid! How soon can you get that fixed up?'

'Can I have about ten days? An idea has occurred to me how we might make the invitation to "Vandal" from the Ministry even more attractive to the Germans. Mind you, I feel sure that Madrid will leap at the proposition even without that. But it occurs to me that we have an opportunity to build up the personality of "Vandal's" influential friend at the M of I without "Vandal" himself having to say who he is. The Germans will do it themselves by brilliant deduction.'

He happened to know, Reid explained, that the head of the Iberian section at the M of I was at this very moment on a visit to Spain and Portugal. The official and he had been friends since their days at Stonyhurst together. 'If "Vandal" reports that his M of I pal is temporarily abroad, we can arrange that Kühlenthal learns he is in Madrid. Kühlenthal and his crowd will then put two and two together and assume that the head of the region and "Vandal's" unconscious sub-agent are the same chap. That should impress them considerably. We can then arrange to have the poor devil recalled to London. Then, when he has returned, "Vandal" can report how he met his M of I friend on his return to London and how he had been asked to join his section as a translator. What do you think?'

Wild liked the scheme. That same evening (May 5, 1944) Jorge Antonio reported almost as an afterthought at the end of his message, that O-15 (his code-number for his M of I contact), was temporarily abroad and therefore unavailable as a source of information.

On May 20, after the M of I man had been recalled and his departure had presumably been observed and reported by the Lisbon K.O., Jorge Antonio told Kühlenthal in his signal that evening how his M of I friend had offered him a job with the Ministry as a translator. 'O-15 has just returned from Madrid and Lisbon where he has been making propaganda preparations for the opening of the second front. At his invitation I called on him in his office. He then asked whether I would be prepared to assist him at the Ministry by doing translation work for him. He offered me a generous salary and said I could do the job at home in my spare time from the fruit importer's office. I accepted provisionally, but said that I must consult my Covent Garden boss. This was in order that I could ask you for your advice. I dislike very much the idea of betraying the Führer by working for the British. O-15 said I would have to sign the Official Secrets Act, as some of the material I would be called on to translate was classified as secret. So it will be no disappointment to me, if you advise that I should reject this proposal.'

Reid was proved correct in his prognostication that Kühlenthal would leap at the chance of getting his V-man into the M of I. He told Jorge Antonio to forget his scruples and sign the Official Secrets Act. It was all in a good cause, he said. As for Bedell Smith and Eisenhower, they were equally delighted to agree to the scheme of the deception artists to let 'Vandal' scoop the invasion. Indeed Bedell Smith suggested that 'Vandal' should signal Madrid not two hours before the expected touch-down but four.

*   *   *

On the evening of June 5, 1944, just a month after Reid had his inspiration, Jorge Antonio, Roger Sneath,* and the Seaforth Highlander colonel who chaired the 'Double-cross' Committee, all met Reid at his house. After a modest but beautifully prepared meal, with which they drank the last magnum of Château Ausone 1934 from Reid's cellar, the four of them set forth in a War Office Humber for the house in High Barnet where Jorge Antonio's transmitter, and its Royal Signals operator, were installed. When they

* The American lieutenant-colonel, who headed the intelligence section of the Deception Unit.

arrived, the operator was just receiving the evening call from Madrid.

Kühlenthal's radio was transmitting routine traffic; administrative arrangements for 'Cato's' network, technical details in connection with his radio link—call signs, frequencies, and that sort of thing.*

There was no sign of tension or expectancy about the German transmission, nothing to suggest the operator or his superiors were aware that the great invasion Armada was on its way at last and that Hitler was about to face the show-down with the Western Allies he so longed for. For Kühlenthal's operator the night of June 5, 1944, was clearly a night just like any other night.

A few minutes before midnight he had completed his messages. 'Anything more from your end?' he asked, using an agreed one-group symbol. 'Not yet,' replied the Royal Signals sergeant and repeated it for emphasis. 'Not yet.'

'Well, good night then.'

It was normal practice for Madrid to close down at midnight.

For the best part of ten days Reid and Jorge Antonio had been searching for a pretext on which to ask Kühlenthal's man to keep open to receive signals in the early hours of the morning instead of going off duty at midnight as was his habit. Clearly Jorge Antonio could not say: 'Stand by for the next few mornings. I am expecting important developments.' That would have given the show away.

Fortunately Kühlenthal himself supplied the pretext. Three days earlier he had asked Jorge Antonio to report urgently, whether the formations in Scotland were on the move. Was the 52nd Division still in Glasgow? Jorge Antonio replied he hoped to transmit a report answering this query late on Sunday night or in the early hours of Monday, June 5. Would Alfonso please have his post ready to receive all night, should it prove necessary? Kühlenthal promised.

But, as all the world knows, Eisenhower had to postpone the in-

---

* The radio of the Madrid K.O. had been installed with the approval of Generalissimo Franco's allegedly neutral government on the terrain of the Spanish Army's Signal Corps. It operated under the cover of the Spanish Army. An agreement to this effect had been reached with the Spanish General Staff on March 16, 1944, and was communicated to the Wehrmachtführungs-stab on April 8, 1944. 'The Abwehr Signals units employed in Spain will to outward appearances operate under orders of the Spanish General Staff and receive its special protection.'

vasion for twenty-four hours because of bad weather in the Channel.
At 1930 hours on June 4, Jorge Antonio signalled Madrid that his
man in Glasgow was now uncertain, exactly, when he would have
the required information. Jorge Antonio said that because he was
aware how urgently the information was wanted he was preparing
to stand by to relay it that night and, if necessary, during the night
of Monday to Tuesday as well. Would Madrid please confirm that
they would make reciprocal arrangements? Back came the signal
that Madrid would be watching on Monday night and Tuesday
morning unless they were advised to the contrary.

Reid and Jorge Antonio, relying on the proverbial German efficiency, congratulated themselves that their revised arrangements were
foolproof. There could be no slip-up now.

Alas, their joy was premature.

By 1.56 am on June 6, the enciphering of the message was complete. Under Montgomery's plan the first battalions to land were
expected to swim ashore in their amphibious DD tanks by 6.30 am
at the latest. H-hour for Jorge Antonio's message had accordingly
been fixed for 2.30 am, although Commando and Parachutist
formations were expected to be dropping from the sky and going
into action just around the same time. The four deception plotters
and the radio operator waited nervously. At 2.29 am the Seaforth
Highlander looked at his watch. 'All right, Sergeant,' he said, 'let
them have it!'

The sergeant pounced on his key to call Madrid. He called and he
called. No answer. He called again. Still no answer.

'I don't get it,' he said. 'Normally Fritzy answers right away. I'll
try again in fifteen minutes.' He tried again at 2.50 am, at 3 am and
at fifteen-minute intervals after that until 4 am. No reply from
Kühlenthal's man in Madrid.

At first there was general consternation. The great opportunity
had been lost. 'The trouble is,' said Carlos Reid bitterly, 'life in
Madrid really only begins at midnight. Kühlenthal's operator is
probably at Chiquotes having a copita with his friends!'

'Well,' drawled Roger Sneath with Texan practicality, 'the situation is not all that bad. We can now flavour the message with some
additional details which for security reasons we could not have included in the original signal. That'll make them feel that much

worse at having missed the transmission, when at last they do receive it. After all, our purpose is not so much to give them the news of the landing as to impress them with the efficiency of "Vandal's" network and the speed and accuracy of its information.'

When the message was at last put over to Madrid it had everything a German intelligence man could have wished for—the embarkation, the direction of the assault, and even the identities of some of the formations taking part. Vehicles of most of the units bound for Normandy were embarked at Tilbury and the London Docks where Jorge Antonio's man could quite plausibly claim to have observed their insignia. From the Allied viewpoint there was no objection to giving this information to the Germans. They were bound to pick it up anyhow within the first twenty-four hours of the landing. All it would do was to confirm Kühlenthal's and Roenne's respect for V-man 'Cato's' efficiency and enterprise. In addition the message contained its bit of melodrama to appeal to the old soldier's appetite for stories of adventure.

This was supplied by the Gibraltarian waiter, the fictitious agent whom Reid and Jorge Antonio had described as being stationed at Hiltingbury, a big assembly camp for the invasion troops. Jorge Antonio had been very angry with the Gibraltarian three weeks earlier when he had (allegedly) caused him to give a false invasion alarm. (The troops in the camp had left to embark for the Channel rehearsal and the Gibraltarian had mistaken the rehearsal for the real thing. When the men all returned forty-eight hours later he had sheepishly confessed his mistake.) Jorge Antonio had wanted to fire him. But the tender-hearted Kühlenthal had prevailed on him to keep him on. Now the Gibraltarian had redeemed himself. He had come across with completely convincing details of the genuine embarkation of the troops. What was more he had risked his freedom to bring the news out of the Security Zone. 'I cannot risk letting him return to the camp,' said Jorge Antonio. 'His disappearance must have been noticed.' Fortunately the Swansea seaman turned up trumps. He knew of a remote farm in the Cambrian mountains where the Gibraltarian could go into hiding.

In his next message on June 6 Jorge Antonio did not refer to the bungled reception of his great scoop. On the contrary he behaved as though he was still unaware there had been a slip-up. The main content of his message was a graphic description of the Ministry of Information, where he himself now worked, on the morning of D-day and the crisis created by the failure of Churchill, General Eisenhower, and the Belgian Premier to conform to the PWE directive which requested everyone to refrain from references to further assaults.

'. . . I arrived to find the department in complete chaos. Everyone was speculating about how much importance should be attached to the attack which was launched this morning in France. All sections of the Ministry were handed copies of the directive sent out this morning by the Political Warfare Executive. This is a committee with access to SHAEF, the Chiefs of Staff, as well as the Foreign Office. It lays down how the important events in the news are to be handled in publicity. I find the directive very significant, especially so if it is compared with the speeches of the Allied leaders. I therefore transmit its text verbatim.'

TOP SECRET
Political Warfare Executive.
Special Directive on the Offensive in Northern France.
    1. The offensive launched today by General Eisenhower represents another important step in the Allied attack on the fortress of Europe.
    2. It is of the utmost importance that the enemy be kept in the dark as to our future intentions.
    3. Care should be taken to avoid any reference to further assaults and diversions.
    4. Speculation regarding alternative assault areas must be avoided.
    5. The importance of the present assault and its decisive influence on the course of the war should be clearly stated.★

'Together with the directive,' Jorge Antonio continued, 'my departmental chief handed me copies of speeches by Eisenhower, Spaak, and Churchill, which at that moment had not yet been broadcast. After reading these speeches I asked my chief for a fur-

---

★ The PWE directive duly made its appearance on the table of Colonel Krummacher at the Führer headquarters along with other documents to be submitted to the Führer. It is mentioned in appendix 2 of the OKW War Diary for June 10, 1944. See Schramm, *Kriegstagebuch des OKW*, IV, Vol. 1, page 331.

ther interview and told him that I considered the directive to be in complete contradiction to the speeches. It was inevitable, I said, that these speeches would be quoted and used as the basis for comment by the world press. For instance in Eisenhower's speech there is a passage in which he says: "Frenchmen! A premature uprising may prevent you from being of maximum help to your country at the critical hour. Be patient. Prepare!" And still more important is the following passage: "This landing is but the opening phase of the campaign in Western Europe. Great battles lie ahead." The Belgian Prime Minister said: "Preliminary operations for the Liberation of Europe have begun. The first assault is the certain signal for your deliverance." And also: "The moment of supreme combat has not yet come."

'My chief told me that I had spotted the one inevitable weakness in the policy which had been laid down. He explained that in the first place, it was essential that Eisenhower should keep the people from rising too early in areas which were not yet to be involved in operations, but at the same time it was equally necessary to hide all this information from the enemy. He said he did not think the enemy would be able to draw any definite conclusions from these speeches, but he thought they nevertheless constituted such a contradiction to the directives as to create a difficult situation internally. He went on to say that the Director General himself had raised the point made by me. Nevertheless, he felt that if the task were performed intelligently, it should be possible to focus public attention on the present attack and divert it from any suggestion of future plans. Precisely this, he said, was the work with which he himself was entrusted.'

On June 7 Jorge Antonio signalled Kühlenthal more news about the give-away PWE directive and the difficulties it had caused. 'The PWE directive has now been amended so as to allow certain limited speculation in general terms about future operations.' But the Prime Minister was still being difficult, said Jorge Antonio. 'In spite of recommendations made to Churchill that his speech should contain every possible reserve, he said in the House of Commons that the assault was "the first of a series of landings in force upon the European continent".

'Brendan Bracken, the Minister of Information, tried to dissuade him from making this statement. But Churchill told him that in his political position he was obliged to avoid distorting the facts and that he was not going to allow his speeches to be discredited by coming events.'

SHAEF's Deception Unit permitted five hours to go by before putting another signal from Jorge Antonio on the air to Madrid. In this he said that his sub-agents in Scotland had not yet given him any detailed reports and he had summoned the Venezuelan to London for a conference. From what he had learned at his ministry he could however state definitely that the fleet had not left the Clyde. Nor had the troops embarked. He had the general impression however from what he had been able to gather at the Ministry that the enemy were hiding some insidious plan behind this landing. He then launched into a paean of self-praise. 'Fortunately this first operation has been robbed of the surprise which the enemy wanted to achieve with it, thanks to the information I was able to pass to you. Comparing the time at which the landing took place with the time at which I sent my warning message I am proud to see that it must have arrived in time to prevent our High Command from being caught unawares.' He added that the Gibraltarian had left that morning accompanied by the Swansea seaman who was arranging for him to be hidden in a safe place, as already reported.

Poor Kühlenthal! Hardly had he received this signal, when another one was handed to him. This was the thunderclap he had been dreading ever since he had discovered that 'Cato's' great scoop had not been delivered on time. Now 'Cato' was living up to the reputation of his irascible Roman namesake. 'I have just learned,' he said with all the flaming fury of the old senator, 'that my important signal of June 6, 0230 hours, was not transmitted until 0830 hours. Marinello [code-name of Jorge Antonio's radio operator] claims that he called you throughout the night but that no-one was listening at your end to receive his message. If what I suspect is the case and Marinello has failed in his duties, then I am determined to abandon the service until I can find some other arrangement. Were it not for my faith in the Führer and the vital importance of his mission to save Europe from the twin tyrannies of Bolshevism and Anglo-American plutocracy, I would this very day give up my work, conscious as I am of my failure.'

To Kühlenthal it looked as though his whole organisation in Britain was breaking up. He just could not afford to lose 'Cato', chief of 'Operation Ganelon', Germany's most successful spy ring. He must do his damnedest to smooth the ruffled feathers of his temperamental agent, assuage his Spanish pride, and get him functioning again. On the very next transmission he tried to reassure his V-man.

'I have read your messages and I sympathise with your disappointment. It would be difficult if not impossible to find out who is to blame. After closing down on Monday at 2350 hours we listened as arranged every full hour up to 0300 hours and again from 0700 hours. Your message was received at 0800 hours. It is possible that in spite of our staff having listened with attention atmospherics and other interference on Tuesday morning stopped us getting Marinello's call before 0800 hours. But even supposing the worst and that Marinello failed to call us don't forget that, according to what you yourself have told me, Marinello is not aware of his mission. It would be only human if Marinello after his long day's work felt very tired. He cannot be blamed for thinking that this message, of whose vitally important content he had no idea, could be delayed for a few hours while he took a nap. I wish to stress that your work over the last few weeks has made it possible for our command to be completely forewarned and prepared. The message of sub-agent six* would have made little difference had it arrived three or four hours earlier. I reiterate to you, as responsible chief of the service, and to all your fellow workers our apprectiation of your splendid and valued work. I beg of you to continue with us in the supreme and decisive hours of the struggle for the future of Europe.'

Jorge Antonio, alias 'Cato', replied: 'Marinello reports that on the night of the crisis he called at 0230 for half an hour, that he repeated his calls at fifteen-minute intervals until 0700 hours without result. Your doubts regarding Marinello's understanding of the urgency of the message I cannot accept. He had been instructed that it was of extreme urgency that the message should be transmitted that night. I am not prepared to accept negligence even if he was tired. I too am

* The Gibraltarian.

exhausted but I do my duty. In future I will see that someone else is present during important transmissions.'

Kühlenthal sent no reply to that.

One reason why he did not do so may have been that at 0006 hours on June 8 Jorge Antonio had sent Madrid a news flash which showed that V-man 'Cato' was still working for Germany with undiminished devotion and watchfulness. In that flash Jorge Antonio reported that the Guards Armoured Division was about to be sent into the bridge-head and that from the same source from which he had this intelligence he had learned that the 3rd British Infantry Division had already taken part in the assault.

In sending this message Jorge Antonio was complying with a request to the SHAEF Deception Unit from Montgomery as overall commander of the landing operation. General Gerow's 5th US Corps had run into exceptionally heavy German resistance on Omaha Beach. Montgomery hoped that an announcement of the imminent arrival of the Guards Armour might draw German forces in front of the British and Canadian lines and thus relieve the pressure on the Americans. By coupling the false news of the Guards' departure with the verifiably accurate news of the participation of the 3rd British Infantry Division in the assault the SHAEF Deception Unit hoped to get the report accepted as a whole.

It was.*

Kühlenthal thought the report so urgent that he sent it direct to Paris instead of routing it, as normal, via Berlin. Colonel Meyer-Detring, Rundstedt's G2, sent him a message on June 9, saying that Rundstedt regarded the message about the Guards as exceptionally important. He would be glad to have more like it.

The stage was now set for Jorge Antonio to send the message which the Reid plan of May 5 provided should be sent forty-eight hours after the invasion had started. At 1930 hours on June 8 he called Madrid: 'Have had a very busy and anxious day. Hope to give you what I consider to be my most important report to date. Trust you will be standing by to receive at 22 hours GMT.'

---

* Situation Report West No. 1290 of June 8 1944: 'A reliable Abwehr source reports that the British Guards Armoured Division, now in the area of Worthing, will embark on the third day of the invasion. One must therefore expect this division to appear shortly.'

At 0007 hours on Friday, June 9, Jorge Antonio's Royal Signals Sergeant in the secret house in High Barnet began to tap out the message. He went on transmitting without pause until 0209 hours GMT. The length of this transmission should have been enough by itself to make the Germans suspect it. One hundred and twenty-two minutes during which, had the transmission been the genuine product of an *enemy* agent, the Radio Security Service of Brigadier Gambier Parry† would have had ample time to locate the transmitter and arrest its operators several times over. But the unreality of the situation did not arouse the suspicions of Kühlenthal or his colleagues on this occasion any more than it had on previous ones.

Jorge Antonio began by reporting that his three best agents—the ones whom Kühlenthal in his reports to Berlin referred to as 'Freddy, Dick and Desmond'—had arrived in London to deliver their reports in person. He then launched into what in effect was a summing up of his reports over the last fortnight and held a kind of review of all the major formations in south and south-east England—British and American, genuine and imaginary. He also referred to landing craft which had been found on the rivers Deben and Orwell. He added that the information about the landing craft came from a hitherto untried source and proposed that the Germans should send over a Luftwaffe reconnaissance patrol to check the reliability of the source. Alas, the Luftwaffe did not bite. It had no teeth. Instead Kühlenthal replied eight days later: 'With reference to the report about the barges, you may consider this as confirmed.' Clearly the Luftwaffe had not wanted to admit their inability to carry out a reconnaissance.

In compliance with the scheme outlined in the Reid memorandum of May 5, Jorge Antonio then proceeded to give Kühlenthal his conclusions.

. . . The present operation, though a large-scale assault, is diversionary in character. Its object is to establish a strong bridge-head in order to draw the maximum of our reserves into the area of the assault and to retain them there so as to leave another area exposed where the enemy could then attack with some prospect of success. I do not like to state my views, unless I am confident of having

---

† Later Major-General Sir Richard Gambier Parry.

strong justification for them. The fact however that the massive
concentration of forces in east and south-east England remains
inactive suggests that these forces are being held in reserve for
other large-scale operations. The constant aerial bombardment
which the sector of the Pas de Calais has been undergoing and the
disposition of the enemy forces, would indicate the imminence of an
assault in this region which offers the shortest route to the final
objective of the Anglo-American illusions: Berlin. An assault here
could be supported by constant bombardment from the air. The
bases of the enemy air fleets would be conveniently close to the
battle area. They would fly their attacks in the rear of our forces
facing the enemy landing in the West of France. I learned yesterday
at the Ministry of Information that there were seventy-five*
divisions in this country before the present assault began. Supposing
they were to use twenty to twenty-five divisions on the present
assault they would still have fifty divisions available for the second
strike.

I trust you will submit my reports for urgent consideration by
our High Command. Moments may be decisive at the present
time. Before they take a false step through lack of full knowledge
of the facts they ought to have at their disposal all the present
information. I transmit this report with the conviction that the
present assault is a trap set with the purpose of making us move all
our reserves in a rushed strategic re-disposition which we would
later regret.

Jorge Antonio's wish was fulfilled. A very much shorter (and
better!) text† of his message was teleprinted from the RSHA in
Berlin on June 9 both to the office of Colonel Meyer-Detring, Field
Marshal von Rundstedt's G2 at St Germain, and to Colonel Krummacher, Hitler's G2, at the Führer headquarters where it arrived at
2220 hours. Krummacher read it and underlined the phrases
'diversionary manœuvre', 'purpose to entice enemy reserves into
bridge-head in order to then launch decisive assault in another

---

* In his interview of May 28, 1944, with Baron Hiroshi Oshima, the Japanese
ambassador to Berlin (see page 132), Hitler had estimated that eighty Allied
divisions were being held in readiness for the invasion. The Deception unit
had read the deciphered text of the ambassador's dispatch. It was thought
courteous therefore that Jorge Antonio's figure should approximately confirm
the Führer's.
† I have quoted text of the teleprint in Chapter 1, on page 18.

place'. By way of comment Krummacher added the following: 'Underlines the opinion already formed by us [bisherige Auffassung] that a further attack is to be expected in another place.' And after 'another place' he wrote in brackets 'Belgium?'

Both Jodl and Hitler saw the report and scribbled their paraphs* on it to show they had read it. The RHSA praised the report in a message to the K.O. Madrid: 'The dispatch is believable. The reports received in the last week from the "Ganelon" enterprise have been confirmed almost without exception and are to be described as especially valuable. The main line of enquiry must now be concentrated on the enemy group of forces in eastern and south-eastern England.'

But gratifying as was this evidence of the respect with which Hitler and his generals treated the strategic counsel given them by the electronics student from Madrid University, what mattered more was its effect on the German dispositions in the field of battle. This was cataclysmic.

On June 8, two days after the landing, Hitler had at last given way to the imprecations of Rundstedt and Rommel that reinforcements should be sent to Normandy by the 15th Army guarding the Pas de Calais sector where Hitler expected the main Allied assault. Pressure from the Allies in the bridge-head had increased to such severity that Hitler had reluctantly ordered that all troops of the 15th Army that were instantly available—five infantry and two Panzer divisions with 300 tanks—should move south to reinforce the German defences in the Normandy bridge-head.

The divisions from the 15th Army were already on the move, when at 0730 on the morning of Saturday, June 10, Jorge Antonio's magic took effect. Rundstedt countermanded his previous order with a drastic 'As you were' after receiving a telephone call from Colonel-General Wilhelm Keitel who was at the Führer headquarters on the Obersalzberg.

'As a consequence of information which has just been received,' said the signal from Rundstedt's headquarters, 'C-in-C West has proclaimed a second degree alert for 15th Army in Belgium and northern France. The move of the 1st SS-Panzer Division will there-

---

* Jodl's paraph consisted of a J with a stroke through it, Hitler's of the three letters 'erl', presumably standing for 'erledigt'= 'dealt with'.

fore be halted. It will take up position in the area previously held by the 19th Luftwaffe Division.'* 15th Army, as well as all units in Belgium and Holland, were ordered to stand by night and day.

On the same page that these dramatic moves are indicated in the OKW War Diary another interesting note is recorded: 'By June 12 seventeen enemy formations had been identified, seven of them American. It could be assumed therefore that the Montgomery Group would not undertake a second operation. A second landing east of the bridge-head was still to be expected either in the area Calais–Le Havre or between the mouth of the Schelde and Dunkirk.'

And the beauty of it was, that thanks to the FUSAG myth Hitler did indeed go on expecting it.

*   *   *

Allied agents picked up the news of the countermanded troop moves. Major-General Kenneth Strong, who was Eisenhower's G2, included it in his 'Sit.Rep.' (situation report), and there Eisenhower saw it. The Supreme Allied Commander rang the colonel.

'You've seen today's G2 report, Noël?'

'I have indeed, General.'

'Nice going! Which of your chaps was it—the Dutchman or the Spaniard?'

'I'd say it was a combined operation!'

'Well, congratulations to the whole of your group.'

'Thank you, General, I'll pass them on.'

When he passed them on to Reid that stalwart very properly—and characteristically—decided the occasion called for a celebration. As a result, the evening of June 12 saw Jorge Antonio and Reid dining very agreeably in a small black-market restaurant in Soho. Its *patron* was a Basque nationalist. At Reid's request he had prepared a Spanish meal for them: 'Huevos escalfados Bilbaina' (poached eggs served cold on a layer of chopped onion, tomatoes,† and beans), followed by 'Pollo de Pamplona' (Pamplona chicken).

---

* *Kriegstagebuch des OKW*, IV, Vol. 1, page 313.

† By rights they should have been pimentos, but pimentos were unobtainable in wartime London.

Alsasua, Jorge Antonio's birthplace, was in the province of Pamplona and Jorge Antonio appreciated the delicacy of the compliment, especially when Agostin, the *patron*, served a fruity red wine from the Basque vineyards with it, which Carlos Reid and he drank out of the same porron, pouring it expertly into their mouths from ever greater heights. They finished three porrons without either of them scoring a miss. The other guests in the restaurant applauded and Carlos and Jorge Antonio felt very good.

In Madrid, General Kühlenthal was also celebrating. He was rejoicing at the praise he had won from the RSHA for V-man 'Cato's' splendid dispatches. The sequel to Kühlenthal's celebration however was less happy. In fact it was dangerous. Dangerous to 'Cato' and his 'Orchestra'.

11

D-day Surprises

On June 5, 1944, 'Fortitude South' had been in operation for the best part of six weeks. With its 'orchestra' of SHAEF-controlled Abwehr spies, its carefully placed displays of dummy landing craft, and its concert of bogus signals traffic, it had intoned for the Führer's benefit the seductive saga of the great Allied Armada waiting in East Anglia to smash itself to destruction in a foolhardy assault against the strongest sector of the Atlantic Wall. Now as D-day dawned the deception artists revealed that together with their colleagues in 21st Army Group★ they had prepared as a supplement to 'Fortitude' an ingenious assortment of tactical devices to assure that the landing in Normandy should take the Germans unawares.

Goering had assured Hitler that surprise was impossible. His network of ninety-two radar stations in northern and north-western France, he had maintained, would make it utterly impossible for the invaders to arrive unannounced. 'We shall have ample warning, mein Führer!' he said, folding his thin lips in that shark-like smile of his. Between Boulogne and Cherbourg, he boasted, there were six long-range radar stations of the most modern design. They were so sensitive that they would detect an aircraft taking off from southern England while it was still taxiing to the take-off! And added to these six long-range spies were four more super-stations responsible for Luftwaffe fighter control and radio intelligence. 'They'll not be caught napping. And they cannot be fooled. I guarantee it.'

But the Reichsmarschall was wrong. The Germans *were* caught napping and they *were* fooled.

In the week before D-day every one of Goering's big radar bastions was heavily and accurately attacked by either the RAF or the US

★ 21st Army Group had been made responsible for visual and tactical deception.

Air Force. And during the night preceding the landing the remaining smaller stations which were charged with such tasks as ship detection, fighter control, and the direction of coastal artillery were blinded by jamming. All were eliminated except a few stations operating north of the Seine. These had been deliberately spared.

They had been spared in order that they should be able to report a number of simulated bomber flights specially laid on for them by the Deception Unit's air liaison. The most important of these bogus movements was the simulation on the enemy radar screens of a continuous stream of aircraft which the German observers would interpret as an Allied air fleet flying in for airborne landings.

The electronic hoax, when carried out, was as successful in spoofing the Germans as that other one which carried Montgomery's wireless signals from his genuine headquarters by landline to a fake headquarters in Kent whose radio traffic was duly located by the German monitors. The air fleet hoax caused Air Fleet III (the Luftwaffe command in northern France) to sweep the skies over Amiens and its environs for three hours, from 0100 hours until 0400 hours on June 6 to no avail. They found nothing. But while the night fighters hunted for the will-o'-the-wisp air fleet over north-eastern France, the Allied Naval Armada, with its transports and landing craft, was approaching the Normandy beaches, and the Allied air fleets were carrying out their airborne landings. Both were able to perform their tasks without interference from the Luftwaffe.

What had projected the mirage on to the German radar screens and sent the night fighters chasing after non-existent bombers was a new electronic device called 'Mandrel'.* It had been perfected several months earlier but had been specially held in reserve so that it could be sprung as a surprise on the Germans on D-day.

About the time that the airborne landings were taking place on the right and left flanks of what was to become the bridge-head, the situation map in Rundstedt's war room at St Germain, which recorded the sites of the reported landings, showed what seemed to be a most threatening rash of parachutist drops north-east of the Seine between Le Havre and Rouen. Was this the beginning of the expected assault in the north? Only when dawn broke was the truth

---

* The Strategic Air Offensive, Vol. III, page 150.

discovered. The 'enemy parachutists' were dummies. The same kind of dummies, fitted with delayed action fire-crackers to simulate the crackle of small-arms fire, as had been used by 'A' Force in the Western Desert for their 1940 raid on the Siwa oasis.

A diversion similar to that of the dummy parachutists north of the Seine was performed by two tiny parties of commandos from the 1st SAS regiment—an officer and two men in each—who dropped on the other flank of the landing. They came down near Isigny at the south-eastern end of the Cherbourg peninsula. Their main armament consisted of Tommy guns, hand grenades, Very pistols, and record-players. The record-players put out recordings of small-arms fire interspersed with soldier's oaths, while the Very pistols lit up the sky for miles around. Hundreds of dummy parachutists with fire-crackers were dropped all around the genuine parachutists and helped to give the impression to the Germans that a large force of paratroops had landed among them. They added to the confusion already created by the American airborne landing a little farther west.*

The most elaborate of all the D-day deception operations was carried out by Admiral Sir Bertram Ramsay's Allied naval force. As part of 'Fortitude', Allied aircraft had since June 1 been attacking the fortifications between Calais and Le Havre, and in case their bombing of the Seine bridges should indicate an intention to cut communications with Normandy they also bombed the bridges across rivers and canals to the east of Calais. More important still, they had not only been going for the coastal guns but also for the beach defences and underwater obstacles. To the Germans this bombing of the beach defences was welcome confirmation that the assault was to be expected in the well fortified Pas de Calais. To strengthen this impression still further, Ramsay on the evening of June 5 sent the main body of the vast invasion fleet—500 men-of-war escorting hundreds of troop transports and landing craft—up the Channel in a demonstrative west-to-east progress. From Falmouth, Plymouth, Dartmouth, Southampton and the other ports, big and little, where they had been standing by in readiness for

* Two men from this commando party managed to find their way to the beach-head by June 20. A considerable feat this, for they were in uniform. The rest were taken prisoner.

D-day, the ships sallied forth and joined in the procession. Ramsay was counting on their being observed by the Germans watching from the French coast opposite.

But it was only the first stage of the procession which Ramsay wanted the Germans to observe. He did not want them to see what happened when the convoy reached the point south of the Isle of Wight known to the Navy as 'Piccadilly Circus'. For at this point the convoy abruptly turned south and sailed down a passage which had been swept clear of mines to the Bay of the Seine. Ramsay counted on this change of direction being hidden from the Germans by the darkness. But to make sure that the Germans would believe the convoy was still heading for the Pas de Calais a 'grand deception' was put into operation.

It was carried out by thirty-four small vessels of the Royal Navy and 105 aircraft of the RAF. Shortly after the sun had gone down and the Channel was shrouded in darkness eighteen of the Navy ships set out for Cap d'Antifer, a headland just north of Le Havre. Behind them they towed captive balloons which its scientific advisers had assured the SHAEF Deception Unit would produce 'big ship echoes' on such of the enemy radar sets as had been left in action. Above the fleet of small ships and their balloons circled a squadron of Stirlings. Minute by minute they dropped successive showers of 'Window' from their bomb bays. 'Window' was the code-name for the strips of metallised paper which had been so successful in producing deceptive readings on the German radar screens during the big bombing raids on the Reich. The aircraft circled in a continuous geometrical pattern producing an image on the German radar screens of a large convoy approaching across the Channel. Similar manœuvres were executed by another detachment of ships and aircraft off Boulogne, while a third group of Flying Fortresses and Stirlings equipped with 'Mandrel' produced the radar mirage which suggested to the Germans that an airborne force was on its way to the Amiens–Boulogne–Calais area.

The Navy's electronic feint succeeded. When the first invasion alerts were sent out they went only to the formations of the 15th Army, the force covering the 'Fortitude' area around the Pas de Calais. The 7th Army, which held Normandy and Brittany, was alerted only after the first landings had taken place in its sector. The Führer was so infuriated by this latest breakdown of his intelligence arrangements that he ordered an inquest. But it was never held. Probably it was quietly forgotten in all the confusion of the Normandy battle. Nor indeed was there much point to a post mortem, for even the weather had conspired against the German intelligence men. The German meteorologists had pronounced on June 4 that bad weather in the Channel ruled out an invasion for the next fortnight.

On the strength of this report Field Marshal Rommel left for Germany the next day in order to spend his wife's birthday with her at home. He also planned to visit Hitler on the Obersalzberg.

Colonel von Roenne was equally caught out. He issued a report on June 5 which contrary to his normal custom ignored the invasion preparations in England and devoted itself exclusively to the Mediterranean and the Balkans. But in a special appendix Roenne warned that by alternating rumours of a postponement of the invasion with others threatening imminent attack the Anglo-American enemy was trying to wear down German watchfulness. They were, he said, doing their best to foster among the defenders a condition of blasé disbelief in the invasion which would be psychologically favourable to a surprise attack.

Rommel's headquarters in its weekly 'survey of the over-all situation', also issued on June 5, said: 'Systematic intensification of enemy air-raids and increased mine-laying in own' (i.e. German-occupied) 'harbours indicates an advance in the enemy's preparations for invasion. Concentration of air attacks on coastal defences between Dunkirk and Dieppe and on Seine and Oise bridges confirms our presumption as to the area chosen by the enemy for his large-scale landing. . . . Air reconnaissance shows no great increase of landing craft in the Dover area. Other harbours of England's south coast were not visited by reconnaissance aircraft. Survey of harbour moorings on entire English south coast by air reconnaissance is urgently required.'

As if to justify Roenne's criticism of the scepticism being shown by officers and men in the Western armies concerning the imminence of a cross-Channel invasion,[*] General Richter, commander of

[*] In Roenne's letter to Colonel Meyer-Detring quoted on page 143.

the 716th Infantry Division at Caen, drew an appreciative guffaw from his officers when he addressed them at his weekly staff conference on the evening of June 5. He was speaking at just about the time when Ramsay was sending his ships out on their west–east progress through the Channel.

'I have received a warning,' said Richter with a humorous grin, 'that the invasion will be launched between the 3rd and the 10th. I should perhaps add, gentlemen, that we have received similar warnings every full-moon period and every no-moon period since April.' His staff loved it. But within an hour of General Richter's conference breaking up, a British minesweeper sighted the coast of the 716th Division's front at Arromanches. Maybe a German lookout sighted the British ship in return. No one, however, reported its presence to the general, let alone its significance.

But despite this heedlessness the invasion did not come as a complete surprise to all the German staffs. Some of them had two to three hours' warning before the first paratroopers dropped down on them. They had London's 'Special Operations Executive' and the French Service of the BBC to thank for that.

The first warning that something was brewing came to the Germans from the BBC. At 2115 hours the French service of the BBC broadcast an ominous-sounding announcement: 'Today the Supreme Commander directs us to say this: "In due course instructions of great importance will be given to you through this channel. But it will not always be possible to give these instructions at a previously announced time. Therefore you must get into the habit of listening at all hours." '

When this was reported to them by the monitors the officers at Rundstedt's headquarters sat up. But C-in-C West's Chief of Staff, General Blumentritt, pooh-poohed their suspicions. 'What kind of a general, my children, would announce a forthcoming invasion over the radio? You can forget it.'

But when on top of the BBC announcement reports came in of of extensive jamming of radar stations, of American reconnaissance aircraft broadcasting weather reports from over France, Rommel's headquarters at Army Group B decided to send out a 'Most Urgent' signal ordering troops to stand by ready for action. But the alert from Army Group B, sent out at 2220 hours, went to only one army. This, as I have said, was 15th Army, which held the Pas de Calais sector, the target indicated by 'Fortitude'. None went to the 7th Army which held the sector where the landing would in fact take place.

Issuing an alert order to the 15th Army was a case of coals to Newcastle. For 15th Army's Chief of Staff, Major-General Rudolf Hoffmann, notified by his watchful G2, Lieutenant-Colonel Helmuth Mayer, had already ordered the alert for 15th Army on his own responsibility. He had done so as a consequence of another item on that same 2115 BBC transmission for France which had caused the commotion at Rommel's and Rundstedt's headquarters.

And when Abwehr officers these days are criticised for having failed to give a warning of impending invasion they indignantly counter 'But we did!', and they tell the story of the 15th Army alert to prove it. It is an impressive story and one which does credit to the Abwehr officers. So I tell of this German triumph with pleasure, all the greater as it is an excellent story in itself.

As early as April 1944 Colonel Oscar Reile, the head of Section III in the Paris Abwehr staff, had called the attention of Rundstedt's G2, Colonel Meyer-Detring, to the so-called 'personal messages' being transmitted most evenings by the French service of the BBC. The messages, read out by BBC announcers, had intriguing texts like 'Victor calling Victorine: The Professor's trousers badly need a patch.' Or 'André calling Octave: Regret Mimi's little hand still frozen.' These messages were code instructions from the French section at the SOE headquarters in London to individual guerilla groups of the French resistance organisation. Colonel Oscar Reile and his men at the Abwehr headquarters in Paris had penetrated SOE's somewhat amateurish organisation in France to quite a substantial extent. They had also managed to turn round some of its operatives and play them back on section F in Baker Street. Now Reile was able to tell Meyer-Detring that one of his French V-men had managed to obtain the text of a code message which London intended for its railway sabotage gangs throughout northern France on D-day. It was important that operations should not start before D-day. So London would give its saboteurs the word 'Go!' with a 'message personnel' over the BBC French service.

The code text consisted of a couplet from Verlaine. The first verse

'*Les sanglots longs des violons d'automne . . .*' told the railway saboteurs that the invasion was imminent and that they must stand by and listen for the other half of the couplet. When this was read by the announcer it would mean: 'The invasion begins at midnight. Take action tonight.'

Reile commented that, provided London did not change the message, it would provide a reliable warning of the invasion D-day. Colonel Meyer-Detring agreed. He ordered that the text of the code message should be circulated to all army G2 officers.

And now on the evening of June 5 the great moment had arrived. On three successive nights the monitors at the headquarters of 15th Army had heard and recorded the first verse of the Verlaine couplet in the BBC's 2115 transmission—on June 1, June 2, and June 3. (This was the reason for the G2 prediction so derided by General Richter.) One night, that of the 4th, had gone by without a Verlaine message. But at the end of an abnormally large number of '*messages personnels*' put out in the 2115 transmission on June 5, there it was: the other half of the couplet. 'Ursule calling Naomi', the monitor recorded, '. . . *blessent mon cœur d'une longeur monotone.*'

There was no 'monotonous length' about the German monitor's reaction.* He immediately reported the message to his chief, Lieutenant-Colonel Mayer. Mayer reported it to the Army's Chief of Staff, Major-General Rudolf Hoffmann. And Hoffmann in a series of urgent teleprints ordered an 'alert' for the whole of the 15th Army. The time was 1215 hours. Mayer also telephoned his news to the headquarters of C-in-C West and Army Group B. But once again nobody bothered to alert 7th Army. And 7th Army had no inkling of what was going on until 84th Corps reported to it at 0120 hours on June 6: 'As from 0030 hours paratroop landings in the east and north-west of Caen, at St Marcouf, Montebourg, on both sides of the Vire and on the east coast of Cotentin.' No one was very much excited. But this time at least the alert was ordered throughout the 7th Army area. At a quarter past two Major-General Max Pemsel, the Chief of Staff of the 7th Army, telephoned to Lieutenant-General Hans Speidel at Rommel's headquarters.

'Engine noises,' he told Speidel, 'are audible from the sea on the

---

* Gert Buchheit, *Der Deutsche Geheimdienst*, pages 348 and 349. M. R. Foot, *SOE in France*, pages 304 and 388.

east coast of the Cotentin. Admiral Channel Coast reports that ships have been located by radar off Cherbourg. The indications are that the operation is of a large-scale character.'

Speidel disagreed about the size and importance of the operation. And so did Rundstedt. He gave orders that Pemsel should be informed, that 'C-in-C West does not consider this to be a major operation'. Queen Victoria could not have put it better.

At 0250 Admiral Channel Coast reported. He was apologetic. He had no intelligence about the size of the Allied naval forces engaged, because most unfortunately his radar had broken down. In fact the whole of the German early-warning system in the Channel area appeared to be paralysed.

But even this suggestive piece of intelligence did not persuade the Field Marshal to change his mind about the scale of the operation. Perhaps he did not want to commit himself to a view contrary to the Führer's conviction, sedulously fostered by the Allied deceivers, that the first assault would be nothing more than a feint. The main assault, Rundstedt claimed, was still to come.

*   *   *

Apart from its contribution to the success of the invasion by keeping the 15th Army out of the Normandy bridge-head, 'Fortitude' was responsible for many helpful by-products.

Grand Admiral Doenitz, for instance, convinced like his Führer that the main assault would be against the Pas de Calais, ordered the new DM1 pressure mine (which he boasted enemy minesweepers could not clear without getting themselves blown up) to be laid between Le Havre and Ostend. Not until the third day were pressure mines dropped by the Luftwaffe in the mouths of the Vire and Orne rivers. Even then the waters in front of the unfortunate 7th Army's invasion beaches were left unprotected.

Goering, sharing Hitler's view that the first landing would be nothing more than a feint, delayed moving Luftwaffe reinforcements to Normandy. He wanted to see where the main blow would fall before he committed his precious aircraft and their crews. As a result, only 319 sorties were flown by the Luftwaffe over Normandy on June 6. And most of the aircraft engaged on them were either shot down or driven off. Not until June 7 did Luftwaffe reserves begin to arrive in northern France from the Reich. When they did they found that the airfields intended to receive them had been so badly wrecked that they could not land there. The runways were a chaos of churned-up bomb-craters, the hangars and ancillary buildings a charred mass of tangled girders and rubble. The Luftwaffe would have been disastrously outnumbered in any case. But this delay meant that Allied supremacy in the air met no challenge at all from the Germans during the vital first forty-eight hours when, as Rommel had said, the Germans had either to win the battle of the beaches or give up hope of defeating the invasion.

Then there were the fuel dumps. In anticipation of the invasion the Germans had wisely built up extensive stocks of oil and petrol for their armour and mechanised transport. The fuel dumps, however, had almost all of them been sited north of the Seine in the 15th Army area. When the Allies landed, Rundstedt tried to refill his forward fuel dumps in Normandy by sending up railway tankers with supplies from the GHQ reserves near Paris. But the railways had been put out of action by the Allied bombers and SOE's gangs of guerilla saboteurs. So the fuel supplies had to go up to Normandy by road. Road convoys, however, could only travel by night. Rocket-firing fighter-bombers shot up everything using the roads by day. The amount of fuel reaching the 7th Army in the night convoys was therefore nothing like enough to sustain the battle. Shortage of fuel held up the German counter-attacks. It hindered the movement of German formations ordered to close the gaps in the German battle line. German troops moving to Normandy from central and southern France made their way on bicycles and in horse-drawn carts. And all this because the reports, planted on the German High Command by the Allied Deception Unit through the V-men 'Cato' and 'Paul' and by means of the bogus wireless transmissions, had misled Hitler and his generals into expecting the main Allied assault north of the Seine and concentrating both their best troops there and their fuel supplies.

Without a doubt 'Fortitude' was a decisive deception. But how much longer could it be kept up? How long before Roenne and Foreign Armies West would begin to suspect the truth?

To most of Eisenhower's staff officers the success and endurance of 'Fortitude' had come as a gratifying surprise. On June 3 that canny Scotsman Major General Kenneth Strong, who was Eisenhower's chief intelligence officer, had cautiously predicted that within a week of the landing in Normandy, three armoured divisions and three infantry divisions of 15th Army would have crossed the Seine and joined in the fighting in the bridge-head. As we have seen, the divisions did indeed set out for Normandy, only to be ordered back to the Pas de Calais after Hitler had read 'Cato's' message of June 9. Only one armoured division in fact crossed the Seine in this early stage of the Normandy battle, the 2nd SS-Panzer Division. When two weeks later the 1st SS-Panzer Division was also sent to Normandy it was no longer possible to cross the Seine. The bridges had all been destroyed and no pontoons were available in Normandy. The 1st SS-Panzers had to travel the long way round by Paris, a most hazardous journey with the fighter-bombers on their tails all the way.

*   *   *

Stubbornly the OKW held on to its belief in the imminence of a major assault from East Anglia by the mythical forces of FUSAG. Colonel von Roenne did his best to encourage them. When information came through which should have made him question the validity of his theory he twisted facts to suit the FUSAG picture. For instance on June 9 he circulated an 'Appendix to situation report No. 1291' in which he tried to explain away the appearance in the beach-head of the 51st British Infantry Division* which he had previously accepted as being located in Cambridge and belonging to FUSAG.

. . . This must not be regarded as a diminution of the force being held in readiness in South-East England. It should be assumed that the division had been transferred to the area of the Montgomery Army-Group before the invasion was launched. The force in South-East England must therefore be considered to remain completely intact. Its imminent employment for further large-scale operations is underlined by the strong concentration of airforce units in the same area. . . .

---

* The 51st Highland Division landed on 'Sword' beach on D-day and was duly identified by the Germans.

Nor did Foreign Armies West or the Wehrmachtführungsstab modify their belief in the threatened strike at the Pas de Calais when it became clear that the Normandy assault was being carried out by an Allied force twice as strong numerically as that of the Germans defending the bridge-head. By June 18 Montgomery had twenty Allied divisions in the bridge-head against eighteen German divisions. (Eighteen was only their nominal strength. In fact the German divisions, made up of the remnants of eighteen divisions, had a fighting strength of ten divisions.) They continued to believe the Allies capable of mounting two assaults of this size. When SS-General Sepp Dietrich warned on June 20, 'Unless reinforcements come soon, the front cannot be held', he received none, even though he was one of Hitler's most trusted companions since the earliest days of the National Socialist movement.* The 15th Army, Hitler ruled, must be kept intact, so that it could deal effectively with the assault of FUSAG when it came, as come it must.

When on June 26 Cherbourg capitulated to the Americans there were more German divisions guarding the 15th Army sector than were opposing the Allies in Normandy. That day Rommel told Rundstedt that all the evidence suggested that the Allies would shortly make 'a thrust from the area north and north-west of Caen towards Paris'. 'This thrust,' he declared, 'will be timed to coincide with a large-scale landing between the Somme and Le Havre.' To be sure that was an interesting variation on the Pas de Calais theme. But from the view-point of the SHAEF deceivers it was still satisfactory. They did not mind where the Germans expected the assault as long as the 15th Army kept out of the bridge-head. And keep out it did.

Rommel wanted to fall back to a new defence line where the German troops would be out of range of the Allied ships' guns which together with the incessant bombing raids of the Allied air forces were in the view of both Rundstedt and Rommel making it very doubtful whether the Germans could continue to hold out in the bridge-head. Rundstedt and Rommel together urged Hitler that before it was destroyed the 7th Army should make an ordered

---

* In the early thirties, before Hitler's access to power, Sepp Dietrich, a former cavalry sergeant of the first war, had commanded Hitler's personal bodyguard of thugs and gunmen.

withdrawal towards the Seine, where with the 15th Army to support it, it could fight a defensive but mobile battle.

But as in Russia and in Italy Hitler, the veteran of the first war's static trench warfare, held on to his strategic panacea of No Retreat. 'Stand where you are,' he ordered, 'and then counter attack.' On June 20 accordingly he laid on a new offensive. Two SS-Panzer divisions which had been transferred to France from Poland would join the 2nd SS-Panzer Division and the 1st SS-Panzer Division—withdrawn at last from 15th Army (where its place had been taken by other formations)—in a 'do-or-die' attempt to cleave a corridor to the coast and 'Dunkirk' the isolated British. What with the demoralisation he counted on the V–1 Flying Bomb attack to produce, Hitler calculated that in sheer desperation the Allied command would be forced to launch their attack on Calais and the launching sites.

Nor was Hitler's guess about Allied reactions to the V–1 entirely off the mark. There *was* a school of thought in the British cabinet which advocated an attack on the Pas de Calais to eliminate the V–1. It was led by Herbert Morrison, the Home Secretary.

But what Hitler did not know was that the trusted V–men who had sold him on the idea of the impending Calais assault were already helping to undermine the effectiveness of his V–1. Nor did he even guess that in the face of Morrison's pleading Churchill* had gone out of his way to tell Eisenhower on June 18 that there could be no question of changing Allied strategy in order to capture the V–1 bases. To assure the success of the overall plan of campaign London would continue to endure the bombardment as long as was necessary.

---

* Winston S. Churchill, *The Second World War*, Vol. VI, page 40.

12

'Cato' Arrested!

As early as December 1943 the Abwehr had decided that 'Cato' and his network should have the honour of acting as spotters when the Führer launched his secret weapon and began to hammer London with his V-1 Flying Bombs. They were to report the fall of the shots. Special arrangements were made with Kühlenthal so that when the time came—in December 1943 the bombardment was expected to begin early in January—spotter signals received from 'Cato' should not go first to Berlin but should be transmitted direct from Madrid to the headquarters of the 65th 'Special Duties' Corps in France. The 65th Corps had been put in charge of the bombardment by the Führer.

On December 15, 1943, Jorge Antonio himself was given a friendly hint by Kühlenthal of the treat in store for him. 'Circumstances make it imperative,' signalled the general, 'that you should move your home outside the capital, preferably to the northward. This warning is strictly confidential and for your eyes only. In taking the necessary precautions your collaborators must in no circumstances be allowed to suspect the reason for them. Should the threatened action begin, you must ensure that your collaborators maintain contact with you.'

Was that message evidence of the kindliness and humanity of the old general? Did he want Jorge Antonio and his comrades to get out of London, 'lest they be consumed in the iniquity of the city' when Hitler's wrath demolished it like Sodom and Gomorrah? Or was he only anxious to preserve his valuable V-man? Probably it was a bit of both.

Kühlenthal, of course, was not responsible for the miscalculation about the beginning of the bombardment. That was Hitler's.

On December 23, 1943, Colonel-General Keitel at Hitler's behest ordered Lieutenant-General Erich Heinemann, the commander of the 65th Corps, to open the long-range bombardment of London in mid-January. Heinemann promptly replied that this was quite impossible. And it became more impossible still as the RAF and the US Air Force in daily and nightly bombing raids smashed up missile sites and missiles. That did not, however, stop Jorge Antonio from fishing for information with a series of probing enquiries to his boss in Madrid.

Like this one which he sent on February 22, 1944, when he reported that the boarding house in which his radio operator now lived in London had been bombed in the Luftwaffe raid of the previous night. 'Please let me know whether these raids are forerunners of other more intensive attacks, so that I can make immediate dispositions for the protection of the service. If one must expect graver developments like the rocket, I would have the transmitter moved to a safer place, making it appear that the present raids are my reason for doing so. This would enable me to persuade those of my collaborators living in Greater London to move to a safer area without alarming them.' But Kühlenthal, who must have had the greatest difficulty in getting permission to send even that discrete warning of December 15, did not reply to this or to any of Jorge Antonio's other enquiries about the timing of the Great Retribution.

Nor did Kühlenthal send a warning, when four months later, on June 13th, the V-1 bombardment at last began in earnest. But this time he did apologise for not having done so. 'We had not been warned of the imminence of the project, owing no doubt to the High Command being fully occupied with the enemy landing.'

Now, however, Jorge Antonio himself came in for a bombardment. Queries from Kühlenthal. Urgent requests for information as to where the V-1 missiles had landed and when. These questions placed the deception team in an uncomfortable dilemma. On the one hand they did not want to give the Germans information which would enable them to correct their aim, on the other they did not want to expose their V-men as frauds by having them transmit reports which a successful reconnaissance flight could reveal to the Germans as false. Nor could they just keep silent. What were they to do?

Fortunately the brilliant and imaginative Dr R. V. Jones, the

Director of Scientific Intelligence at the Air Ministry, came forward to help them with his expert advice. Dr Jones, as a result of his service with Air Intelligence, had considerable experience with agents' reports of where bombs had fallen. This had shown him that agents could as a rule be trusted to give an accurate report about the site of what in the jargon of the air-raid precaution services was referred to as an 'incident'. But they were far less reliable, Dr Jones had found, when it came to reporting the time at which the 'incident' had taken place. He therefore suggested to the Deception Unit that it should allow its V-men to report the correct location of a number of genuine 'incidents'. 'But,' he added, 'they should report only those where the missiles have overshot Central London. At the same time they should attribute to these bombs that have overshot the timing of others known to have fallen short. This procedure has two advantages. Firstly the Germans will have no evidence that the V-men have misled them. Secondly this mixture of truth and falsehood may well induce them to reduce the range of the missiles, so that many more of them will fall short than are doing so at present.'

Needless to say the deception artists were delighted. Here was an almost classical piece of tactical deception and from a scientist, who though he was an experienced intelligence officer and had made invaluable contributions to electronic deception, had, so far as they knew, never ventured into tactical or strategic deception before. Equally impressed was Duncan Sandys, Churchill's dynamic young son-in-law, who had recently been made chairman of the 'Crossbow Committee'.* He took up Dr Jones's suggestion with characteristic verve. On his own responsibility he authorised the deception team to go ahead with the scheme without waiting for approval from the Cabinet. Sandys did not want to waste any time on such formalities. Quite right too. Had they had to wait for the cabinet's ruling, the reports of the V-men might well have lost their freshness and spontaneity. They might have appeared to the Germans as what they really were—something that had been cooked up after careful calculation.

The results of the Jones scheme were highly gratifying. Of the

---

* 'Crossbow' was the code-name for the V-1 and V-2 weapons. The 'Crossbow Committee' had been set up by Churchill to study intelligence about the weapons, and devise the best defence against them.

numerous 'incidents' reported to the 65th Corps by a 'very reliable V-man' not one was south of the Thames. All the Flying Bombs reported by him had fallen in the outskirts of London, well to the north, north-west, and north-east of the metropolis. In reality 75 per cent of the missiles had landed south of the river. Colonel Max Wachtel, commandant of the Flying Bomb regiment, on receiving the report did exactly what Dr Jones had said he would do. He shortened range, and the mean point of impact moved even farther south.

Still without cabinet approval, Jorge Antonio relayed a report from the Swansea seaman, whom allegedly he had posted as an observer in Southampton. It told of 'extensive damage in the harbour area'. The object of this report was to divert the Flying Bomb attack to small targets which would be difficult to hit and where such damage as they did would be comparatively slight.

General Heinemann was taken aback by the Southampton report. Hitler had given specific orders that only London was to be attacked and he saw himself faced with the gravest displeasure from the All Highest. Presumably at Heinemann's request Kühlenthal now queried Jorge Antonio. Had not the Swansea seaman made a mistake? But Jorge Antonio stuck to his story. On July 3 he amplified it. As a result of damage done to their airfield by Flying Bombs, a squadron of fighters had been moved from Southampton to an emergency airfield which had not been used since the Battle of Britain.

Colonel Wachtel, who all along had wanted to 'have a bash' at the south coast invasion bases, was much impressed by these reports. If this kind of dislocation could be inflicted by Flying Bombs which were off target, how much greater he argued would their effect be if they were aimed deliberately in a concentrated attack. So he secretly gave orders for V-bombs to be aimed at Southampton. They were—and did as good as no damage. Hitler, however, got wind of this disobedience and in a stern message to Heinemann re-affirmed his decision that London was to be the sole target.

But the missile attacks on Southampton made trouble not only for Heinemann and Wachtel. They also made trouble for the Deception Unit. For when Lord Cherwell, Churchill's scientific adviser and a member of the 'Crossbow Committee', heard how the

Germans were being lured into wasting their missiles he was so pleased with the ingenuity of the scheme that he decided to have a go himself.

'I would press you,' he wrote to Herbert Morrison, the Home Secretary, 'to consider the possibility of commiserating with an unnamed "south coast town" on the heavy losses sustained, or in some other way indicating that the attack had been a success.' The proposal, Lord Cherwell argued, promised to save the lives of hundreds of Londoners every week at the cost of at worst only a few lives in the coast towns.

Herbert Morrison was shocked. So far he had not been aware that deception was interfering with the German aiming of their V-bombs and causing the lives and limbs of one lot of Britons to be spared at the expense of those of another. Morrison commented on the Cherwell proposal that 'politically it would be dangerous in the extreme!' Such a public statement, he insisted, would be at variance with the truth. It would soon be known to be untrue, and 'doubts would be cast upon the accuracy of Government statements generally'.

Churchill unfortunately was abroad at the time that Herbert Morrison put the matter before the cabinet. As a consequence it was ruled that the deception artists should confine themselves to 'confusing' the enemy as to where his missiles had landed. They should not attempt to make him alter his aim in any particular direction.

In my opinion this was one of the silliest British decisions of the war. For the 'incident' charts on the wall of Noël Wild's office in Norfolk House showed clearly how, under the influence of the reports from the SHAEF-controlled V-men, the mean point of impact of the missiles was moving farther and farther away from Central London. They were landing in the south-east, many of them in open country. Lord Cherwell, Duncan Sandys, and Dr Jones were a united front of infuriated protest. As for Jorge Antonio, as far as he was concerned the cabinet's ruling was sheer murder!

Embarrassing queries kept arriving from Kühlenthal. Once more the deceivers were in dire trouble.

'The best thing,' said Roger Sneath, 'would be for "Vandal" to disappear for a while until this thing has blown over. But how? He can't just go into hiding. He has to be somewhere where he can't communicate with Madrid, where even his own sub-agents cannot reach him.'

'Sounds like gaol,' someone joked.

'Excellent!' said Wild. 'The very place. He must go to prison. The police must pick him up on suspicion of being an enemy spy while he is snooping around somewhere enquiring about a V-1 incident.'

And that was how they did it.

Jorge Antonio's message of July 3 about the Flying Bomb on the Southampton fighter airfield was the last Madrid heard from him for some time. When his operator came through on July 5, Madrid, after deciphering the signal, found it was in English, not Spanish as normally used by V-man 'Cato'. It was from a female sub-agent of 'Cato's' known as 'The Widow'.* She was called 'The Widow' because she was the widow of that sub-agent of 'Cato's' who had resided in Bootle and had fallen sick and died in November 1942 at the very moment when he should have been able to observe and report the embarkation of the troops for North Africa. The widow had been having a difficult time and, with the approval of Kühlenthal, 'Cato' had taken her on as a kind of secretary. She had been enciphering his messages for him and doing a thousand and one other jobs for which 'Cato' with the vastly increased burden of his intelligence work could not find time.

Now 'The Widow' informed Madrid that Jorge Antonio had been arrested but that so far as she knew the other members of the network were safe. She had contacted the Venezuelan and he was already on his way to London to take charge, as 'Cato' had arranged that he should, if anything ever happened to himself. Madrid acknowledged the signal and ordered the Venezuelan to preserve radio silence and remain strictly under cover until further notice. The radio operator was to keep up his radio watch and hold himself ready to receive instructions should there be any.

A week went by. And then on July 12 the Venezuelan came through with the sensational news: ' "The Widow" has just informed me that our chief was released on July 10 and is back at his home. My instructions from him are to return at once to Glasgow and await orders there.'

---

* Like all of Jorge Antonio's sub-agents, 'The Widow' was, of course, purely fictitious.

No further message reached the anxious Kühlenthal until he received a letter from Jorge Antonio which the BOAC steward (or whoever in real life was playing the part of courier) had placed in the Lisbon bank's safe-deposit box. The letter was dated July 14, 1944.

It told an extraordinary story.

Around lunch-time on July 4 Jorge Antonio had found himself in El Vino's, a Fleet Street bar largely frequented by journalists. There was a lot of talk about a Flying Bomb which had dropped early that morning in the Commercial Docks, in the East End of London. So Jorge Antonio had gone to dockland to have a look round and find out what had happened. He had started asking a man in the crowd questions. 'Quite casual questions,' Jorge Antonio said. To his horror the man he had picked turned out to be a policeman in plain clothes. Rather imprudently Jorge Antonio tried to swallow a piece of paper while the policeman's back was turned, but the policeman caught him at it.

The constable had already been suspicious of him because of his foreign English. But trying to swallow the paper was the last straw. Jorge Antonio was arrested and taken to the station. But here he had one piece of luck. The policeman was over-zealous, and in his eagerness to catch a spy he detained Jorge Antonio without a warrant for a longer period than was legally permitted.

Another prisoner pointed this out to Jorge Antonio. On this man's advice he wrote a letter of protest to the Home Secretary informing him of the mistake that had been made. He also wrote to his boss at the Ministry of Information.

'I do not know whether it was just the fact that I had written these two letters which impressed the police, or whether the letters themselves had produced a reaction in the Home Office and the M of I. A dramatic change came over the attitude of the police to me. The superintendent of the station sent for me and I was able to explain what I was doing in Bethnal Green. I had had a conversation a few days earlier, I said, with my departmental chief at the Ministry in the course of which I had questioned the efficacy of the defence measures used by the British against the Flying Bomb. When I heard on July 4 that one had dropped on the Commercial Docks I decided to go there and see whether my criticisms were justified.

And that, I told him, was what I was doing when the plain-clothes man arrested me.

'Fortunately my friend at the M of I was able to corroborate everything I had said about our conversation, and very soon after I was released, as the superintendent put it, "without a stain on my character". When I said good-bye the superintendent apologised to me and said that his officers had been over-zealous in the performance of their duties. I did not understand half of what he said. But I could see he was sincerely sorry. In my own relief at being set free I rather overdid my gratitude. I thanked him for his hospitality! That must have sounded utterly ridiculous.'

The effect of Jorge Antonio's arrest on Kühlenthal and his new masters at the RSHA was exactly what Noël Wild and his friends had hoped. All other agents who had been asked to act as observers for General Heinemann were told to stop their snooping for bomb damage and confine themselves to their normal fields of intelligence. 'Paul', for instance, was ordered: 'Discontinue all reports on damage caused by Flying Bombs and send us only reports about location of troops etc.' Jorge Antonio received a similar message after Kühlenthal had received the letter describing his arrest and subsequent release. With almost maternal concern General Kühlenthal begged him to 'cease all investigation of the new weapons'.

Jorge Antonio's was an excellent story and Kühlenthal must have enjoyed reading it almost as much as Wild, Sneath, Reid and Jorge Antonio had enjoyed inventing it. But they had still another treat in store for the old gentleman. M.I.5 arranged that an official letter should be sent to Jorge Antonio from the office of the Under-Secretary of State at the Home Office. It was a true masterpiece of Whitehall officialese—as, of course, it should have been, seeing that it was drafted by a genuine Home Office official.

It began aggressively enough by rejecting Jorge Antonio's complaint. He had only himself to blame, it said, because his conduct at the Surrey Commercial Docks on the afternoon referred to was bound to arouse the suspicion of any police officer doing his duty. But having administered this reproof and admitted that enquiries had established Jorge Antonio's innocence the official conveyed an unqualified apology.

For once I cannot blame Erich Kühlenthal for being taken in. This letter had every appearance of being perfectly genuine. In every detail it was evidence of V-man 'Cato's' consummate skill in bluffing the British.

Jorge Antonio wasted no time in getting it delivered to his master in Madrid. On July 23 he received Kühlenthal's answer. 'In my possession all the documents you mentioned. Shocked by the story of your detention. We send cordial congratualations to you on your liberation. The security of the service requires a prolonged period of inactivity on your part without any contact with your collaborators.' He added that in the event that important military information should crop up the Venezuelan should take over the job of communicating it to Madrid.

The piece of news, however, which caused the greatest gratification to the SHAEF team General Kühlenthal kept for a special message he sent Jorge Antonio the following day.

'With great happiness and satisfaction I am able to advise you that the Führer has conferred the Iron Cross on you as a reward for your outstanding distinguished and meritorious service. This is a decoration which without exception is granted only to front line combatants. We all send you our most sincere and cordial congratulations.'

Jorge Antonio sent a becomingly emotional and modest reply: 'I cannot at this moment, when my feelings overwhelm me, express in words my gratitude for this decoration granted by our Führer to whom humbly and with deepest respect I express my gratitude for the high distinction he has bestowed on me and of which I feel myself unworthy as I have never done more than what I consider the fulfilment of my duty. Furthermore I must state that I regard this decoration as being won not by me personally but by all my comrades who have one and all given of their best from a sense of true devotion to our Führer. We shall continue to do so until final victory crowns the Führer's efforts. Heil Hitler!'

It was a longish message for a man to send who had been told to keep radio silence and take a long rest. Jorge Antonio, however, had no intention of resting. He was eager to get on with the new phase of the FUSAG deception. But the award of the Iron Cross did most certainly make a satisfactory ending to his stint as a spotter for Hitler's Flying Bomb regiment!

Neither Jorge Antonio's retirement from the V-1 Spotter Service or the cabinet's veto on SHAEF's attempts to trick Colonel Wachtel put an end to the Deception Unit's nefarious interference with the V-1's range and direction, for on the same day that Jorge Antonio had bowed out Schellenberg and his SD had entered the ring. They parachuted two young volunteers from the Waffen-SS into East Anglia to act as V-men. Their mission was to demonstrate to Hitler the superiority of the 'young' SD over the old sweats of the Wehrmacht's Abwehr when it came to doing a job that required courage, dash, and brains. In other words, transmitting radio reports of where and when the Flying Bombs had landed, and what damage they had done.

Alas for Schellenberg's illusions. 'Zig' and 'Zag', as the Deception Unit later code-named the two young heroes, were captured immediately after landing. But they certainly showed brains, for they at once agreed to collaborate with their captors. Within less than twenty-four hours of being picked up they were sending reports to the 65th Corps which followed the identical formula recommended by Dr Jones. Once again there was no time to seek special cabinet approval, for that would have left a suspicious hiatus between the SS men's arrival in Britain and the time they went into action.

When Morrison learned, as he inevitably did learn, that despite the cabinet veto, the SHAEF deception team were continuing their efforts to 'correct' Colonel Wachtel's aiming, there was a major crisis. Morrison, furiously indignant, once more took the matter to the cabinet.

'Who are we,' the Minister of Home Security rhetorically asked his fellow ministers, 'to act as God? Who are we to decide that one man shall die because he lives on the south coast, while another survives because he lives in London?'

Morrison's view won the day. But as this matter involved the handling of agents, it was not mentioned in the official record. The decision therefore never reached Dr Jones—officially.

'Zig' and 'Zag' continued saving the lives of Londoners until the whole bombardment—V-1 and V-2—came to an end.

13

Problems

In the seven weeks after D-day during which they kept the FUSAG hoax alive the SHAEF deceivers lived in an almost continuous state of alarm lest German intelligence should learn some give-away fact which would reveal to them the hollowness of the threat pinning down the 15th Army.

Looking back today most of them would agree that their fears were groundless. Once Hitler had fallen for the 'Cato' message of June 9 and countermanded the move of those 15th Army formations to Normandy, he was committed to accepting the hoax as fact. There was no going back for him. The Führer could change his mind once and still be the Führer, but he could not change it a second time without standing revealed to his increasingly sceptical army as an incompetent ditherer. Furthermore, once the Führer had decided that the threat against Calais was real, who was there among the military experts advising him with the courage to speak up against his decision?

That was the beauty of Carlos Reid's plan of May 4—as perfect a piece of psychological calculation as had ever been devised. Reid had arranged that Jorge Antonio's message clinching the deception should reach his German clients on the third day after the landing, at a time when they would still be trying to make up their minds about the Allied intentions. He intended the message to be the straw that would tip the balance, tip it in favour of the Führer's known belief that the first landing would be nothing more than a diversion, that the main assault must be expected later, in the Pas de Calais. It did exactly that.

Once the die had been cast and the 15th Army divisions had been ordered back to their staions it was very difficult to move them out again. For the German Army had lost its mobility. You could not order troops to cross and recross the bridgeless Seine.

To the Deception Unit, however, things did not look as simple as that. They were confronted with a whole chessboard of problems.

One problem, a legacy of the period before D-day, faced them in the first days after the landing. In the weeks before D-day severe security restrictions had been imposed in order to prevent secrets of the Allied invasion preparations being leaked to the enemy. Mail services to neutral countries had been suspended at the end of March. On April 1 travel to Ireland was halted. Certain coastal areas were closed to all but local residents. No visitors were allowed. On April 6 all leave was stopped for the fighting services. On April 18 a ban was imposed on travel to and from the United Kingdom. Most drastic measure of the whole series: on April 24 an order was issued prohibiting diplomatic communications in cipher or by diplomatic courier. The ban was universal and affected Allies and neutrals alike. Needless to say the neutrals resented it. The Foreign Office, deeply apologetic over what they agreed was a high-handed curtailment of traditional diplomatic privileges, promised that the restriction would be lifted as soon as the emergency necessitating it was ended.

Colonel John Bevan, in his capacity as head of the London Controlling Section, attended the meetings of the Home Defence Executive at which these restrictions were drafted. At his suggestion various modifications were adopted which took care of the interests of the cover plan. For instance Bevan arranged that the visitors' ban should be extended to areas of east and south-east England affected by 'Fortitude South', which would otherwise not have been included.

In these early discussions, however, insufficient attention was paid to the need to keep the restrictions in force after the landing, if the threat of the second assault was not to lose reality. The omission was natural enough. The SHAEF deceivers themselves at that time had no great hopes of the hoax holding out for more than a few days after the landing in Normandy had taken place. The consternation of the Home Defence Executive when the deception staffs asked that this should be put right was predictable.

At a meeting of the Executive on May 17, Bevan urged on behalf of the deception staffs that the curtailment of the diplomatic communications should be continued for at least a month after D-day. His demand came as a bombshell. The representative of the Foreign Office was immediately up in arms.

'We would never have agreed to the ban in the first place,' he declared, 'if we had not understood that it would be terminated as soon as "Overlord" had been launched. Once it is known that we have landed on the continent, it will be quite impossible to ask the neutrals or our allies to agree to a continuation of this unprecedented curtailment of their diplomatic rights. I must warn you that if you persist with this proposal the Foreign Office will appeal to the cabinet.'

So Bevan took the matter to his bosses, the Chiefs of Staff. They, however, had already received a minute from the Foreign Secretary, Sir Anthony Eden, in which he said that it would be impossible to maintain the diplomatic ban for any length of time after D-day. Eden, who would have made a first-class diplomat, had he not been the Foreign Secretary, proposed an astute compromise. The embassies and legations, he suggested, should be informed officially two days after the landing had taken place that the ban had been lifted. Obstacles would, however, be put in the diplomats' way which would have the practical effect of preventing diplomatic communications leaving the country for a full week after D-day.

This proposal, of course, in no way met the needs of the SHAEF Deception Unit which for the purpose of keeping the Pas de Calais hoax alive was not so much concerned with the reality of preventing diplomatic communications as with giving the appearance that the British were trying to prevent them. They wanted the German High Command to believe that the ban on diplomatic communications was being kept alive because the main assault was still to come. However, the Chiefs of Staff accepted Sir Anthony Eden's compromise.

On May 30 the Home Defence Executive held another meeting. Colonel Bevan once more went into battle. The lifting of the ban on diplomatic communications, he argued, was bad enough. It would, however, be an absolutely disastrous blow to 'Fortitude' if —as was being proposed—all the other restrictions were lifted at the same time. He therefore urged that the remaining restrictions should not all be lifted simultaneously but that their removal should be staggered so as to take place by instalments. This was accepted. It was also agreed that such security restrictions as remained should be reviewed approximately twelve days to a fortnight after the landing. Most of those present at the meeting believed that by then there would be no further need for them, as 'Fortitude' would have come to the end of its life.

Nevertheless, the SHAEF deceivers now found themselves in an awkward predicament. The Germans, they felt, would be bound to ask why the ban on diplomatic communications was not being maintained for the second and more important assault on the Pas de Calais. That was just the kind of inconsistency a wide-awake intelligence officer was bound to spot.

The job of rescuing them from this dilemma fell to Jorge Antonio. Less than a week after the landing he radioed Madrid that the ban on diplomatic communications had provoked a major clash between the British Chiefs of Staff and the Foreign Office. He had learned this from his girl friend, the Whitehall secretary. The Chiefs of Staff argued, he told Kühlenthal, that the impending assault by FUSAG made it imperative to keep the ban on diplomatic communications in being. To this the Foreign Office had countered that they would only be able to keep the neutrals in line if they could tell them why the ban had to be continued. The Chiefs of Staff thereupon preferred to dispense with the ban rather than disclose their operational intentions to the neutrals and through them to the enemy. And thus for the time being the Foreign Office had won the day—much to the irritation of the soldiers.

I would say that this was about as neat a way out of the difficulty as could have been devised by anyone. But, like some of the deception artists' other most skilful ploys, it missed. Not because of any intrinsic defect, nor because Jorge Antonio's signal was not read, or had gone astray in the labyrinth of the RSHA—as had happened on other occasions—but because it was too subtle for the somewhat obtuse minds of Hitler's G2 staff.

There is no reference to Jorge Antonio's message in the situation reports of Foreign Armies West. With that department the message presumably just failed to register. But it does turn up in the files of

Colonel Friedrich Adolf Krummacher, the G2 at the Führer-hauptquartier. Obviously the message had meant nothing to him. Probably he wondered why on earth the great 'Cato' had bothered to send it. For he had scribbled in the margin: *'Von keinem Interesse'* ('Of no interest').

It was a good thing, though, that Jorge Antonio had qualified his announcement of the victory of the Foreign Office over the Chiefs of Staff with a hedging 'for the time being'. For Eisenhower was not prepared to abandon the interests of 'Fortitude' to the neutral diplomats and their Whitehall champions as lightly as had the British Chiefs of Staff. When the Supreme Commander learned what had happened he made a personal intervention and succeeded in getting the ban on diplomatic communications prolonged to June 21. (Jorge Antonio duly reported this prolongation to Madrid, slightly amplifying his previous story. But again without result!) Eisenhower also persuaded the War Cabinet to keep the other security restrictions in operation up to the end of the month. Even beyond that, if good reasons could be shown for doing so.

Two of the restrictions were of particular interest to the protagonists of 'Fortitude': the visitors' ban and the cancellation of leave for the fighting services. Herbert Morrison, as Home Secretary, was, of course, particularly anxious to lift the visitors' ban which was unpopular with the public. To appease it the ban was lifted, but only from the coastal districts west of Southampton. In deference to 'Fortitude' it was agreed to continue banning all visits to the FUSAG area between Southampton and the Wash up to August 1. In fact the ban remained in force throughout August. Not until September 6 did 'Paul' signal the Germans that it had been suspended.

SHAEF strongly resisted the suggestion that leave should be restored to the fighting services. They even opposed a proposal that an exception should be made in favour of 'non-operational' units. Their reason for doing so was convincing. 'The Germans,' said Bevan, 'will not necessarily appreciate the difference between operational and non-operational units. If they learn of leave having been granted to troops in Britain they will immediately doubt the seriousness of Allied preparations in East Anglia.'

But in the end the SHAEF deceivers took pity on the troops and agreed that leave should be restored from August 15. But when

'Paul', who was allegedly with the headquarters staff of FUSAG, signalled his controller that it was expected that 'leave for short periods would soon be restored' he took the precaution of adding: 'This does not apply to the forces in FUSAG.'

*   *   *

At the same time as these problems were testing the judgment and ingenuity of the SHAEF deceivers a flock of others were presenting themselves. And like the difficulties over the security restrictions they too arose out of 'Fortitude's' unforeseen longevity.

When around the middle of May such evidence as was available had begun to indicate that 'Fortitude' was being accepted in the Führerhauptquartier the Deception Unit decided to revise the plan. The aim of this revision was to keep the German belief in the imminence of a second assault alive up to the end of June. But by the middle of June even that date looked too unambitious. The deception planners now believed the hoax could be made to last well into July. This brought fresh complications, for a number of formations included in General Patton's bogus FUSAG were perfectly genuine. Like Patton's own 3rd Army they were due to cross the Channel early in July. They had only been included in FUSAG because it was calculated that 'Fortitude' would have expired long before their presence in Normandy could embarrass the hoax.

Now, therefore, it was necessary to write the Normandy-bound formations out of the script along with FUSAG's Normandy-bound commander. In fact it was going to be necessary to go in for some of that 'regrouping' which George 'blood-and-guts' Patton affected to despise as effete and pedantic. Poor George Patton! Thank goodness he had no idea of what the deceivers were doing to the Army Group with whose command they had notionally entrusted him.

Wisely (and fortunately) the SHAEF Unit had provided for just such an eventuality and they had suitable replacements in the shape of fictitious divisions and corps waiting in the wings, or more accurately in Scotland and the Midlands. For example, in place of the two corps of the Canadian Army which were scheduled to move

to Normandy—the 2nd Canadian Corps and the 12th—SHAEF
brought the imaginary 2nd British Corps to East Anglia to fill at
least part of the gap. The 2nd British Corps was one of the imaginary
formations with which the Germans had become familiar when, as
part of the equally fictitious 4th Army in Scotland, it was expected
to take part in the no-less-fictitious expedition to Norway.* Jorge
Antonio, in a message sent shortly before D-day, had allowed one
of his observant sub-agents to report it as being on the move in a
southerly direction. The V-man had located its headquarters at
Louth in Lincolnshire with its two divisions at Skegness and Horn-
castle. Now the idea was to suggest to the Germans that Eisenhower,
unhappy about the slow progress of the Normandy assault, had
decided to reinforce Field Marshal Montgomery's 21st Army Group
with two of FUSAG's Canadian Corps and replace them at FUSAG
with 2nd British Corps and other formations from the 4th Army.

To help put across this regrouping, the Wireless Deception units
were ordered to make appropriate changes in their Fake Signals
programme. On June 4 the signals unit representing the 2nd British
Corps got into signals contact with that representing FUSAG.
On June 14 1st Canadian Army Signals fell silent. On June 16 the
unit representing 2nd British Corps closed down at Louth and
opened up again almost immediately in the Dover area. All of this
would have been most convincing had the Germans been listening.
There is, I regret, no evidence that they were.

But now the V-men went into action. 'Paul' was the first to score.
On June 11 Foreign Armies West recorded in Situation Report
West No. 1293:

... The same source whose reports on the location of the British
2nd Army Corps and the 58th British Infantry Division in Scotland
have been confirmed, reported on June 7 that these formations
were located in the Doncaster area. As these two formations had
been observed by another reputable source to be on the move in a
southerly direction from north of the Solway Firth, it may be
assumed that they are about to go into position in southern or
eastern England. ...

On June 16 Jorge Antonio reported that one of his sub-agents

---

* See Chapter 8.

(a member of the highly efficient 'Freddy, Dick, and Desmond' trio) had identified troops in Kent with the insignia of the 2nd British Corps and the 58th Division. Jorge Antonio, basking in his new-found authority as a strategic commentator, added: 'I regard the mention of these insignia by this agent as highly significant. It is evidence that all the troops observed by my deputy [the Venezuelan] in Glasgow–Motherwell have now been moved south.' After an 'Enemy appreciation West' (No. 1299) in which he stated that the 2nd British Corps was now considered to belong to FUSAG, Colonel von Roenne on June 19 included Jorge Antonio's dispatch in these terms:

... From south-east England come further reports that the FUSAG formations are closing up towards the south-east coast. The hitherto unconfirmed transfer of the formations of the 2nd British Army Corps to Kent fits in with this concentration in the south-east. Also deserving of attention is a report from a particularly reliable source that FUSAG is to be supported by strong formations of heavy bombers. This suggests an intended assault on strong fortifi-cations and would indicate the mid-Channel (Pas de Calais) area. A date for the intended assault is still lacking.

In my mind's eye I can see Colonel von Roenne standing in front of his big 'Order of Battle' map of Britain with flag pins and coloured pencils in his hands. Lovingly, he sticks in flags to represent the non-existent British 2nd Corps and its two subordinate divisions. He pencils them into exactly the area where Lieutenant-Colonel Roger Sneath (who was in charge of the false order of battle in the SHAEF Unit) wanted the Germans to place them: Kent.

In anticipation of the departure of further genuine divisions from FUSAG for Normandy the SHAEF Deception Unit decided that they would pass information to the Germans through the V-men showing that these formations had been transferred to other commands. At the same time the V-men would report the arrival of new American formations from the United States which were being used to reinforce FUSAG. These newly arrived formations were without exception bogus.

Their numbers, flashes, and other points of identification had been supplied by the War Department in Washington along with bogus 'historical background' for each unit. Like the War Office in London, Washington had forwarded 'a bank' of phony formations to Colonel Bevan's LCS and Colonel Bevan, in performance of his functions as co-ordinator of deception, had allocated a quota of phonies to each deception unit. This way it was impossible for two or more Allied deception units to use the same phonies at the same time! A wise precaution.

One of the first of FUSAG's new units 'created' in this way by Washington with the assistance of LCS and the SHAEF Deception Unit was the 59th US Infantry Division. This division will not be found on any American roll of honour. But it features prominently in the situation reports of Colonel von Roenne's Foreign Armies West. The 59th was introduced to von Roenne by Jorge Antonio when he reported that the 28th US Infantry Division, which according to him had been undergoing amphibious training with (the fictitious) 'F' Force in the neighbourhood of Harwich, had been relieved by the 59th.

The 28th, said Jorge Antonio, was returning to its normal location near Dover. Roenne's Situation Report No. 1292 registered the replacement in Harwich of the 28th by 'a new Infantry division which is said to have arrived recently in England'. In a subsequent report Roenne said, 'The 59th US Infantry Division is probably the American Infantry Division of unknown number which was hitherto believed to be in Scotland but which had not been confirmed there for some time.' So the colonel was still drawing on his imagination!

Another bogus division added to FUSAG at this time was the 2nd British Airborne Division which popped up at Skegness on the east coast of Lincolnshire and promptly got into wireless touch with the 2nd British Corps. 'Paul' had already reported finding this division at Grantham. On June 11 in Situation Report No. 1293 Foreign Armies West made its own contribution to the fictitious history of this bogus airborne division:

According to an Abwehr source which has been reporting accurately for some time the British 2nd Airborne Division, which had hitherto been presumed to be in the Mediterranean, is located in the region of Grantham (thirty kilometres east of Nottingham). It therefore seems possible that this formation, parts of which have had considerable battle experience, has been transferred to England in exchange for the 4th British Airborne Division. The 4th Airborne had been assumed to be located in Dorset though not with any certainty. Thus the increasingly frequent reports from the Middle East that the 4th British Airborne Division is in Egypt gain in probability.

Fascinating this habit Roenne's unit had developed of embroidering the fake intelligence planted on it by the Allies with further fakes of its own concoction. Did they do it in order to impress their superiors with the wide range of their knowledge? I suppose so.

But the SHAEF-controlled V-men did not confine themselves to reporting the arrival of mere corps and divisions from the United States. Even before D-day Jorge Antonio and his colleagues had been preparing the ground for the establishment in FUSAG of a bogus 14th US Army. One of Jorge Antonio's sub-agents, who had allegedly been sent to Liverpool to investigate a report of preparations to attack Bordeaux, discovered nothing to confirm the Bordeaux expedition. Instead he found American troops arriving in large numbers. This Jorge Antonio passed on to Madrid and it duly appeared in the Foreign Armies West bulletin. So did a report from 'Paul': 'I have heard that a new American army is being assembled in the West of England and is coming under the control of FUSAG.' Shortly after Jorge Antonio discovered from his unconscious sub-agent, the omniscient American sergeant, that the 14th US Army was to join FUSAG. Foreign Armies West devoured it all omnivorously.

*   *   *

The 'regrouping' of FUSAG had made excellent progress. But one all-important element was still lacking—a new commander. Patton was itching to fly to Normandy to take over his genuine command. The deception team could hardly expect a soldier of his 'up-and-at-'em' temperament to remain content for long with the notional command of a phantom army.

General Eisenhower accordingly signalled General Marshall in Washington, asking him to nominate a high-ranking officer of suitably wide renown to take the place of Patton in command of FUSAG.

All arrangements to implement the revised cover plan can be made here except that a suitable notional commander for FUSAG is not available in this area. Desire therefore to suggest for your consideration that some well-known officer such as McNair, de Witt, or another of corresponding reputation be ordered to this theatre without delay. The names I have given you are suggested because they have been fairly well publicised throughout the world. While I had thought of using Simpson for this purpose, I feel that his name will not be of sufficient significance to the enemy. If you find it impossible to comply, I will have to start immediately to build up Simpson as best I can.

I would be most grateful for a radio reply as time is pressing and I cannot over-emphasise the importance of maintaining as long as humanly possible the Allied threat to the Pas de Calais area, which has already paid enormous dividends and, with care, will continue to do so.

On July 10 General Bedell Smith received a memorandum from General Eisenhower.

I have just received a telegram to the effect that General McNair* is soon to be here. You will note from the telegram that General Marshall intends to say in Washington that McNair has left to take an important command in the field. Please send a short wire to General Marshall saying that I fully concur with his idea of making such an announcement. Through a 'leak' I think we could let out something on roughly the following lines:

(a) We should convey to the enemy certain information which we are sure the enemy can verify as authentic, thus giving an atmosphere of plausibility. I suggest something like the identification of certain units in France.

(b) A story that Patton has lost his high command because of displeasure at some of his indiscretions, and that as a result he is reduced to army command.

(c) That the most capable and most experienced senior American commander has been brought in to take over Patton's Army Group.

(d) That owing to the damage inflicted to landing craft by the storm some weeks ago, the next expedition has been slightly delayed and that it is now estimated that it will take a certain length of time

---

* Lieutenant-General Lesley J. McNair, Commander-in-Chief of the Ground Forces in the United States.

to launch it. (This time should not be so long as to make the enemy think he could bring divisions into the 'Neptune' area and get them back to the threatened point, but should be long enough to help to assist in carrying on the deception.)

(e) The location of McNair's headquarters should probably be given and he should be directed to make a tremendous show of activity.

When Noël Wild was shown this directive he chortled with pleasure. For there could have been no greater tribute to deception than that the Supreme Allied Commander should himself take a hand in it!

*   *   *

Jorge Antonio, still lying low after his Flying Bomb escapade, was .out of touch with his transmitter when in mid-July the Deception Unit prepared to implement the Supreme Commander's directive. In the absence of the Spaniard the job was given to the Dutchman. By virtue of his appointment to the FUSAG headquarters at Wentworth 'Paul' would in any case have been the natural choice.

It was high time that the story was put across to the Germans, for General Patton had now been in Normandy since July 6. And although 3rd US Army was not due to go into action until August 1, and there was thus theoretically plenty of time before the Germans would discover its presence in Normandy together with that of the FUSAG commander, the impetuous Patton was becoming restless and impatient. As he sat in the old apple orchard near Bricquebec where he had established his command post, he became obsessed with the fear that the war would be over before he got into it.*
All the glory would go to others, while he was forced to sit idle watching the cider apples growing.

He protested to General Bradley against the slow pace of the Allied advance. He told everyone in earshot (and that included newspaper men) that two armoured divisions, preceded by a heavy artillery concentration using airbursts, could cut straight down the west coast to Avranches without any need to wait for an air blitz. On this form it was clearly only a matter of days before security

* General George S. Patton, Jr., *War As I Knew It*, page 95.

was breached and the Germans would learn that Patton, the super-general whom they were expecting to lead the FUSAG assault on the Pas de Calais, was not only in France but south of the Seine in the bridge-head. If they were not to deduce from this that the assault on the Pas de Calais was off, action had to be taken at once.

And indeed the SHAEF deceivers were none too soon. On July 18, the very day on which 'Paul' transmitted his message, the publicity-starved general had agreed with his public relations officer that war correspondents accompanying his 3rd Army should be briefed on the role he and his army were about to play in the planned break-through to Avranches and beyond. Bradley, furious with Patton for this new proof of his egotistic contempt for discipline, ordered an even stricter censorship veto to be clamped down on any mention of Patton's presence in Normandy or that of 3rd Army. But the news was out, and even before 'Paul's' message could make the Foreign Armies West situation report, the *Pariser Zeitung*, a newspaper for the German occupation forces in France, printed and published in Paris, came out with the banner headline the general had so longed for: 'PATTON'S ARMY IN THE BRIDGE-HEAD!'

If there had been a Pulitzer prize for V-men's dispatches, 'Paul's' dispatch of July 18 would have been a close runner-up to Jorge Antonio's of May 9.

I learned at Wentworth [he reported] that FUSAG has undergone important changes because of the necessity to send immediate reinforcements to Normandy. The Supreme Commander General Eisenhower decided, I gather, that it was urgently necessary to send a portion of the troops belonging to FUSAG to Normandy to form part of a new army-group there. These forces will be replaced in FUSAG by fresh units arriving from America and by British reserves. I have no exact details. But I can confirm that FUSAG will include the 9th US Army, the 14th US Army, and the 4th British Army. I suspect that Eisenhower and Patton were in severe disagreement over these FUSAG changes. This is shown by the fact that Patton has been displaced as Commander-in-Chief of FUSAG by another senior American general, General McNair. I have discussed the changes with my colonel. They have caused quite a stir at our headquarters. The colonel tells me that Montgomery had demanded immediate reinforcements in Normandy. He demanded them so urgently that it was necessary to send units

228

THE COUNTERFEIT SPY

from FUSAG which were immediately available in the south of
England, notably the 1st Canadian Army and a large portion of
the 3rd American Army. The fresh units which have recently
arrived for FUSAG from the United States will take over from
those which have been sent to Normandy. The Staff command of
FUSAG remains unchanged. The 14th United States Army has
already moved to East Anglia to the location previously occupied
by the 3rd US Army. Their headquarters are at Little Waltham,
near Chelmsford.

No reference was made to 'Paul's' dispatch by Foreign Armies
West until July 27. But before that there had been several reports
indicating that FUSAG formations were finding their way to the
bridge-head as reinforcements and that as a result the threat from
the 'Patton Army Group' was becoming less immediate. This did
not stop von Roenne issuing admonitions to his superiors in the
High Command not to underestimate the FUSAG threat and the
prospect of a second landing. Appendix 1320 of July 8, 1944,
contained a typical warning:

The strongly augmented enemy forces in the bridge-head should
not lead us to overlook the fact that the enemy continues to dispose
over all the means needed to carry out a new landing operation.
The strengths of the forces in south-east England particularly as
regards the close combat formations of the Anglo-Saxon Air
Force makes these preparations especially clear. The retention of two
light close-combat Air Corps as well as of one heavy Close-combat
Air Corps underlines this and points to the target being in the
Channel area.... Worthy of special note is the continued reinforce-
ment of the 3rd US Army which is being augmented by for-
mations from the 1st Canadian Army. This has resulted in the 3rd
American Army now being almost twice the strength of the
Canadian. This change in the dispositions may be a reaction to the
V-1 missiles. If this is so, the move would be evidence for a special
operation to seize the V-1 launching sites. Increased attention should
therefore be paid to the area Dunkirk–Boulogne.

The first mention of reinforcements leaving FUSAG for 21st
Army Group in the bridge-head and thus weakening its potential
as an assault force appears on July 10. But no sooner has he said this
than Roenne recalls the Pas de Calais threat.

. . . Summing up it would therefore seem that the Montgomery Army Group no longer disposes over any substantial reserves. The tendency for Patton formations to be used to reinforce the bridge-head . . . points in the same direction and underlines that the operations in Normandy with the forces originally provided have not led to the expected success in the time allotted. The Patton Army Group between Brighton and Humber disposes over more than thirty large formations including four airborne divisions. . . . Qualitatively this Patton army group is inferior to that under Montgomery. . . . The Patton Army Group is no longer entrusted with the decisive role. . . . It is expected to co-operate with the Montgomery Group in the near future in closest operational proximity. It is important to note that the 43rd British Division, which until a short time ago still belonged to the Patton Army Group but is now in the bridge-head, was supplied with maps not only for the Normandy area but also for that of north-east France and Belgium.

A nice touch that. But was it a plant by the 21st Army Group deception team? Or was it due to Roenne's own anxiety to bolster the fading assault threat? His next words rather suggest that.

Despite the fact that the maps covered the whole area between Antwerp and Le Havre, one must see in them evidence for the enemy intention to stage a second large-scale assault against this region.
The thinning out of the 1st Canadian Army has not yet attained dimensions which would rule out an attempted landing in the Somme area. . . . For an authoritative gauging of the enemy intentions a thorough reconnaissance of the Thames–Dover region for naval vessels of all kinds is indispensable in order to ascertain preparations for an assault against the Calais–Boulogne sector.

Roenne's report of July 13 makes much of the lifting of the visitors' ban for the coastal area between Portsmouth and Land's End. He argues that this shows the enemy's resources in this area are exhausted. The exhaustion of Montgomery's resources, he claims, is emphasised by the transfer of a further American division —the 35th—from the Patton Army Group to Normandy. But even so he still has hopes of an assault on the Pas de Calais. The increased activity of sabotage groups of the Resistance in the Belgian area, he claims, points to this. And on July 15 he is still harping on the threatened assault, when he insists that despite the stiffening of the Montgomery Army Group in the bridge-head with close-combat aircraft and military formations the strength of the airforce formations in England is sufficient for a landing operation against the eastern Channel coast. And he suggests that the introduction of large formations of the Patton Army Group into the bridge-head is due to the continued closure of the captured harbour of Cherbourg to all but small ships which has prevented expected reinforcements being sent to Normandy through that port.

But on July 21, three days after the dispatch of 'Paul's' signal and three days after the announcement in the *Pariser Zeitung* of Patton's arrival in the bridge-head with the 3rd Army, Roenne shows doubts about the assault on the Pas de Calais. He stresses the arrival in the bridge-head of further FUSAG formations (the 4th US Armoured Division, the 5th US Infantry Division), and says that this is evidence that the Montgomery Army Group enjoys priority in the enemy plans. And then for the first time he concedes that: 'The recognisable diminution of the Patton forces causes a far-off separate landing operation to lose probability.' In other words the Patton Group might still land north of the Seine, close alongside the Normandy bridge-head (say somewhere like Le Havre), but not as far away as Calais, let alone Belgium.

A first indirect reference to 'Paul's' dispatch comes on July 24 when Foreign Armies West report No. 1336 mentions 'a reliable V-man in Great Britain' reporting that 4th Army had moved from Scotland to the area north of Brighton. 'This army is said by the same source to have taken the place of the 1st Canadian Army in the FUSAG force.'

At last on July 27 the information in 'Paul's' dispatch makes its way into Colonel von Roenne's bulletin No. 1339:

Captured documents, borne out by credible Abwehr reports, show that US 3rd Army, which was hitherto accepted as being located in the area north of London, has been transferred as a second American Army Staff to northern France. In its place are to be assumed the staffs of the American 9th Army (hitherto listed as being without known location) or of a newly introduced 14th

US Army. Of the Corps commands the staff of the 15th Army Corps as well as of another Army Corps (the 12th or the 20th Army Groups) have been transferred to France. Abwehr sources have now provided information about the arrival in England of the new troop transports from the USA which had been announced for July. It can be accepted that during July one infantry division and one armoured division (numbers unknown) have been shipped to Britain. . . .

In a comment on this news Roenne said on the same day:

. . . The Patton Group is gradually losing the capacity to carry out large-scale operations, and it is therefore improbable now that it will be used at short notice to attack a strongly fortified coastal sector. FUSAG, while continuing to lose further formations to the Normandy bridge-head, will continue to be held in readiness to attack a German-held coastal sector, whenever such a sector may appear to have been denuded of its defenders. In the opinion of the department the Patton Army Group no longer constitutes an acute danger. But it is to be expected that it will be brought up to its full strength once more by the introduction of fresh drafts from the USA. . . . It will probably consist of two armies. The British 4th Army in south-east England will form one part, along with either the 9th or the 15th US Army to form the other in the area between the Thames and the Wash.

On July 29 and 31 Foreign Armies West put out further analyses of the military situation, stressing the improbability that FUSAG in its weakened state would undertake a landing operation at short notice. And at the beginning of August Hitler authorised Field Marshal Günther von Kluge, the new Commander-in-Chief West, to draw on the 15th Army for infantry to reinforce the counter-attack he had ordered von Kluge to mount against the enemy break-through at Avranches.

'Fortitude' was dead at last. It had served its purpose for seven weeks during which it had pinned down Hitler's best divisions in the Pas de Calais and prevented them from going to the aid of their comrades in the bridge-head. Now only shattered remnants of the German forces in France were left to oppose the Allied drive to Paris and the German frontier. There was nothing more left for 'Fortitude' to do. The FUSAG myth, however, lived on.

The SHAEF deceivers themselves had killed 'Fortitude'. The appearance of the FUSAG divisions in Normandy had been too much for them, and if they wanted to preserve the credibility of their agents for the future they could not continue to maintain the threat of the second assault as immediate.

Hitler and his staff never discovered they had been hoaxed. They believed the more flattering story that Eisenhower had fully intended to launch a large-scale assault against the Pas de Calais, but that the need to reinforce the armies in Normandy, caused by the unexpectedly obdurate resistance of Hitler's troops, had compelled him to change his plans.

When a few weeks after all this Colonel Wild found himself in Paris, a torn page of the *Pariser Zeitung* in his lavatory at the Crillon Hotel caught his eye. It carried the article announcing Patton's arrival in Normandy with the 3rd Army.

'Whereas the enemy army group which has so far been fighting in the bridge-head', he read, 'was called the "South-Western Invasion Army", because before being transported to France it had been located in the south-west of England, these new divisions belong to the "South-Eastern Invasion Army". Their employment shows to what extent the German defence in Normandy is depleting enemy forces.'

The colonel saved that piece of newsprint from its unsavoury fate. He carefully folded it. With a huge grin of satisfaction he put it in his wallet. I believe he still has it today.

14
Two Deaths

Before General Marshall ordered him to fly to England to assume notional command of the phantom FUSAG Lieutenant-General Lesley J. McNair had been in charge of the training of the American Ground Forces in America. It was entirely natural therefore that he should want to visit the bridge-head to see for himself how the men he had prepared for the invasion were conducting themselves in battle. McNair, however, unlike his predecessor, took 'Fortitude' seriously and was fully conscious of the need to preserve security and not to depart from the role prescribed for him by the cover plan.

So when shortly after his arrival in England he met Colonel Wild at the SHAEF headquarters almost the first thing this very senior and eminently distinguished American general said to the British colonel was: 'Look here, Colonel, you're my boss in this thing. Is it all right with you if I pop over to Normandy for a couple of days to have a look around?'

'Perfectly, General, so long as you don't propose to get into the fighting line yourself,' Wild laughed. 'It wouldn't do for the new FUSAG commander to get himself captured or attract attention to his presence on the wrong battlefield in some other way.'

McNair promised, and Colonel Wild thought no more about it. He knew that Eisenhower was flying over to watch the launching of 'Cobra', as the Normandy break-out was code-named, and he assumed that McNair would be accompanying Eisenhower. Nothing would be allowed to happen to Eisenhower, and so it was safe to assume that nothing would happen to McNair. Alas, that assumption was to be proved false.

'Cobra' provided for the enemy to be stunned and paralysed by the saturation bombing of a rectangular area three and a half miles wide and one and a half miles deep. It lay just south of St Lô on the other side of the long straight road running from St Lô to Périers. The rectangle was to be the area through which the Americans made their break-out. Once the bombers had knocked out the Germans, the plan was for the Americans to crash through what was left of the enemy in the rectangle with infantry, motorised cavalry, and armour. Then they would drive on to Coutances, fifteen miles to the south-west, in the hopes of clearing the way for the break-through to Avranches and the open country beyond. If 'Cobra' succeeded it would decide the battle of Normandy. McNair wanted to watch it being launched.

At dawn on Monday, July 24, McNair joined a battalion belonging to the 9th US Infantry Division in a position a mile back from the rectangle. The bombardment began punctually at 0940 hours. Fighter-bombers, 350 of them, swooped low over a 250-yard strip of the St Lô–Périers road. The strip was within immediate vision of McNair's binoculars. The fighter-bombers fired at the German posts along the road with rockets and machine guns. McNair from his foxhole studied the American troops around him. From the way his eyes shone it was clear he liked what he saw—the relaxed and confident expressions of the men, the cool, dispassionate expertise with which they watched the airforce at work. McNair had deliberately picked a battalion of the 9th because the day before the 9th had been victims of one of those tragic accidents which can shatter the morale of even the most battle-hardened veterans. A covey of American heavies had dropped their bombs a mile short of their target. They fell right among the men of the 9th. But McNair was delighted to see the incident had not affected the GIs around him.

After twenty minutes of the cavorting merry-go-round of the diving, swooping, and rocket-firing fighter-bombers the first wave of the heavies flew in at 1000 hours to bomb the rectangle. McNair watched them through his binoculars—Flying Fortresses and Liberators. There were to be almost 2000 of them with 4000 tons of explosives. And then quite incredibly it happened again. The bombers did not fly in parallel with the road, as Bradley had arranged with the Air Force. Instead they flew in vertically and once more spilled their load on the American line before they bombed the Germans in the rectangle. A direct hit killed General Lesley J. McNair in his foxhole.

Colonel Harry A. Flint, commander of the 39th Infantry Regiment of the 9th Division, was killed at the same time. He and General McNair were both buried two days later on July 26. But while 'Paddy' Flint was given a big military send-off with an army commander, three corps commanders, an army Chief of Staff, and all the cavalrymen at headquarters to act as pallbearers,* Lesley McNair's funeral was a small and very private affair as befitted an officer on an important secret mission. Only General Bradley, General Hodges, General Patton, Major-General Quesada,† and McNair's personal aidé were present.

★   ★   ★

General McNair's death clearly posed yet another problem for the SHAEF Deception Unit. It was of the greatest urgency that FUSAG should be provided with a new commander in his place and equally that the Germans should be informed by 'Paul' before an account of McNair's death reached them which did not fit in with the requirements of the cover plan.

'Paul's' message to his controller in Hamburg was brief and effective. 'I have learned that General McNair has been killed in Normandy', he signalled on July 26 within a few hours of the general's funeral. 'He had gone there to consult with General Montgomery and to inspect the German coastal defences.‡ Here at FUSAG this loss is considered very serious. It is thought that a successor will be appointed immediately to command the FUSAG operations.' Two days later the news was released to the press.

In the meantime Eisenhower had once more addressed himself to General Marshall. He asked him to appoint another general officer from the United States to replace McNair. Marshall replied with a promptness which showed how highly he regarded the

---

* George S. Patton, *War As I Knew It*, page 95.

† Major-General E. R. Quesada, Commanding General, 9th Tactical Air Command.

‡ The implication was that he was inspecting the defences to get an idea of what he would be up against in the Pas de Calais.

contribution made by 'Fortitude' to the success of the invasion. General de Witt, signalled Marshall, would be immediately available to take command of the 1st United States Army Group.

General John L. de Witt was a distinguished officer. For the last two years he had been Director of the Army and Navy Staff College in Washington. At the time of Pearl Harbour he had been made chief of the Western Defence Command with the special task of dealing with the war against Japan.

This time the news of the appointment was given to *The Times* in London while a similar announcement was issued in Washington. 'Lieutenant-General John de Witt is now in the United Kingdom to fill the assignment previously held by General Lesley McNair....' Foreign Armies West reported the news of General McNair's death in a note on August 5.

According to a reliable report Lieutenant-General L. J. McNair, who was killed on a visit to the front, had been slotted to assume command of the 1st US Army Group in England in the place of Lieutenant-General Patton. Lieutenant-General Patton, it would appear, has taken command of the 3rd US Army in Normandy. There is no news so far about the new commander of FUSAG in Great Britain. . . .

This item was followed on August 8 by the news of de Witt's appointment.

According to an official American announcement Lieutenant-General John L. de Witt has been appointed as successor to Lieutenant-General L. J. McNair who was killed during a visit to France. Lieutenant-General de Witt commanded the 4th US Army in the United States up to 1.9.1943 and after that he was commander of the Army and Navy Staff College. He is considered to be an exceptionally brilliant organiser. Presumably Lieutenant-General de Witt has assumed command of the 1st US Army Group in Great Britain (FUSAG).

And on the following day Foreign Armies West commented:

The probable appointment to the command over FUSAG of an exceptionally highly regarded officer, General de Witt, is a proof that the enemy High Command attaches special importance to this Army Group which apart from its airborne formations comprises around thirty-two large formations. An immediately imminent new landing in the Channel area is now as before considered unlikely; should however further German forces be withdrawn from the Channel front this possibility would become a probability once more.

So although Hitler had withdrawn some divisions from the 15th Army, FUSAG was still a spook which for the OKW was no phantom but a very real threat.

★   ★   ★

Alexis von Roenne's end was inevitable. Once Gestapo and SD began rounding up the opponents of Hitler after the failure of the attempt to assassinate him at the Führer Conference of July 20, 1944, such an outspoken critic of the régime and its strategic genius as Roenne was bound to be in trouble. The amazing thing is not that he was arrested but that Himmler's myrmidons should have left Colonel of the General Staff the Freiherr Alexis von Roenne at liberty and in charge of the Foreign Armies West Department as long after the abortive *Putsch* as they did.

SD investigators interviewed him several times during the first fortnight following the attempted coup, but they always let him go again. Roenne even continued to issue his daily bulletins of military intelligence. Perhaps Gestapo-Chief Heinrich Müller, who headed the investigation, hoped to lull Roenne into a false sense of security in the expectation that he would become indiscreet and lead the sleuths trailing him to some hitherto unsuspected ramifications of the conspiracy. If that was his hope, he hoped in vain. When Gestapo Müller discovered that this somewhat outworn ploy was getting him nowhere he decided to wait no longer.

The last bulletin of the Foreign Armies West Department to appear over Roenne's signature was issued on Tuesday, August 8. On the following morning two SD officers arrested the colonel in his office. In a car they conveyed him from the underground 'Zeppelin' citadel of the Army High Command at Zossen to the RSHA headquarters in Berlin. While Roenne was being interrogated there, his former deputy, Lieutenant-Colonel Bürklin, was promoted to full colonel and put in charge of the department. On

August 17 the first bulletin appeared above Bürklin's signature as chief of the department.

Roenne was perfunctorily tried by the People's Court along with other German officers and civilians accused of complicity in the attempt on the Führer's life. And like the 4,790 fellow victims of Hitler's lust for revenge he too was sentenced to death.

His turn to be hanged (hanging was considered a dishonourable death for a German officer, an officer sentenced to death was entitled to a firing squad) came on October 12. Together with Dr Carl Langbehn, a lawyer who had made several trips to Switzerland in the hopes of establishing contact with the Americans, Colonel Count Rudolf Marogna-Redwitz, the Roman Catholic Prelate Otto Müller, and six other Germans whose names are not known, Roenne was led into a low-ceilinged whitewashed cellar under Berlin's Plötzensee prison. As at all the hangings, a special camera team of the official UFA newsreel stood by to make a sound film of the hanging for Hitler to gloat over. A warder who was present has described the scene.

'An iron rail had been fixed to the ceiling. Suspended from it were ten hooks of the kind that butchers use to hang up the carcasses of the animals they have slaughtered. In one corner of the room stood the film camera. A two-man crew had been sent to operate it. Also a lighting engineer to attend to the arc lights. Against the wall stood a table with a bottle of French cognac, a carafe of water, and several glasses. The brandy was for the witnesses, not the condemned. Present apart from myself and another warder were the hangman with two assistants and the Reich Attorney General.

'The prisoners were brought in. They were dressed in prison uniform and were fettered hand and foot. The hangman made them line up in a row, one behind the other. As he and his assistants slipped a noose round each man's neck he made comic grimaces and cackled out a long stream of facetious remarks in broad Berlin dialect. He was renowned as a comic.

'As each man's turn came the hangman and his assistants hustled him a few steps forward, lifted him up, slipped his noose over the hook, and jerked him down, breaking his neck.

'The whole thing took about twenty-five minutes during which

the film camera whirred incessantly. That evening, like every other
evening, Hitler had a special showing of the day's hangings in his
private film theatre at the Reich Chancellery.'*

Friends of Roenne told me years after the war that he could have
escaped his fate had he chosen to defend himself. But this courageous
officer, true to the highest traditions of the much maligned Prussian
aristocracy, felt that loyalty to his friend Klaus von Stauffenberg†
demanded that he should admit with complete candour that like
Stauffenberg he had become convinced the interests of his fatherland
demanded the removal of its evil genius.

Many of the condemned men were, like Roenne himself, devout
Christians. To add a special touch of refinement to his revenge
Hitler therefore ordered that none of them were to be allowed the
spiritual consolation of a visit from a priest or a pastor. Visits from
clergy, whether Roman Catholic or Protestant, were strictly
forbidden. But that did not prevent the prisoners from finding their
own spiritual consolation, as is shown by the letters of farewell
many of them wrote to their families.

Alexis von Roenne, too, wrote to his mother, and this letter was
published after the war in *Neue Kirche*, the news sheet of the
Protestant community in Westphalia, on November 23, 1947.
To anyone who like me has read the intelligence bulletins with
which this passionately sincere patriot attempted to warn the
German High Command of what was in store for the German Army
in France, or has studied his courageous report damning the in-
sufficiency of the much vaunted Atlantic Wall, and the letter in
which he urged his friend Beelitz to use his influence to persuade the
OKW to withdraw from Italy and other minor theatres of war in
order that the German Army should concentrate its forces where the
decisive battle was about to be fought, this devoutly religious letter
with its message of comfort for his mother and his wife and their
two children is a profoundly moving document.

---

* From *20 Juli 1944*, Bundeszentrale für Heimatdienst, Bonn, pages 181 and
182.
† Klaus Count Schenk von Stauffenberg, an officer of the General Staff like
von Roenne, had placed the bomb under Hitler's map table in the war-
room at the Führerhauptquartier. He was the organiser of the Officers'
Revolt.

My dear Mama!

Today for a special reason [presumably that he had been told to prepare himself for his execution] I have the urgent desire to write to you once again. I know that despite your intense longing and joy to go to our Saviour you are at times tortured by the fear of death. And so I want to tell you that our Lord can wipe away that fear, if only we ask him.

For the last week I have now been awaiting death day by day—just now for instance I am awaiting it for tomorrow. The Saviour in his unlimited mercy has freed me from all fear. I pray and think all day long of almost nothing but Him. At the same time of course I think of my dear ones. I eat with good appetite, enjoy the sunshine, and have only tried to loosen my ties with the world in so far as I no longer read anything. I keep my thoughts clear of anything to do with military or political affairs and keep myself entirely at the disposition of the Saviour. I go to bed early—in prayer—sleep quietly and as firmly as a child all night and on waking turn immediately to Him and am completely free and in addition—apart from thinking of my little family—a completely happy person. I had been trying to develop thoughts which would give me the strength and joyfulness to die. Suddenly He showed me two ways of achieving it.

Above all I was to represent my death to myself with complete realism and compare it with His! That at last helped me. The sinless one was martyred to death for many hours by those he had saved. With me on the other hand it is a momentary happening which in any case must be faced by me some time and possibly under much more painful conditions. Those two beautiful verses, 'When once I must part . . .' and 'And let me see Thine image in Thy throes of death . . .' They made me feel ashamed of my inhibitions and I became free of fear. And then He showed me that the moment of death is the first moment of blessed rest in God's peace. I have held fast to this thought, and now for days I am looking forward to my departure and homecoming with complete calm and freedom. I have full confidence that the short last happening will be illuminated by His indescribable grace.

I write of all this in such detail, my beloved mother, because on His behalf I can therewith give you a small help. For me since the beginning of this time of grace there is no doubt that I owe this undeserved mercy in large part to the long years of your prayers for me. I simply cannot put my thanks to you in words. I hold your prayers for me to be the biggest gift of your endless love for me. I beg you with all my heart, that you may for the rest of your time on earth transfer these prayers to my two children. Oh, please do it with the same love and loyalty you showed for me. It is an immeasurable treasure which you would confer upon my little flock. It needs it so badly.

It was very hard on me to be separated from you all without news of you. But at the same time I had the consciousness of our being so closely bound together before God's throne and the unimportance of our time on earth. And all the greater became the joyful prospect of never being parted again on the other side.

I send you my greetings with the whole of my heart and commend you to the power of God and his Blessing. Let Him lead you on His gentle path into His Kingdom even as He leads me to Paradise as he did the malefactor.* I know you will not cease to care for my loved ones. For this I thank you and for all the infinite love I thank all of you and above all you, my darling mother, from the bottom of my heart. Richer and more deepfelt love from its mother no child ever enjoyed than

thine A.

Alexis von Roenne's hanging made no difference to the SHAEF deceivers. They knew nothing about it. In fact they had no idea of the set-up at the Foreign Armies West Department, although it should have been easy for them to learn all about it from one of the many staff officers captured by the Allies. (One of the rare criticisms I would make about the way the SHAEF unit conducted their brilliant operation.)

Bürklin carried on from where Roenne had left off. He also failed to spot the fakes by the SHAEF-controlled agents, though he did, as we shall see, become suspicious of some of the freelance agents like Kramer and 'Josephine'. Oddly enough he and his colleagues in the Abwehr SD decided these agents must be in the pay of the Allies!

But never, never did any of the German high-ups so much as suspect that FUSAG was a Trojan Horse, conjured up by Eisenhower's 'con-men commando' to trick them into defeat. Or that Jorge Antonio was anything but a fanatical devotee of the Führer.

---

* St Luke 23 :39 to 43.

15

Kühlenthal Rescues 'Cato'
from M.I.5

Walter Schellenberg, that ambitious go-getter of the RSHA, is hardly a witness whose evidence on matters concerning his despised rivals of the Abwehr historians could be expected to accept on his mere say-so. Yet when in his memoirs* he describes his shock at the fantastic lack of security in the Abwehr's Madrid KO I am prepared to believe him.

After all, the whole story of General Kühlenthal's relations with the young Spaniard whom the Abwehr code-named 'Cato' shows an amazing disregard for the ground rules of espionage. One only needs to consider how the Germans used the services of the mythical BOAC steward as a courier without checking on him or trying to discover who was collecting their V-man's mail for him from the Lisbon bank. Then there is the incredible way they fell for Jorge Antonio's clumsy fakes, when he first started sending them reports from Lisbon while pretending he was in England. For example those in which he referred to the 'Portuguese Embassy at Brighton'† and described 'a litre of red wine' as the favourite tipple of the Liverpool dockers. Those two instances alone would have made me for one suspect that Kühlenthal might be trying a double bluff. But he was not bluffing. Conclusive proof of this is provided by the repeated praise of Jorge Antonio as a 'reliable V-man' in the captured

---

* Schellenberg, *Memoiren*, page 198.
† In a guide book to the British Isles which Jorge Antonio used in Lisbon to give him the necessary background for his fake reports from England he had found Brighton described as 'London's San Sebastian'. As foreign embassies traditionally followed the Spanish Government from Madrid to San Sebastian during the summer months, Jorge Antonio assumed the Portuguese diplomats would similarly move their London embassy to Brighton!

files of the Foreign Armies West Department. Also by Hitler's reaction to the 'Ganelon' reports in his strategic decisions. I am therefore ready to believe Schellenberg when he says that the carelessness with which Germany's Secret Service performed its job in Madrid 'made his hair stand almost on end'.

. . . Our Secret Service [writes Schellenberg] had established a kind of headquarters in the back room of a Madrid drinking shop. Leading members of the organisation met their multifarious agents there and conducted their business with them in its convivial surroundings. After the agents had been paid for their services, it was customary to celebrate with drinks all round. Everyone present joined in. By way of precaution they had recruited the owner of the pub as a member of the service. They even went so far as to promote him to be their treasurer. He kept the accounts and looked after their precious fund of foreign currencies—US dollars, Sterling, Swiss francs, and so forth. Thus the cash-box of the Reich Secret Service rested on the cashier's desk of the bodega. When the *patron* was drunk—a by no means rare occurrence—he as often as not put his hand in the Abwehr cash-box instead of the pub's till and paid out change to the customers in foreign notes. The receipts for the money paid to the agents he used to make out on bills carrying the name and address of the bar. No wonder that the local police were informed of everything that went on in this cosy little tavern. In the end the police were themselves taken into partnership, and they too joined in the drinking parties. . . . That those entertained at these parties included characters who reported everything they learned to the Enemy did not bother anyone. I decided to allow the boon companions to carry on undisturbed. What they reported was all nonsense anyhow, and I thought it a good idea to let the Enemy go on listening in to them, while we quietly built up a new team to do the real work. In any case, it was high time we strengthened Group VId, which covered the Anglo-American sphere. We already had a first-rate contact in London. . . .

I wonder whether Schellenberg ever came to regret having spared those Secret Service roysterers in Madrid's 'cosy little tavern'. With the knowledge we have today it is easy to see he would have been well advised to shut the place down, pay off the Spanish V-men, and send their German spymasters packing.

'Home to the Reich' should have been the watchword for them.

For their drink-loosened tongues were almost certainly responsible for a mysterious leakage that very nearly 'closed the case', as Secret Service parlance puts it, of that 'contact' in London of whom both Schellenberg and Kühlenthal were so proud.

*   *   *

Officially my friend David Walker was the Lisbon correspondent of London's mass-circulation tabloid the *Daily Mirror*. Unofficially he was a secret operative of Britain's SOE (the Special Operations Executive). David had the job of disseminating rumours in Lisbon which were designed to have a detrimental effect on Germany's war effort. They were called 'sibs' or 'whispers' and had been specially thought up by a committee in London which consisted of representatives of the Political Warfare Executive, SOE itself, the various intelligence departments of the fighting services, and the Ministry of Economic Warfare.

Every week David was sent a list of 'sibs' which he and a group of agents under his control were expected to put around in suitable places. David took a special pleasure in planting his 'sibs' on agents known to be selling information to the German intelligence. As a news man himself—and one with a distinguished Fleet Street reputation—it was perfectly in character for him to be swopping stories with his foreign colleagues.

One of David's most cherished clients was a certain Jan Jindric, an Austro-Czech journalist, who had managed to persuade both Abwehr and SD that he had a network of 'contacts' spread over the entire anti-Hitler world, especially Britain, the USA, and the Middle East. He pretended to the Germans that the intelligence service of Dr Benes's Free Czech Government in London permitted him to use its diplomatic couriers and gave him access to their secret reports. This of course was pure invention. The Czechs were very security-minded and in any case did not trust Jindric one milli-metre. Jindric nevertheless was a highly competent operator, and a very expensive one, as the Germans discovered very early in their dealings with him. They paid out tens of thousands of escudos for his fakes.

In the last few months, however, as a direct result of the competition from the SHAEF-controlled V-men, his reputation with his German masters had been on the wane. Not even a lucky guess, which had enabled him on May 31, 1944, to forecast correctly the date of the invasion, had succeeded in restoring his prestige. The vague generalisations of his reports contrasted unfavourably with the sharp detail presented in the SHAEF-fed reports of 'Cato' and his fictitious team of on-the-spot observers. Maybe, too, Jan had been including too many of David Walker's 'sibs' in the diet which he served up to the Germans. They were becoming doubtful of his reliability. They even began to suspect him of being the member of an international ring in Allied pay which was trying to plant false intelligence on them.

Knowing a bit about the atmosphere in which the Third Reich's services worked, I would not put it outside the bounds of possibility that Hitler's scathing denunciation of the Abwehr agent who had correctly predicted the date and place of the invasion (see page 17) had first put Himmler's obsequious SD on to investigating Jindric.

But the real irony of the situation was that Jan Jindric's predicament was the direct result of the German spymasters' own methods. They had been in the habit of permitting favoured agents like Jindric in Lisbon and his counterpart Kramer in Stockholm to read their intelligence summaries. They did this in the hope that Jindric and Kramer would use their own (non-existent*) networks to amplify, contradict, or confirm the reports in the summaries. The inevitable result was that Jindric and Kramer, each basing his reports on the same German intelligence and neither having the benefit of the SHAEF deceivers' careful editing and co-ordination, produced reports closely resembling each other. The Germans deduced that this was evidence of collusion between them, collusion under the orders of the perfidious British and Americans. Nor did Jindric and Kramer stand up too well under questioning.

How fortunate it was for Jorge Antonio and 'Paul' that neither of them ever had to face a personal confrontation of the kind that Jindric and Kramer were forced to undergo. If Kühlenthal pressed Jorge Antonio with awkward questions he could always find a pretext to avoid an embarrassing answer. If necessary he could even

---

* The gullible Germans did not suspect the bogus nature of these networks until July 1944 at the earliest.

get himself arrested, as Jorge Antonio did, when Kühlenthal was pressing him too closely over the Flying Bomb hits. But Jindric could not retire into unavailability.

And so it was a depressed and gloomy Jindric that travelled to the Spanish capital on July 30, 1944, in the hope of meeting his friends of the Madrid K.O. and enlisting their help to blow away the clouds that hung over him in Lisbon. Exactly what happened in Madrid is not clear. Jindric did meet an Abwehr man in what later he described as 'a bar'. Whether this was the 'cosy tavern' described by Schellenberg I have been unable to discover. But it would not surprise me, if it was. The undeniable fact however is that Jindric returned to Lisbon in a much more optimistic frame of mind than when he had set out for Madrid.

Almost the first thing he did was to call up David Walker and suggest to him that they should meet in a little restaurant they both knew and liked in Lisbon's Old City. 'I think I have something for you that might make a good story for the Mirror.'

The 'something', however, turned out to be not so much for the Daily Mirror as for M.I.5. Jindric revealed that in return for a substantial reward he was prepared to put the Mirror on the tracks of a master spy operating in Britain as the head of an extensive network of agents supplying the Germans with military intelligence.

'If the Mirror could publish the information leading to his arrest that would be worth quite something to your editor?' Jindric's approach to David was that of a free-lance tipster to an accredited correspondent. In all probability he suspected him of being an agent and had sought him out for this reason. But they both continued to talk on the basis that they were two bona-fide journalists.

As a newspaperman David Walker was discouraging. 'It's not the sort of thing English newspapers go in for in real life. The news-hawk who tracks down the spy is strictly fiction. And then you should know that in England we have very severe laws of libel. I doubt whether any editor would care to accuse a man of being a German spy.'

'Not even a foreigner?'

'No, Jan. Not even a foreigner!'

'Well, there must be someone among the British here who would be interested to know this—and pay for the information. I would have to have money, and protection too. I could not stay here. The

Germans would kill me, if they found out I had caused their man to be caught. . . . I would have to have money, as well as my passage to Australia, and a guarantee of permission to settle there. I have relatives in a place called Bendigo.'

David was good at his job. And after a lot more of this kind of badinage he got Jindric to the point, where he hinted that the German spy was a Spaniard working in London's Ministry of Information. His position there, Jindric said, gave him access to a great deal of valuable information. But the spy's main importance was that he had organised a very extensive spy-ring. If the British went about it with their customary skill, they ought to be able to round up the lot.

Jindric's story—though of course David had no idea of this when he reported it to the rabbit-toothed Old Etonian who was Schreiber's opposite number in Lisbon and represented M.I.6—pointed straight at Jorge Antonio.

For Wild, Reid, and the 'Double-cross' Committee Jindric's denunciation of the 'Spanish spy in the Ministry of Information' posed a most disagreeable problem. Had Kühlenthal, or some confidant of his in the Madrid K.O., betrayed his prize V-man to Jindric through careless talk—perhaps in a fit of drunken boasting at the 'cosy tavern'? (The tavern and its indiscretions were no secret from the British and Americans, as Schellenberg had rightly suspected.) Had the Abwehr men merely been trying to demonstrate to the expensive Jindric that they had much better-informed sources at their disposal against whose reliable information they could check his? (Not a ploy a completely sober case officer would use with an agent, but conceivable in the course of a conversation in 'the bibulous tavern'.) Or was it a deliberate leak, intended to test the British reaction? For obviously, if the Germans were behind the denunciation, even if they were not old Abwehr hands but members of the rival SD group, jealous of the kudos Kühlenthal had derived from 'Cato's' triumphs, they would be watching carefully to see what the British would do. If M.I.5 received the denunciation and then did nothing, the plain inference would be that the V-man was under British control. If the British locked him up, or merely pretended to lock him up, that too would be the end of Jorge Antonio as a V-man.

Appropriately it was Charlie Reid who, as Jorge Antonio's case officer, thought up the procedure by which to extricate Jorge Antonio and M.I.5 from their difficulty. What he devised was a far from ideal solution. For though it fooled the Germans, it did not bring Jorge Antonio back into operation. All it achieved was to stop the Germans from becoming aware that for all these years the agent they called 'Cato' had been conning them and their all-powerful master on behalf of the Allies. Needless to say that was most important. For to expose 'Cato' would have exposed the whole of Allied Deception and that would have been most undesirable, even though it had already achieved its main objective. For it might have alerted the Germans to any future deception by SHAEF-controlled V-men.

*   *   *

It was at the beginning of August that the news reached the SHAEF Deception Unit that a German agent was offering information about the spy-ring led by Jorge Antonio. At that time Jorge Antonio himself, in compliance with Kühlenthal's orders, was still lying low. Only the Venezuelan, to whom he had (notionally) handed over the direction of the organisation, and 'The Widow' knew how to contact him. Kühlenthal believed 'Cato' was still doing his job at the Ministry of Information and the Covent Garden fruit importers but was not seeing any of his informers.

In accordance with the Reid plan the Venezuelan now broke the news to Madrid that on his last trip to Lisbon the courier (who by this time had become a conscious sub-agent) had learned of Jan Jindric's desertion of the Führer's cause and of his intention to buy the good-will of the British by telling them what he had learned about the existence of a German spy-net in Britain. The Venezuelan attached a message for 'Alfonso' from Jorge Antonio to whom he said he had given this piece of bad news.

'I appreciate of course that ours is not the only organisation working for the Führer in Britain, but I sincerely hope it is the most efficient, and I am sure that none is more dedicated to the cause', said the ostensibly 150 per cent Nazi Jorge Antonio. 'But if I assume that it is us that this traitor wishes to denounce to the enemy, I beg you not to have him liquidated immediately, as he so richly deserves. Any act of violence committed against him would only confirm in the opinion of the British whatever information he may have already passed to them. Instead I suggest for your consideration, that at the earliest opportunity this man—I understand he is a Czech Communist working from Lisbon—should have it conveyed to him in as casual a manner as possible, that the agent about whom he had heard is no longer in Britain but has already returned to Spain. This would deprive of its value whatever information about me this reptile was about to give to the British. Presumably he would realise this and desist from his plans. But even if he did inform the British I suggest that in order to substantiate the report that I have returned to Spain you should send a series of letters to my London firm which I shall write and date as though coming from Spain. I will send them to you by our courier. In the meantime I will go into hiding at the same hill farm in Wales where we have safely concealed other members of the organisation from the English.'

Kühlenthal immediately signalled his agreement to Jorge Antonio's suggestions. Did he feel any compunction at having allowed his most valuable V-man to be exposed to such danger by loose talk? I do not suppose so. For the Kühlenthals of this world seldom have the imagination to realise their own mistakes. But enquiries have established with a considerable degree of probability that it was Kühlenthal himself whose celebration of the telegram from the RSHA on June 10 congratulating him on the reports of the 'Ganelon' organisation had caused him to talk a little too freely to his friends and colleagues in the 'cosy tavern' when celebrating Jorge Antonio's triumphs. But then, who can blame a general for rejoicing over a victory with his friends?

Erich Kühlenthal's anxiety about Jorge Antonio was allayed when he heard that the police had visited the Covent Garden fruit importers a number of times during October enquiring about the whereabouts of Jorge Antonio. 'But', said the Venezuelan, 'they appeared to be quite satisfied when shown the letters he had written from Spain. The sergeant merely laughed and said that someone must have slipped up at the Immigration Office in failing to register his departure properly.'

Clearly Kühlenthal and his associates were as ignorant about

conditions in Britain in 1944 as they were in 1940. For how otherwise could they have believed that Scotland Yard would permit an
alien to leave Britain without so much as an exit visa? However they
did, and that was all that mattered.

Jorge Antonio wrote Kühlenthal a number of letters describing
with graphic detail the ghastly primitivity of the Welsh hill farm
in which he and the Gibraltarian lived with a flock of chickens,
four starving steers, and an aged Welsh couple. But he sent no
further military reports to the Germans. His work for them and the
SHAEF Deception Unit had come to an end.

And so too had that of the unit as a whole. 'Paul' with the aid of
the Venezuelan and the remnants of Jorge Antonio's 'orchestra'
now conducted by the Venezuelan had laid on a scare about a
FUSAG landing at Emden or Wesermünde. Noël Wild and Roger
Sneath had done their best to help with the 'Anvil' landing in the
South of France. But that deception was conducted mainly by
agents working from French North Africa and Italy.

'Paul' left his job with FUSAG and was posted to the headquarters of the Dutch Army. In the middle of September he as good
as gave the Germans notice. 'Paul' told his German masters that
his work at the Dutch Army headquarters was now taking up all his
available time. He could not get around to observe what was going
on as he used to. He never told them he was giving up. But his
messages became fewer and fewer. And on January 2, 1945, he sent
his last signal.

For all practical purposes that was the end of the deception
operation that had begun when Sir Archibald Wavell launched the
unit he called 'A' Force way back in 1940. It had done more than its
share of helping to win the war and save all of us—and in that 'us'
I include the Germans—from that incarnation of evil, Hitler's
Third Reich.

*   *   *

Financial postscript: When all the money came to be added up which
General Erich Kühlenthal had been sending 'Cato' over the years
to finance his 'orchestra' of fictitious sub-agents it was found to
amount to a total of £73,586 17s. 6d. I would like to have been able
to report that Jorge Antonio was allowed to keep it. That, however,

is not the way the minds of Treasury bureaucrats work. HM Government took the lot.

The 'Twenty Club', however, decreed that Jorge Antonio should be given a 'golden hand-shake' of £10,000 when he left the service. Jorge Antonio, who had been entirely genuine in saying that he joined the struggle against Hitler not for money but because he believed Britain to be the last bulwark of Democracy, could only be made to accept it after Carlos Reid had used all his arts of persuasion.

★   ★   ★

Jorge Antonio did not return to Spain, when soon after VE-day he left England. Wisely he accepted that while he had helped the Allies to win the war against Hitler, there would be no help from them for him in his private crusade against Generalissimo Franco's police state. So now at the age of thirty-four he gave himself up once more to that wanderlust that had first seized him four years before when he set out in the sardine boat for Gibraltar. Four years he had been pent up in an office dreaming up exciting adventures for himself and his 'orchestra' of bogus James Bonds with which to hoax the Germans into war-losing moves. Now he was going to have some real adventures and see the world.

He travelled across Canada and Australia, working now as a ranch hand, now as an electrical engineer. In Darwin he fell in love and married a beautiful young New Australian, the daughter of Portuguese immigrant parents. Politics, deception, and all the rest of it were by now entirely forgotten. Instead he devoted himself to making money.

And then the wanderbug got into him again. Possibly with an eye to an eventual return to Spain, he and his young wife set out for Portuguese Africa. This time, however, he seemed settled for good. In Angola,★ using his gifts of psychological perception and imagination, he built up a prosperous public relations firm along with an import-export business.

Suddenly in 1959, when the two children his wife had borne him

---

★ For the same reason that I have refrained from identifying 'Cato' more closely, I am not revealing the town or the particular region of Angola where he set up in business.

were hardly out of their kindergarten, Jorge Antonio succumbed to another attack of malaria. And this time it killed him.

As for General Erich Kühlenthal, he returned to Germany when he thought Chancellor Adenauer had made it safe for him to do so. He died in 1956 at the age of seventy-six without ever having learned the truth about 'Cato' or the FUSAG hoax.

Like Hitler himself, Kühlenthal was unwittingly an 'Ally of the Allies.'

Index